53. *The A to Z of the Druzes* by Samy S. Swayd, 2009.
54. *The A to Z of the Welfare State* by Bent Greve, 2009.
55. *The A to Z of the War of 1812* by Robert Malcomson, 2009.
56. *The A to Z of Feminist Philosophy* by Catherine Villanueva Gardner, 2009.
57. *The A to Z of the Early American Republic* by Richard Buel Jr., 2009.
58. *The A to Z of the Russo-Japanese War* by Rotem Kowner, 2009.
59. *The A to Z of Anglicanism* by Colin Buchanan, 2009.
60. *The A to Z of Scandinavian Literature and Theater* by Jan Sjåvik, 2009.
61. *The A to Z of the Peoples of the Southeast Asian Massif* by Jean Michaud, 2009.
62. *The A to Z of Judaism* by Norman Solomon, 2009.
63. *The A to Z of the Berbers (Imazighen)* by Hsain Ilahiane, 2009.
64. *The A to Z of British Radio* by Seán Street, 2009.
65. *The A to Z of The Salvation Army* by Major John G. Merritt, 2009.
66. *The A to Z of the Arab-Israeli Conflict* by P. R. Kumaraswamy, 2009.
67. *The A to Z of the Jacksonian Era and Manifest Destiny* by Terry Corps, 2009.
68. *The A to Z of Socialism* by Peter Lamb and James C. Docherty, 2009.
69. *The A to Z of Marxism* by David Walker and Daniel Gray, 2009.
70. *The A to Z of the Bahá'í Faith* by Hugh C. Adamson, 2009.
71. *The A to Z of Postmodernist Literature and Theater* by Fran Mason, 2009.
72. *The A to Z of Australian Radio and Television* by Albert Moran and Chris Keating, 2009.
73. *The A to Z of the Lesbian Liberation Movement: Still the Rage* by JoAnne Myers, 2009.
74. *The A to Z of the United States–Mexican War* by Edward R. Moseley and Paul C. Clark, 2009.
75. *The A to Z of World War I* by Ian V. Hogg, 2009.
76. *The A to Z of World War II: The War Against Japan* by Ann Sharp Wells, 2009.
77. *The A to Z of Witchcraft* by Michael D. Bailey, 2009.
78. *The A to Z of British Intelligence* by Nigel West, 2009.

79. *The A to Z of United States Intelligence* by Michael A. Turner, 2009.
80. *The A to Z of the League of Nations* by Anique H. M. van Ginneken, 2009.
81. *The A to Z of Israeli Intelligence* by Ephraim Kahana, 2009.
82. *The A to Z of the European Union* by Joaquín Roy and Aimee Kanner, 2009.
83. *The A to Z of the Chinese Cultural Revolution* by Guo Jian, Yongyi Song, and Yuan Zhou, 2009.
84. *The A to Z of African American Cinema* by S. Torriano Berry and Venise T. Berry, 2009.
85. *The A to Z of Japanese Business* by Stuart D. B. Picken, 2009.
86. *The A to Z of the Reagan–Bush Era* by Richard S. Conley, 2009.
87. *The A to Z of Human Rights and Humanitarian Organizations* by Robert F. Gorman and Edward S. Mihalkanin, 2009.
88. *The A to Z of French Cinema* by Dayna Oscherwitz and MaryEllen Higgins, 2009.
89. *The A to Z of the Puritans* by Charles Pastoor and Galen K. Johnson, 2009.
90. *The A to Z of Nuclear, Biological and Chemical Warfare* by Benjamin C. Garrett and John Hart, 2009.
91. *The A to Z of the Green Movement* by Miranda Schreurs and Elim Papadakis, 2009.
92. *The A to Z of the Kennedy–Johnson Era* by Richard Dean Burns and Joseph M. Siracusa, 2009.
93. *The A to Z of Renaissance Art* by Lilian H. Zirpolo, 2009.
94. *The A to Z of the Broadway Musical* by William A. Everett and Paul R. Laird, 2009.
95. *The A to Z of the Northern Ireland Conflict* by Gordon Gillespie, 2009.
96. *The A to Z of the Fashion Industry* by Francesca Sterlacci and Joanne Arbuckle, 2009.
97. *The A to Z of American Theater: Modernism* by James Fisher and Felicia Hardison Londré, 2009.
98. *The A to Z of Civil Wars in Africa* by Guy Arnold, 2009.
99. *The A to Z of the Nixon–Ford Era* by Mitchell K. Hall, 2009.
100. *The A to Z of Horror Cinema* by Peter Hutchings, 2009.
101. *The A to Z of Westerns in Cinema* by Paul Varner, 2009.

OTHER A TO Z GUIDES FROM THE SCARECROW PRESS, INC.

1. *The A to Z of Buddhism* by Charles S. Prebish, 2001. *Out of Print. See No. 124.*
2. *The A to Z of Catholicism* by William J. Collinge, 2001.
3. *The A to Z of Hinduism* by Bruce M. Sullivan, 2001.
4. *The A to Z of Islam* by Ludwig W. Adamec, 2002. *Out of Print. See No. 123.*
5. *The A to Z of Slavery and Abolition* by Martin A. Klein, 2002.
6. *Terrorism: Assassins to Zealots* by Sean Kendall Anderson and Stephen Sloan, 2003.
7. *The A to Z of the Korean War* by Paul M. Edwards, 2005.
8. *The A to Z of the Cold War* by Joseph Smith and Simon Davis, 2005.
9. *The A to Z of the Vietnam War* by Edwin E. Moise, 2005.
10. *The A to Z of Science Fiction Literature* by Brian Stableford, 2005.
11. *The A to Z of the Holocaust* by Jack R. Fischel, 2005.
12. *The A to Z of Washington, D.C.* by Robert Benedetto, Jane Donovan, and Kathleen DuVall, 2005.
13. *The A to Z of Taoism* by Julian F. Pas, 2006.
14. *The A to Z of the Renaissance* by Charles G. Nauert, 2006.
15. *The A to Z of Shinto* by Stuart D. B. Picken, 2006.
16. *The A to Z of Byzantium* by John H. Rosser, 2006.
17. *The A to Z of the Civil War* by Terry L. Jones, 2006.
18. *The A to Z of the Friends (Quakers)* by Margery Post Abbott, Mary Ellen Chijioke, Pink Dandelion, and John William Oliver Jr., 2006.
19. *The A to Z of Feminism* by Janet K. Boles and Diane Long Hoeveler, 2006.
20. *The A to Z of New Religious Movements* by George D. Chryssides, 2006.
21. *The A to Z of Multinational Peacekeeping* by Terry M. Mays, 2006.
22. *The A to Z of Lutheranism* by Günther Gassmann with Duane H. Larson and Mark W. Oldenburg, 2007.
23. *The A to Z of the French Revolution* by Paul R. Hanson, 2007.
24. *The A to Z of the Persian Gulf War 1990–1991* by Clayton R. Newell, 2007.
25. *The A to Z of Revolutionary America* by Terry M. Mays, 2007.

26. *The A to Z of the Olympic Movement* by Bill Mallon with Ian Buchanan, 2007.
27. *The A to Z of the Discovery and Exploration of Australia* by Alan Day, 2009.
28. *The A to Z of the United Nations* by Jacques Fomerand, 2009.
29. *The A to Z of the "Dirty Wars"* by David Kohut, Olga Vilella, and Beatrice Julian, 2009.
30. *The A to Z of the Vikings* by Katherine Holman, 2009.
31. *The A to Z from the Great War to the Great Depression* by Neil A. Wynn, 2009.
32. *The A to Z of the Crusades* by Corliss K. Slack, 2009.
33. *The A to Z of New Age Movements* by Michael York, 2009.
34. *The A to Z of Unitarian Universalism* by Mark W. Harris, 2009.
35. *The A to Z of the Kurds* by Michael M. Gunter, 2009.
36. *The A to Z of Utopianism* by James M. Morris and Andrea L. Kross, 2009.
37. *The A to Z of the Civil War and Reconstruction* by William L. Richter, 2009.
38. *The A to Z of Jainism* by Kristi L. Wiley, 2009.
39. *The A to Z of the Inuit* by Pamela K. Stern, 2009.
40. *The A to Z of Early North America* by Cameron B. Wesson, 2009.
41. *The A to Z of the Enlightenment* by Harvey Chisick, 2009.
42. *The A to Z Methodism* by Charles Yrigoyen Jr. and Susan E. Warrick, 2009.
43. *The A to Z of the Seventh-day Adventists* by Gary Land, 2009.
44. *The A to Z of Sufism* by John Renard, 2009.
45. *The A to Z of Sikhism* by William Hewat McLeod, 2009.
46. *The A to Z Fantasy Literature* by Brian Stableford, 2009.
47. *The A to Z of the Discovery and Exploration of the Pacific Islands* by Max Quanchi and John Robson, 2009.
48. *The A to Z of Australian and New Zealand Cinema* by Albert Moran and Errol Vieth, 2009.
49. *The A to Z of African-American Television* by Kathleen Fearn-Banks, 2009.
50. *The A to Z of American Radio Soap Operas* by Jim Cox, 2009.
51. *The A to Z of the Old South* by William L. Richter, 2009.
52. *The A to Z of the Discovery and Exploration of the Northwest Passage* by Alan Day, 2009.

102. *The A to Z of Zionism* by Rafael Medoff and Chaim I. Waxman, 2009.
103. *The A to Z of the Roosevelt–Truman Era* by Neil A. Wynn, 2009.
104. *The A to Z of Jehovah's Witnesses* by George D. Chryssides, 2009.
105. *The A to Z of Native American Movements* by Todd Leahy and Raymond Wilson, 2009.
106. *The A to Z of the Shakers* by Stephen J. Paterwic, 2009.
107. *The A to Z of the Coptic Church* by Gawdat Gabra, 2009.
108. *The A to Z of Architecture* by Allison Lee Palmer, 2009.
109. *The A to Z of Italian Cinema* by Gino Moliterno, 2009.
110. *The A to Z of Mormonism* by Davis Bitton and Thomas G. Alexander, 2009.
111. *The A to Z of African American Theater* by Anthony D. Hill with Douglas Q. Barnett, 2009.
112. *The A to Z of NATO and Other International Security Organizations* by Marco Rimanelli, 2009.
113. *The A to Z of the Eisenhower Era* by Burton I. Kaufman and Diane Kaufman, 2009.
114. *The A to Z of Sexspionage* by Nigel West, 2009.
115. *The A to Z of Environmentalism* by Peter Dauvergne, 2009.
116. *The A to Z of the Petroleum Industry* by M. S. Vassiliou, 2009.
117. *The A to Z of Journalism* by Ross Eaman, 2009.
118. *The A to Z of the Gilded Age* by T. Adams Upchurch, 2009.
119. *The A to Z of the Progressive Era* by Catherine Cocks, Peter C. Holloran, and Alan Lessoff, 2009.
120. *The A to Z of Middle Eastern Intelligence* by Ephraim Kahana and Muhammad Suwaed, 2009.
121. *The A to Z of the Baptists* William H. Brackney, 2009.
122. *The A to Z of Homosexuality* by Brent L. Pickett, 2009.
123. *The A to Z of Islam, Second Edition* by Ludwig W. Adamec, 2009.
124. *The A to Z of Buddhism* by Carl Olson, 2009.
125. *The A to Z of United States–Russian/Soviet Relations* by Norman E. Saul, 2010.
126. *The A to Z of United States–Africa Relations* by Robert Anthony Waters Jr., 2010.
127. *The A to Z of United States–China Relations* by Robert Sutter, 2010.

128. *The A to Z of U.S. Diplomacy since the Cold War* by Tom Lansford, 2010.
129. *The A to Z of United States–Japan Relations* by John Van Sant, Peter Mauch, and Yoneyuki Sugita, 2010.
130. *The A to Z of United States–Latin American Relations* by Joseph Smith, 2010.
131. *The A to Z of United States–Middle East Relations* by Peter L. Hahn, 2010.
132. *The A to Z of United States–Southeast Asia Relations* by Donald E. Weatherbee, 2010.
133. *The A to Z of U.S. Diplomacy from the Civil War to World War I* by Kenneth J. Blume, 2010.
134. *The A to Z of International Law* by Boleslaw A. Boczek, 2010.
135. *The A to Z of the Gypsies (Romanies)* by Donald Kenrick, 2010.
136. *The A to Z of the Tamils* by Vijaya Ramaswamy, 2010.
137. *The A to Z of Women in Sub-Saharan Africa* by Kathleen Sheldon, 2010.
138. *The A to Z of Ancient and Medieval Nubia* by Richard A. Lobban Jr., 2010.
139. *The A to Z of Ancient Israel* by Niels Peter Lemche, 2010.
140. *The A to Z of Ancient Mesoamerica* by Joel W. Palka, 2010.
141. *The A to Z of Ancient Southeast Asia* by John N. Miksic, 2010.
142. *The A to Z of the Hittites* by Charles Burney, 2010.
143. *The A to Z of Medieval Russia* by Lawrence N. Langer, 2010.
144. *The A to Z of the Napoleonic Era* by George F. Nafziger, 2010.
145. *The A to Z of Ancient Egypt* by Morris L. Bierbrier, 2010.
146. *The A to Z of Ancient India* by Kumkum Roy, 2010.
147. *The A to Z of Ancient South America* by Martin Giesso, 2010.
148. *The A to Z of Medieval China* by Victor Cunrui Xiong, 2010.
149. *The A to Z of Medieval India* by Iqtidar Alam Khan, 2010.
150. *The A to Z of Mesopotamia* by Gwendolyn Leick, 2010.
151. *The A to Z of the Mongol World Empire* by Paul D. Buell, 2010.
152. *The A to Z of the Ottoman Empire* by Selcuk Aksin Somel, 2010.
153. *The A to Z of Pre-Colonial Africa* by Robert O. Collins, 2010.
154. *The A to Z of Aesthetics* by Dabney Townsend, 2010.
155. *The A to Z of Descartes and Cartesian Philosophy* by Roger Ariew, Dennis Des Chene, Douglas M. Jesseph, Tad M. Schmaltz, and Theo Verbeek, 2010.

156. *The A to Z of Heidegger's Philosophy* by Alfred Denker, 2010.
157. *The A to Z of Kierkegaard's Philosophy* by Julia Watkin, 2010.
158. *The A to Z of Ancient Greek Philosophy* by Anthony Preus, 2010.
159. *The A to Z of Bertrand Russell's Philosophy* by Rosalind Carey and John Ongley, 2010.
160. *The A to Z of Epistemology* by Ralph Baergen, 2010.
161. *The A to Z of Ethics* by Harry J. Gensler and Earl W. Spurgin, 2010.
162. *The A to Z of Existentialism* by Stephen Michelman, 2010.
163. *The A to Z of Hegelian Philosophy* by John W. Burbidge, 2010.
164. *The A to Z of the Holiness Movement* by William Kostlevy, 2010.
165. *The A to Z of Hume's Philosophy* by Kenneth R. Merrill, 2010.
166. *The A to Z of Husserl's Philosophy* by John J. Drummond, 2010.
167. *The A to Z of Kant and Kantianism* by Helmut Holzhey and Vilem Mudroch, 2010.
168. *The A to Z of Leibniz's Philosophy* by Stuart Brown and N. J. Fox, 2010.
169. *The A to Z of Logic* by Harry J. Gensler, 2010.
170. *The A to Z of Medieval Philosophy and Theology* by Stephen F. Brown and Juan Carlos Flores, 2010.
171. *The A to Z of Nietzscheanism* by Carol Diethe, 2010.
172. *The A to Z of the Non-Aligned Movement and Third World* by Guy Arnold, 2010.
173. *The A to Z of Shamanism* by Graham Harvey and Robert J. Wallis, 2010.
174. *The A to Z of Organized Labor* by James C. Docherty, 2010.
175. *The A to Z of the Orthodox Church* by Michael Prokurat, Michael D. Peterson, and Alexander Golitzin, 2010.
176. *The A to Z of Prophets in Islam and Judaism* by Scott B. Noegel and Brannon M. Wheeler, 2010.
177. *The A to Z of Schopenhauer's Philosophy* by David E. Cartwright, 2010.
178. *The A to Z of Wittgenstein's Philosophy* by Duncan Richter, 2010.
179. *The A to Z of Hong Kong Cinema* by Lisa Odham Stokes, 2010.
180. *The A to Z of Japanese Traditional Theatre* by Samuel L. Leiter, 2010.
181. *The A to Z of Lesbian Literature* by Meredith Miller, 2010.
182. *The A to Z of Chinese Theater* by Tan Ye, 2010.

183. *The A to Z of German Cinema* by Robert C. Reimer and Carol J. Reimer, 2010.
184. *The A to Z of German Theater* by William Grange, 2010.
185. *The A to Z of Irish Cinema* by Roderick Flynn and Patrick Brereton, 2010.
186. *The A to Z of Modern Chinese Literature* by Li-hua Ying, 2010.
187. *The A to Z of Modern Japanese Literature and Theater* by J. Scott Miller, 2010.
188. *The A to Z of Old-Time Radio* by Robert C. Reinehr and Jon D. Swartz, 2010.
189. *The A to Z of Polish Cinema* by Marek Haltof, 2010.
190. *The A to Z of Postwar German Literature* by William Grange, 2010.
191. *The A to Z of Russian and Soviet Cinema* by Peter Rollberg, 2010.
192. *The A to Z of Russian Theater* by Laurence Senelick, 2010.
193. *The A to Z of Sacred Music* by Joseph P. Swain, 2010.
194. *The A to Z of Animation and Cartoons* by Nichola Dobson, 2010.
195. *The A to Z of Afghan Wars, Revolutions, and Insurgencies* by Ludwig W. Adamec, 2010.
196. *The A to Z of Ancient Egyptian Warfare* by Robert G. Morkot, 2010.
197. *The A to Z of the British and Irish Civil Wars 1637–1660* by Martyn Bennett, 2010.
198. *The A to Z of the Chinese Civil War* by Edwin Pak-wah Leung, 2010.
199. *The A to Z of Ancient Greek Warfare* by Iain Spence, 2010.
200. *The A to Z of the Anglo–Boer War* by Fransjohan Pretorius, 2010.
201. *The A to Z of the Crimean War* by Guy Arnold, 2010.
202. *The A to Z of the Zulu Wars* by John Laband, 2010.
203. *The A to Z of the Wars of the French Revolution* by Steven T. Ross, 2010.
204. *The A to Z of the Hong Kong SAR and the Macao SAR* by Ming K. Chan and Shiu-hing Lo, 2010.
205. *The A to Z of Australia* by James C. Docherty, 2010.
206. *The A to Z of Burma (Myanmar)* by Donald M. Seekins, 2010.
207. *The A to Z of the Gulf Arab States* by Malcolm C. Peck, 2010.
208. *The A to Z of India* by Surjit Mansingh, 2010.
209. *The A to Z of Iran* by John H. Lorentz, 2010.

210. *The A to Z of Israel* by Bernard Reich and David H. Goldberg, 2010.
211. *The A to Z of Laos* by Martin Stuart-Fox, 2010.
212. *The A to Z of Malaysia* by Ooi Keat Gin, 2010.
213. *The A to Z of Modern China (1800–1949)* by James Z. Gao, 2010.
214. *The A to Z of the Philippines* by Artemio R. Guillermo and May Kyi Win, 2010.
215. *The A to Z of Taiwan (Republic of China)* by John F. Copper, 2010.
216. *The A to Z of the People's Republic of China* by Lawrence R. Sullivan, 2010.
217. *The A to Z of Vietnam* by Bruce M. Lockhart and William J. Duiker, 2010.
218. *The A to Z of Bosnia and Herzegovina* by Ante Cuvalo, 2010.
219. *The A to Z of Modern Greece* by Dimitris Keridis, 2010.
220. *The A to Z of Austria* by Paula Sutter Fichtner, 2010.
221. *The A to Z of Belarus* by Vitali Silitski and Jan Zaprudnik, 2010.
222. *The A to Z of Belgium* by Robert Stallaerts, 2010.
223. *The A to Z of Bulgaria* by Raymond Detrez, 2010.
224. *The A to Z of Contemporary Germany* by Derek Lewis with Ulrike Zitzlsperger, 2010.
225. *The A to Z of the Contemporary United Kingdom* by Kenneth J. Panton and Keith A. Cowlard, 2010.
226. *The A to Z of Denmark* by Alastair H. Thomas, 2010.
227. *The A to Z of France* by Gino Raymond, 2010.
228. *The A to Z of Georgia* by Alexander Mikaberidze, 2010.
229. *The A to Z of Iceland* by Gudmundur Halfdanarson, 2010.
230. *The A to Z of Latvia* by Andrejs Plakans, 2010.
231. *The A to Z of Modern Italy* by Mark F. Gilbert and K. Robert Nilsson, 2010.
232. *The A to Z of Moldova* by Andrei Brezianu and Vlad Spânu, 2010.
233. *The A to Z of the Netherlands* by Joop W. Koopmans and Arend H. Huussen Jr., 2010.
234. *The A to Z of Norway* by Jan Sjåvik, 2010.
235. *The A to Z of the Republic of Macedonia* by Dimitar Bechev, 2010.
236. *The A to Z of Slovakia* by Stanislav J. Kirschbaum, 2010.
237. *The A to Z of Slovenia* by Leopoldina Plut-Pregelj and Carole Rogel, 2010.

238. *The A to Z of Spain* by Angel Smith, 2010.
239. *The A to Z of Sweden* by Irene Scobbie, 2010.
240. *The A to Z of Turkey* by Metin Heper and Nur Bilge Criss, 2010.
241. *The A to Z of Ukraine* by Zenon E. Kohut, Bohdan Y. Nebesio, and Myroslav Yurkevich, 2010.
242. *The A to Z of Mexico* by Marvin Alisky, 2010.
243. *The A to Z of U.S. Diplomacy from World War I through World War II* by Martin Folly and Niall Palmer, 2010.
244. *The A to Z of Spanish Cinema* by Alberto Mira, 2010.
245. *The A to Z of the Reformation and Counter-Reformation* by Michael Mullett, 2010.

The A to Z of United States–Middle East Relations

Peter L. Hahn

The A to Z Guide Series, No. 131

The Scarecrow Press, Inc.
Lanham • Toronto • Plymouth, UK
2010

Published by Scarecrow Press, Inc.
A wholly owned subsidiary of
The Rowman & Littlefield Publishing Group, Inc.
4501 Forbes Boulevard, Suite 200, Lanham, Maryland 20706
http://www.scarecrowpress.com

Estover Road, Plymouth PL6 7PY, United Kingdom

Copyright © 2007 by Peter L. Hahn

All rights reserved. No part of this book may be reproduced in any form or by any electronic or mechanical means, including information storage and retrieval systems, without written permission from the publisher, except by a reviewer who may quote passages in a review.

British Library Cataloguing in Publication Information Available

Library of Congress Cataloging-in-Publication Data

The hardback version of this book was cataloged by the Library of Congress as follows:

Hahn, Peter L.
  Historical dictionary of United States–Middle East relations / Peter L. Hahn.
    p. cm. — (Historical dictionaries of U.S. diplomacy ; no. 5)
  Includes bibliographical references.
  1. Middle East—Foreign relations—United States—Dictionaries. 2. United States—Foreign relations—Middle East—Dictionaries. I. Title.

DS63.2.U5H3472 2007
327.7305603—dc22   2006035062

ISBN 978-0-8108-7557-9 (pbk. : alk. paper)

∞™ The paper used in this publication meets the minimum requirements of American National Standard for Information Sciences—Permanence of Paper for Printed Library Materials, ANSI/NISO Z39.48-1992.
Printed in the United States of America

For my father-in-law and mother-in-law,
Donald E. and Mary Anna (Wagner) Myers

Contents

Editor's Foreword *Jon Woronoff*	xvii
Acknowledgments	xix
List of Acronyms and Abbreviations	xxi
Map	xxiii
Chronology	xxv
Introduction	xxxv
THE DICTIONARY	1
Appendix: U.S. Presidents and Secretaries of State	173
Bibliography	175
About the Author	205

Editor's Foreword

Although the United States had relatively little to do with the Middle East until the Cold War, that region has since become central to its foreign policy and absorbs a disproportionate share of its action and resources. This has occurred for various reasons, the only constant one being that this is the major source of oil and natural gas. But there have been peripheral, if changing, motives as well, namely, to keep the Soviet Union away, to remove causes of conflict and instability, to increase economic development, and to spread democracy. It could hardly be said that American efforts have been particularly successful, although there were successes—at least temporarily until the next crisis erupted. Meanwhile, for several decades already, the United States has been bogged down in the most intractable of all disputes, the Arab–Israeli conflict, and more recently and without quite knowing why sucked into an occupation of Afghanistan and Iraq.

The purpose of *The A to Z of United States–Middle East Relations* is to shed some light on this very patchy area of American diplomacy. This volume is even more essential than some others because clearly what is missing is light and understanding on the part of the American policymakers and public in general, who do not know much about the region. But it also reveals the trials and tribulations of a region whose own people are not capable of sorting out their problems without the occasional external nudge. Thus, the chronology passes from one event or initiative to the next, following a rather tortuous and confusing trajectory. The introduction also considers the half century or so of history and shows its underlying trends. And the dictionary section is full of entries on events, initiatives, agreements and disagreements, wars and peace settlements, and the persons who crafted or just concocted them as well as the organizations that played an often desultory role.

The bibliography then directs readers toward other useful sources of information and opinions.

This volume was written by Peter L. Hahn, one of the leading authorities on U.S.–Middle East relations. He is professor of history at Ohio State University and executive director of the Society for Historians of American Foreign Relations, and he was recently the associate editor of *Diplomatic History*. Dr. Hahn spends much of his time researching and lecturing on the subjects dealt with here and has written several important books, one considering the earlier period, *The United States, Great Britain and Egypt, 1945–1956: Strategy and Diplomacy in the Early Cold War*; another dealing with the biggest problem, *Caught in the Middle East: United States Policy toward the Arab-Israeli Conflict, 1945–1961*; and, more broadly, *Crisis and Crossfire: The United States and the Middle East since 1945*. Given the incredibly confusing and sometimes baffling situations, he does a masterly job of presenting the facts and tracing the events and making as much sense of them as anyone can.

Jon Woronoff
Series Editor

Acknowledgments

I am grateful to several research assistants who contributed to the completion of this volume. Dustin Walcher, Chapin Rydingsward, Alexander Poster, Susan Dawson, and Paul Chamberlin conducted research and gathered the evidence that I needed to write the entries in the dictionary. Paul and Chapin also contributed significantly to the chronology and the bibliography, proofread the text of all of the dictionary entries, and made numerous, excellent suggestions for improvement. Of course, any errors or omissions that appear in the text are my responsibility.

This book is dedicated to Don and Mary Myers in admiration of their careers as educators and in appreciation for the way they welcomed me into their family a quarter century ago.

Acronyms and Abbreviations

AACOI	Anglo-American Committee of Inquiry into the Problems of European Jewry and Palestine
ADC	American-Arab Anti-Discrimination Committee
ADL	Anti-Defamation League
AIOC	Anglo-Iranian Oil Company
AIPAC	American Israeli Political Affairs Committee
AL	Arab League
ARAMCO	Arabian American Oil Company
AUB	American University of Beirut
AUC	American University in Cairo
CASOC	California-Arabian Standard Oil Company
CENTO	Central Treaty Organization
CIA	Central Intelligence Agency
CPA	Coalition Provisional Authority
DCI	Director of Central Intelligence
EIJ	Egyptian Islamic Jihad
ESM	Economic Survey Mission
IAEA	International Atomic Energy Agency
IDF	Israeli Defense Forces
IGC	Iraq Governing Council
INC	Iraqi National Congress
IPC	Iraq Petroleum Company
JCS	Joint Chiefs of Staff
JVP	Jordan Valley Plan
MEC	Middle East Command
MEDO	Middle East Defense Organization
MEFTA	Middle East Free Trade Area
NAAA	National Association of Arab Americans
NATO	North Atlantic Treaty Organization

NEA	Office of Near Eastern and African Affairs, U.S. Department of State
NSC	National Security Council
OAPEC	Organization of Arab Petroleum Exporting Countries
OIC	Organization of the Islamic Conference
OPEC	Organization of Petroleum Exporting Countries
PA	Palestinian Authority
PCC	Palestine Conciliation Commission
PLO	Palestine Liberation Organization
PNA	Palestine National Authority
UAE	United Arab Emirates
UAR	United Arab Republic
UN	United Nations
UNEF	United Nations Emergency Force
UNMOVIC	United Nations Monitoring, Verification, and Inspection Commission
UNRWA	United Nations Relief and Works Agency
UNSCOP	United Nations Special Committee on Palestine
WMD	Weapons of mass destruction

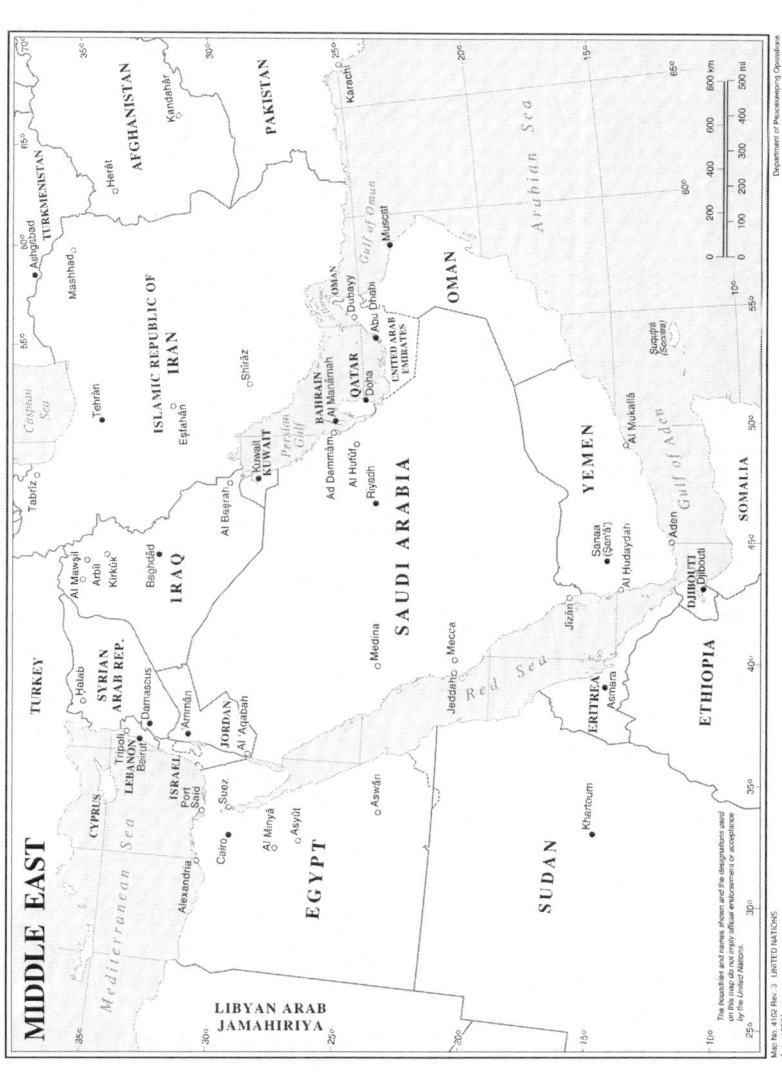

Source: United Nations, map of Middle East, no. 4102 Rev. 3 (August 2004), www.un.org/Depts/Cartographic/english/htmain.htm. Reprinted by permission of the Secretary of the United Nations Publication Board.

Chronology

1866 Daniel Bliss establishes the Syrian Protestant College, later renamed American University of Beirut.

1916 **June:** Arab revolt against the Ottoman Empire begins.

1919 Paris Peace Conference sends King-Crane Commission to Middle East. American missionaries establish the American University in Cairo.

1920 **April:** San Remo agreement gives mandates in Palestine and Iraq to Great Britain and a mandate in Syria to France.

1927 Iraq Petroleum Company, partially owned by American firms, discovers oil near Kirkuk.

1932 Abdel Aziz Ibn Saud establishes the Kingdom of Saudi Arabia.

1933 King Ibn Saud gives Standard Oil of California a 60-year oil concession.

1938 California-Arabian Standard Oil Company strikes oil at Dhahran. Kuwait Oil Company, jointly owned by Gulf Oil Corporation, strikes oil in southeastern Kuwait.

1939 **17 May:** British White Paper limits Jewish immigration into Palestine. **September:** World War II begins.

1941 **26 August:** Britain and Soviet Union occupy Iran. **16 September:** Reza Shah abdicates in favor of his son Mohammad Reza Shah.

1944 **September**: The United States recognizes Lebanon.

1945 **14 February:** President Franklin D. Roosevelt meets Saudi king Ibn Saud. **22 March:** Arab states form the Arab League. **13 November:** Anglo-American Committee is formed to investigate Palestine situation.

1946 **March:** The United States contests the Soviet occupation of Iran. **22 March:** Britain relinquishes its mandate in Transjordan. **April:** The United States recognizes Syria. **22 July:** Zionist terrorists bomb the King David Hotel in Jerusalem.

1947 **14 February:** Britain refers the Palestine question to United Nations. **12 March:** Truman Doctrine pledges aid to Greece and Turkey against the Soviet Union. **29 November:** United Nations approves partition of Palestine. **5 December:** United States embargoes arms shipments to the Middle East.

1948 **14 May:** Israel is established and recognized by the United States. **15 May:** Arab-Israeli War begins; many Palestinian Arabs flee the country. **17 September:** Count Folke Bernadotte is assassinated.

1949 **7 January:** Israel and Egypt declare a cease-fire. **31 January**: United States extends de jure recognition to Israel and Jordan. **24 February:** Egypt and Israel sign an armistice. **23 March:** Israel and Lebanon sign an armistice. **3 April:** Israel and Jordan sign an armistice. **20 July:** Israel and Syria sign an armistice.

1950 **25 May:** Tripartite Declaration regulates Western arms supply to the Middle East.

1951 **2 January:** Arabian-American Oil Company agrees to share profits equally with Saudi Arabia. **28 April:** Mohammed Mossadegh becomes prime minister of Iran and soon enacts nationalization of the Anglo-Iranian Oil Company. **22 July:** King Abdullah I of Jordan is assassinated. **October:** United States and Britain enlist France and Turkey to cosponsor the Middle East Command security pact; Egypt rejects the pact.

1952 **February:** Turkey and Greece join the North Atlantic Treaty Organization. **June:** Middle East Command is renamed Middle East Defense Organization. **23 July:** The Free Officers overthrow King Farouk. **18 September:** Camille Chamoun is elected president of Lebanon.

1953 **August:** Supporters of Shah Mohammed Reza Pahlavi, aided by the United States and Britain, overthrow Mohammed Mossadegh.

1954 **25 February:** Mohammed Naguib resigns as president of Egypt. **2 April:** United States induces Turkey and Pakistan to sign a defense consultation agreement. **17 April:** Gamal Abdel Nasser becomes premier of Egypt. **27 July:** Britain and Egypt sign a treaty to end Britain's military occupation of Egypt in June 1956.

1955 **20 February:** Anglo-American Alpha peace plan is shared with Egypt. **24 February:** Turkey and Iraq sign the Baghdad Pact (Britain, Pakistan, and Iran join in April, September, and October, respectively). **August:** Secretary of State John Foster Dulles publishes the Alpha peace plan. **27 September:** Egypt purchases Soviet weapons through Czechoslovakia.

1956 **19 July:** Secretary of State Dulles withdraws U.S. support for the Aswan Dam project. **26 July:** Egypt nationalizes Suez Canal Company, triggering Suez Crisis. **August–September:** Britain and France mobilize forces against Egypt, and United States seeks a diplomatic settlement of crisis. **29 October:** Israel invades Egypt in collusion with Britain and France. **31 October:** British and French air strikes on Egypt begin. **6 November:** Britain and France agree to a cease-fire in Egypt. **22 December:** Under U.S. pressure, British and French troops withdraw from Egypt.

1957 **1 March:** Israel agrees to remove troops from Egypt. **9 March:** Eisenhower Doctrine is formally approved. **29 June:** The United States provides Jordan $10 million in foreign aid.

1958 **1 February:** Egypt, Syria, and Yemen merge into the United Arab Republic. **4 February:** Jordan and Iraq form a union. **May:** Unrest sweeps Lebanon; officials in Beirut blame Egypt. **14 July:** Iraqi general Abdel Karim Qassim overthrows King Faisal II. **15 July:** President Dwight D. Eisenhower orders U.S. Marines to occupy Lebanon. **17 July:** British troops occupy Jordan to bolster King Hussein. **2 August:** General Fuad Chehab is elected president of Lebanon. **25 October:** U.S. troops leave Lebanon.

1959 **24 March:** Iraq resigns from Baghdad Pact.

1960 **14 September:** Organization of Petroleum Exporting Countries (OPEC) is established. **25 September:** President Eisenhower and Nasser meet for first time in New York City.

1961 **19 June:** Kuwait achieves independence from Britain. **August:** State Department appoints Joseph E. Johnson to propose solution to

Palestinian refugees issue. **5 October:** United Arab Republic dissolves after Syrians protest Egyptian dominance.

1962 **August:** President John F. Kennedy proposes Johnson plan for settlement of Palestinian refugees issue. **September:** Civil war erupts in North Yemen.

1963 **18 November:** Civilian government is overthrown in Iraq.

1964 **28 May:** The Palestine Liberation Organization (PLO) is formed.

1965 **24 August:** Egypt and Saudi Arabia agree to deescalate civil war in Yemen.

1966 **3 January:** U.S. aid released to Egypt. **2 April:** United States agrees to sell jets to Jordan. **21 June:** President Lyndon Johnson meets with King Faisal. **15 August:** Israel downs two Syrian MiGs. **7 November:** Egypt and Syria sign a mutual defense treaty.

1967 **7 April:** Israeli fighters shoot down six Syrian MiGs. **12 May:** Israelis warn of military action against Syria. **14 May:** Nasser orders Egyptian forces to advance into the Sinai. **18 May:** Nasser requests UN forces to leave Israeli–Egyptian border. **22 May:** Nasser announces blockade of the Straits of Tiran to Israeli shipping. **30 May:** Jordan enters mutual defense pact with Egypt. **1–2 June:** Mossad director Meir Amit meets U.S. officials in Washington. **5 June:** Israel attacks Egypt, inaugurating the Arab-Israeli War of 1967 (5–10 June). **22 November:** UN approves Resolution 242, calling for Arab–Israeli peace and Israeli withdrawal from occupied territories.

1968 **16 January:** Britain announces withdrawal of its forces from east of Suez. **27 December:** United States agrees to sell Israel military jets.

1969 **3 February:** Yasser Arafat becomes recognized leader of PLO. **February–August**: War of Attrition intensifies. **1 September:** Libya's King Idris is ousted by Colonel Muammar Qaddafi. **9 December:** Draft of Rogers Plan is announced.

1970 **14 April:** Yemen civil war ends. **June:** Rogers Plan B is presented to Egypt, Israel, and Jordan. **7 August:** War of Attrition ends.

7–12 September: PLO hijacks several Western airplanes and lands them in Jordan. **16 September:** Jordanian forces attack PLO forces in Jordan. **26 September:** Jordan and PLO agree to a cease-fire. **28 September:** Nasser dies of heart attack. Anwar al-Sadat becomes president of Egypt. **5 October:** United States agrees to sell Israel 180 tanks. **13 November:** Hafiz al-Asad seizes control of Syria in a coup.

1972 **February–March:** United States sells military jets to Israel and Jordan. **18 July:** Sadat expels most Soviet advisers from Egypt. **5 September:** PLO murders 11 Israeli Olympic athletes in Munich. **15 October:** Israel attacks Palestinian bases in Syria and Lebanon.

1973 **6 October:** Arab-Israeli War of 1973 begins. **10 October:** United States begins airlift to Israel. **17 October:** OPEC nations announce that they will suspend oil shipments to states supporting Israel in the conflict against Syria and Egypt. **22 October:** Cease-fire takes effect, ending the Arab-Israeli War. UN Security Council passes Resolution 338, calling for peace on the basis of Resolution 242 of 1967. **December:** United States, Soviet Union, Israel, Egypt, and Jordan meet at Geneva.

1974 **18 January:** Egypt and Israel sign a disengagement accord. **13 May:** Syria and Israel sign a disengagement accord.

1975 Civil war erupts in Lebanon. **September:** Secretary of State Henry Kissinger secures Sinai II agreement between Egypt and Israel.

1976 Syria occupies central Lebanon.

1977 PLO begins attacks on Israel from southern Lebanon. **17 May:** Menachem Begin is elected prime minister of Israel.

1978 **March:** Israel invades southern Lebanon to attack PLO and support Maronite regime in Beirut. **17 September:** Israel and Egypt sign the Camp David Accords under the auspices of President Jimmy Carter. **November:** Revolutionary unrest sweeps Iran.

1979 **January:** Shah Mohammed Reza Pahlavi flees Iran as the Ayatollah Ruhollah Khomeini seizes power. **26 March:** Egypt and Israel formally make peace and establish diplomatic relations. **16 July:** Saddam Hussein becomes president of Iraq. **4 November:** Iranian militants storm the U.S. embassy in Tehran and take U.S. personnel hostage. **25 December:** Soviet Union invades Afghanistan.

1980 January: President Carter announces the Carter Doctrine. **24 April:** U.S. attempt to rescue hostages in Iran ends in disaster. **4 September:** Iran–Iraq War of 1980–1988 begins when Iraqi forces invade Iran.

1981 20 January: Iran releases American hostages minutes after President Reagan is inaugurated. **7 June:** Israel stages preemptive strike against Iraqi nuclear reactor at Osirak. **19 August:** U.S. jets shoot down two Libyan fighters over Gulf of Sidra. **6 October:** Anwar Sadat is assassinated by Islamic extremists. **14 December:** Israel annexes Golan Heights.

1982 6 June: Israel invades Lebanon. **12 August:** U.S. envoy Philip Habib brokers deal to evacuate PLO leadership from Lebanon and send in U.S., French, and Italian peacekeepers. **23 August:** Israel influences Lebanese presidential elections to ensure victory for Bashir Gemayel. **16 September:** Bashir Gemayel is assassinated. General Ariel Sharon orders Israeli forces to reoccupy parts of Beirut. **16 September:** Phalangist militias massacre hundreds of civilians at Sabra and Shatila refugee camps; Israeli tribunal later finds Sharon complicit in massacres. **1 September:** President Reagan announces plan to settle Arab–Israeli conflict on basis of UN Resolution 242.

1983 18 April: Suicide bomb at U.S. embassy in Beirut kills 63 persons. **17 May:** Secretary of State George P. Shultz brokers peace deal between Israel and Lebanon. Israeli Defense Forces retreats to southern Lebanon, and UN peacekeepers are deployed to their north. **23 October:** Suicide bomb kills 241 U.S. Marines at barracks in Beirut.

1984 21 February: President Reagan withdraws marines from Lebanon. **November:** President Reagan opens diplomatic relations with Iraq and sends military and economic aid to regime in Baghdad.

1986 24 March: U.S. Navy sinks Libyan patrol boats in Gulf of Sidra. **5 April:** Bomb in West German disco kills two U.S. soldiers. **15 April:** President Reagan orders air strikes on Libya, killing dictator Muammar Qaddafi's adopted daughter.

1987 July: U.S. Navy begins attacking Iranian ships and oil facilities in Persian Gulf. **9 December:** Motor vehicle accident in Gaza sparks

Palestinian intifada, which in turn gives birth to the Islamic Resistance Movement (Hamas).

1988 3 July: USS *Vincennes* shoots down Iranian civilian airliner, killing 290 passengers and crew. **18 July:** Iran accepts UN cease-fire leading to the end of the Iran–Iraq War on 20 August. **30 July:** King Hussein renounces Jordanian claims to West Bank and declares that Amman will no longer represent the Palestinian people. **14 November:** Palestine National Council votes to approve UN Resolutions 242 and 338, implicitly accepting the existence of Israel. Israeli prime minister Yitzhak Shamir rejects Palestinian overture. **14–15 December:** Arafat accepts Israel's right to exist and renounces terrorism; the United States agrees to negotiate with the PLO, but Israel refuses. **21 December:** Explosion of a bomb aboard Pan Am Flight 103 over Lockerbie, Scotland, kills 270 persons.

1990 20 May: Israeli army veteran murders seven Palestinians. **30 May:** Israel thwarts terrorist attack on beach near Tel Aviv. **20 June:** Secretary of State James A. Baker suspends dialogue with the PLO. **2 August:** Iraq invades Kuwait; within days, President George H. W. Bush implements Operation Desert Shield. **29 November:** UN Security Council passes Resolution 678 authorizing member states to use force to liberate Kuwait from Iraqi control.

1991 12 January: Congress authorizes use of force to liberate Kuwait. **17 January:** President Bush orders start of Operation Desert Storm. Allied aircraft launch strikes in Iraq and Iraqi-occupied Kuwait. **24–28 February:** Allied ground offensive liberates Kuwait from Iraqi control. **March:** Secretary of State James Baker launches Arab–Israeli peace initiative. **3 April:** UN Security Council Resolution 687 orders Iraq to disarm and to submit to inspections by the International Atomic Energy Agency and the UN Special Commission. **6 April:** Official cease-fire accepted, ending Persian Gulf War. **30 October–1 November:** United States and Russia cohost the Madrid Conference.

1992 June: Yitzhak Rabin elected prime minister of Israel.

1993 January: Israeli–Palestinian negotiations begin at Oslo. **February:** Islamic terrorists explode a bomb in the parking garage of the

World Trade Center. **27 June:** U.S. cruise missiles hit Iraqi intelligence headquarters in Baghdad to retaliate for Iraqi plot to kill former president Bush. **20 August:** Declaration of Principles on Interim Self-Government Arrangements (Oslo I Accord) is announced. **13 September:** President William J. Clinton witnesses signing of Oslo I Accord in Washington.

1994 **25 February:** American-born Jewish settler kills 29 worshippers at the Mosque of Abraham in Hebron. **May:** Israeli army evacuates Gaza and Jericho. **July:** Israeli prime minister Yitzhak Rabin and King Hussein announce cessation of hostilities between Israel and Jordan. Arafat returns to Gaza and establishes Palestinian Authority. **October:** President Clinton deploys 36,000 U.S. troops to Kuwait. **26 October:** Jordanian–Israeli peace treaty is signed at White House.

1995 **24 May:** Secretary of State Warren R. Christopher brokers preliminary Israeli–Syrian agreement on security issues. **October:** Israel and Palestinian Authority sign Israeli–Palestinian Interim Agreement. **4 November:** Israeli extremist assassinates Prime Minister Yitzhak Rabin.

1996 **20 January:** Palestinian voters elect Arafat as president of Palestinian Authority. **13 March:** President Clinton and the leaders of several other nations meet at Sharm el-Sheikh to condemn terrorism. **24 April:** Palestinian National Council votes to amend charter to excise those passages that call for the violent destruction of Israel. The next day, Israel's Labor Party announces support for Palestinian statehood. **31 May:** Israeli voters elect Prime Minister Benjamin Netanyahu. **25 June:** Truck bomb kills 19 U.S. soldiers at Khobar Towers complex in Dhahran, Saudi Arabia. **August:** Osama bin Laden issues declaration of war against the United States. **September:** President Clinton orders bombing of Iraqi forces near Kurdish town of Irbil.

1998 **7 August:** Al-Qaeda orchestrates simultaneous bombings of U.S. embassies in Kenya and Tanzania. **15–22 October:** PLO chief Arafat and Israeli prime minister Benjamin Netanyahu meet with President Clinton at Wye River Conference Center in Maryland and sign Wye River Memorandum, restarting the peace process. **12–15 December**: President Clinton visits Israel and the West Bank, where he witnesses the Palestinian National Council revoke those portions of its charter calling for the destruction of Israel. **December:** Saddam Hussein halts UN Special Commission arms inspections. In response, President Clinton orders military strikes against Iraqi military facilities.

1999 **7 February:** King Hussein dies in Amman. **March:** President Clinton announces support for Palestinian statehood. **17 May:** Ehud Barak is elected prime minister of Israel. **December:** UN Security Council establishes United Nations Monitoring, Verification, and Inspection Commission to monitor Iraqi weapons programs. U.S. authorities foil terrorist attack on Los Angeles International Airport.

2000 **11–25 July:** Israeli prime minister Ehud Barak and Palestinian president Arafat meet with President Clinton at Camp David to discuss final settlement. Arafat rejects Barak's final offer. **28 September:** Ariel Sharon visits Temple Mount under heavy police guard and announces Israel's intention never to surrender the land that held the Al-Aqsa Mosque, thereby sparking the second Palestinian intifada. **October:** Al-Qaeda bombs USS *Cole* in Aden, Yemen.

2001 **February:** Sharon is elected prime minister of Israel. **30 April:** George Mitchell Commission issues final report calling for Israeli–Palestinian cease-fire. **11 September:** Al-Qaeda terrorists hijack four airliners and fly two of the planes into the twin towers of the World Trade Center in New York City and another into the Pentagon, while the fourth plane crashes in Pennsylvania; nearly 3,000 Americans and others are killed. **7 October:** U.S. and allied forces invade Afghanistan to topple the Taliban regime and capture Osama bin Laden. **November:** Taliban regime collapses. **19 November:** Secretary of State Colin Powell calls for Israeli–Palestinian peace agreement leading to two states living in peace.

2002 **29 January:** President George W. Bush warns that an "Axis of Evil"—consisting of Iraq, Iran, and North Korea—threatens U.S. security interests. **June:** Grand Council of Afghanistan agrees on blueprints for a new government. **24 June:** President Bush outlines plan for a settlement of the Israeli–Palestinian conflict and calls for new Palestinian leadership. **September:** White House releases *The National Security Strategy of the United States*, which declares administration's willingness to wage preemptive war. **12 September:** President Bush calls on the United Nations to pass new resolutions to deal with Iraq. **10–11 October:** Congress grants President Bush authority to use force against

Iraq. **8 November:** UN Security Council passes Resolution 1441, declaring Iraq in breach of previous UN resolutions and warning of "serious consequences" should Iraq fail to comply with weapons inspectors.

2003 March: U.S., British, and Australian forces launch attack on Iraq. **9 April:** Allied forces capture Baghdad. **30 April:** The Roadmap peace plan for Israel–Palestine is released. **1 May:** Mahmoud Abbas is named prime minister of the Palestinian Authority. **July:** The United States appoints Iraq Governing Council (IGC). **13 December:** U.S. soldiers capture Saddam Hussein.

2004 January: U.S. weapons inspectors conclude that Saddam Hussein had abandoned his weapons of mass destruction programs years before the invasion of Iraq. **March:** The IGC approves an interim constitution. **11 March:** Al-Qaeda terrorists bomb commuter train system in Madrid, Spain, killing 191 persons. **28 June:** Coalition Provisional Authority hands control of Iraqi regime over to Iyad Allawi. **11 November:** Yasser Arafat dies.

2005 9 January: Palestinian people elect Mahmoud Abbas as Arafat's successor. **30 January:** Elections for the Transitional National Assembly are held in Iraq. **8 February:** Israel and the Palestinian Authority agree to a cease-fire. **14 February:** Car bomb kills Rafik Hariri in Beirut, triggering mass demonstrations calling for withdrawal of Syrian troops from Lebanon. **April:** Syria withdraws troops from Lebanon. **7 July:** Terrorists detonate four bombs in and around London's public transportation system, killing 56 persons. **October**: Iraqi voters approve constitution. **15 December:** Iraqis elect a parliament.

2006 4 January: Israeli prime minister Ariel Sharon is incapacitated by a stroke. **25 January:** Hamas wins Palestinian elections. **22 February:** Golden Mosque (Al Askari) in Samarra, Iraq, is bombed by Sunni insurgents sparking a wave of violence between Sunnis and Shiites in Iraq. **28 March:** Ehud Olmert is elected prime minister of Israel. **April–May:** U.S.–Iranian showdown ensues over Iran's nuclear activities. **May:** Nuri al-Maliki in named prime minister of Iraq. **8 June:** American bombs kill terrorist Abu Musab al-Zarqawi in Iraq.

Introduction

In the early 21st century, the Middle East emerged as the most troublesome and dangerous part of the world in the eyes of the United States. On 11 September 2001, the al-Qaeda terrorist network inflicted a devastating attack on the American homeland, scarring the psyche of the American people and triggering U.S. military action in Afghanistan. President George W. Bush also launched a preemptive invasion of Iraq. The victory over the regime in Baghdad was quick and efficient, but the jubilation was tempered by criticism that the president had lacked an adequate cause for war and by the emergence of a debilitating insurgency against U.S. troops in Iraq and the new Iraqi government that the United States created and protected. Meanwhile, sustained violence between Israelis and Palestinians that had erupted in 2000 stoked passions and extremism on both sides of that dispute and prevented a resumption of the deadlocked bilateral peace process. Observers in the United States and in the Middle East openly questioned whether some enduring clash of civilizations between the United States and the Muslim world was under way, and some voices on both sides asserted that such a conflict was inevitable or even desirable.

In stark contrast to such deep involvement in the Middle East, the U.S. government took very little interest in the Middle East before 1941. In the 19th and early 20th centuries, American Christian missionaries launched ministries of evangelism and social welfare across the region and in the process established such enduring institutions as the American University of Beirut and the American University in Cairo. In the early 20th century, U.S. businesses, especially those engaged in oil prospecting, added a commercial dimension to the American experience in the Middle East. By the 1930s, U.S. oil firms owned significant shares of the corporations that pumped, refined, and transported the oil of Saudi Arabia, Iraq, Kuwait, and Bahrain to Western markets. Prior to World War II, by contrast, the U.S. government generally deferred to Great Britain and France to rule the Middle East on behalf of the Western world. Those two European powers dominated the heart of the region by exercising League of Nations mandates or perpetuating other forms of colonial control in Egypt, Palestine, Jordan, Iraq, Syria, and Lebanon.

During World War II, the U.S. government shed its traditional disinterest in the Middle East. The threats that Axis armies in North Africa or sympathetic local regimes in the Middle East would capture control of the region and thereby deliver its natural resources, military bases, and lines of communication to Nazi Germany's control or that Germany and Japan would establish a geostrategic link through the Middle East and thereby consolidate their dominance of the Old World motivated U.S. officials to contribute to the defense of the region. By 1945, the U.S. government supplied the British army that successfully defended Egypt against Axis attack, and it built military airfields in Saudi Arabia. The world war also drew attention to the importance of preserving access to the vast oil resources of the Middle East in the unsettled years that would follow the war.

The onset of the Cold War in 1945 and after led the United States to take a much greater interest in the Middle East. As they shaped a strategy for containing the Soviet Union on a global basis, American officials came to see the stability and friendship of Middle East states as vital to their national security interests. Keeping the Middle East in the Western orbit would ensure access to the region's human, strategic, and economic assets and deny these same prizes to the Soviet Union. American officials especially valued the array of military facilities, especially air bases, that the British had established in the Arab states. They calculated that possession of such bases might spell the difference between victory and defeat if a shooting war should erupt against the Soviet Union.

For such reasons, U.S. officials practiced anti-Soviet containment in the Middle East for the duration of the Cold War. Tactics of containment included professions of friendship and dispensation of financial assistance to local states. American officials also erected various security shields in the region, such as the extension of the North Atlantic Treaty Organization to Greece and Turkey in 1952, the establishment of the Baghdad Pact in 1955, and the declaration of the Eisenhower Doctrine in 1957. They also sought, with less success, to erect an interallied military command system that would integrate Egypt and other Arab powers into the Western defense orbit. The United States dispatched covert action officers to effect favorable political change in Iran in 1953 and Syria in 1956–1957. President Dwight D. Eisenhower ordered U.S. Marines to occupy Lebanon in July 1958 in order to quell a popular uprising that portended a reorientation of that country away from the West.

Two fundamental complications beset the U.S. quest to practice anti-Soviet containment in the Middle East. First, leaders in Washington endorsed the creation and survival of Israel even though Arab states and peoples vowed to resist such a state. For a combination of humanitarian, cultural, and domestic political reasons, President Harry S. Truman supported the establishment of Israel in 1948, and his successors, for varying combinations of the same reasons, deemed it impossible to withdraw such support. Certain U.S. presidents, notably Eisenhower and Jimmy Carter, promoted Arab–Israeli peace plans based on mutual concessions and compromise in hope of stabilizing the region and renewing friendship with all parties to the Arab–Israeli conflict. Other leaders in Washington, notably Presidents Richard M. Nixon and Ronald Reagan, viewed Israel as a strategic partner deserving of strong support on behalf of U.S. national security and accordingly showed less interest in Arab sensitivities. Yet consistently through the late 20th century, the U.S. support for Israel alienated many of the other states on whose cooperation U.S. anti-Soviet containment policy depended. Thus, the Soviet Union gained pockets of political influence in such states as Egypt and Syria.

The emergence of Arab and Iranian nationalism posed a second challenge to U.S. Cold War policy in the Middle East. To a certain degree, such nationalism was a by-product of a worldwide upheaval by colonized peoples against their European imperial masters, a rebellion triggered by the turmoil and dislocation of World War II. Yet U.S. officials aggravated the anti-Western dimension of such nationalism, in part by backing Israel over Arab opposition and in part by bolstering or assuming British imperial prerogatives—such as military bases in Arab states—that seemed essential for reasons of national security. Such nationalist leaders as Gamal Abdel Nasser of Egypt and Muammar al-Qaddafi of Libya constantly challenged Western interests in the region.

American officials understood in an academic sense the origins and power of nationalism, and they tried on occasion to mollify or mitigate it with political gestures and concessions. But they also occasionally decided to stifle nationalists, such as in 1953 when President Eisenhower used covert methods to overthrow Iran's anti-Western prime minister Mohammed Mossadegh on the grounds that he made his country ripe for communist exploitation. Eisenhower's action restored to power Shah Mohammed Reza Pahlavi, who ruled Iran on terms friendly to the United States for an additional 26 years. But the legacy of Eisenhower's action also aggravated the anti-American features of the revolutionary movement that captured control of Iran in 1979 and governed it for decades thereafter.

The 1970s and 1980s witnessed a sharp rise in the level of U.S. government involvement in the Middle East. Advocating such plans as the Nixon Doctrine and the strategic consensus proposal, respectively, Presidents Nixon and Reagan sought to promote U.S. security interests by partnering with local powers against creeping Soviet influence. President Carter concentrated his energy on breaking the deep-seated Arab–Israeli deadlock, achieving partial success by brokering the Egyptian–Israeli peace treaty of 1979. Reagan deemed it necessary to use military force in defense of American interests—sending warplanes to attack Libya in retaliation for that state's sponsorship of international terrorism and dispatching naval ships into the Persian Gulf to combat Iran when it rebuffed U.S. efforts to end the Iran–Iraq War—and he organized a major, effective covert operation to undermine the Soviet occupation of Afghanistan.

The end of the Cold War set the stage for a concentrated burst of U.S. military operations in the region. In the Persian Gulf War of 1990–1991, President George H. W. Bush led the United States, in conjunction with a broad international coalition, in a major military engagement designed to reverse Iraq's conquest of Kuwait. After rushing forces into Saudi Arabia to deter Iraqi expansion into that country, Bush organized a multinational counteroffensive that liberated Kuwait. The president elected not to liberate Iraq, opting instead for a long-term policy of containing Iraq through a mixture of financial sanctions, compulsory disarmament, and restrictions on military mobility. This containment policy was extended by President William J. Clinton into the early 2000s. In the process of containing Iraq, the United States developed new security partnerships with Saudi Arabia and the United Arab Emirates.

The end of the Cold War and the victory in the Persian Gulf War also created an opportunity for the United States to promote Arab–Israeli peacemaking. The U.S. victory in the gulf earned the government in Washington a degree of credibility in the minds of Middle East leaders, while the collapse of the Soviet Union removed the patron state of Arab radicals and thereby rendered them open to Western peacemaking proposals. The George H. W. Bush administration broke the ice by arranging the Madrid Conference of October 1991, which set a precedent for peaceful negotiations that stretched across the decade. In 1993, Israel and Palestinian leaders reached an agreement to negotiate their differences within a finite time frame, and in 1994, Israel and Jordan signed a formal peace treaty. American officials also pressed hard for a Syrian–Israeli treaty and for political and economic interaction between Israel and other Arab states.

Meanwhile, the United States also confronted a growing problem with terrorism. Although terrorism had declined on a global scale since the 1980s, the United States experienced an increase in major terrorist attacks by Islamic fundamentalists in the 1990s. The al-Qaeda network, which originated under the leadership of Osama bin Laden as a resistance movement against the Soviet occupation of Afghanistan in the 1980s, essentially declared war on the United States and such Middle East states as Saudi Arabia in the 1990s. In 1993–2000, al-Qaeda operatives struck at U.S. assets in the United States, Kenya, Tanzania, Saudi Arabia, and Yemen, and, most infamously, they perpetrated the 11 September 2001 attacks on the U.S. homeland. Clinton's initial strategy of combating terrorism through intelligence, law enforcement, and minimal military activity gave way after 9/11 to a more assertive and aggressive war on terrorism announced by President George W. Bush. The U.S. invasion of Afghanistan in 2001 scattered al-Qaeda's leadership and crushed the Taliban regime that had given it sanctuary.

President Bush also made the controversial decision to link the antiterrorism initiative with the older policy of containing Iraq. In the shadow of 9/11, he articulated the fear that Iraqi leader Saddam Hussein might develop weapons of mass destruction and provide them to terrorist groups, with catastrophic consequences for the American people. Although critics at home and abroad charged that the circumstances did not warrant a preemptive strike, a broad cross section of the American people, shell-shocked by 9/11, gave the president wide latitude. In March 2003, Bush ordered an invasion of Iraq that quickly demolished Saddam Hussein's regime. In an offensive lasting three weeks, U.S. and allied forces dismantled the government, scattered the army, and occupied the capital. The dictator himself became a fugitive and was caught hiding in a crude cellar near Tikrit in December 2003.

American euphoria over the rapid conquest of Iraq soon gave way to despair over a violent insurgency that swept the country. Tactical missteps by American officials—such as understaffing the U.S. occupation forces and disbanding the Iraqi army—allowed insurgents to organize an armed resistance contesting American plans for reconstruction of the country. Insurgents killed thousands of U.S. troops, foreigners working for the U.S. occupation authorities, and UN and relief workers and a much greater number of Iraqis who cooperated with the U.S. occupation. Despite such challenges, U.S. officials worked assiduously to build a stable, democratic government in Iraq, holding elections to determine Iraq's leadership and to approve a constitution written by an elected Iraqi assembly. By early 2006, however, the insurgency had fomented intersectarian violence between Shiite and Sunni Muslims that threatened to erupt into full-scale civil war.

The early 2000s also witnessed a spike in Israeli–Palestinian violence that gravely endangered the long-term American ambition of promoting Arab–Israeli peace. The violence swept across Israel and the occupied territories and stymied the Roadmap peace plan proposed by an international coalition and promoted by the United States. The death of Palestinian leader Yasser Arafat in 2004 seemed to ease tensions, and Israeli prime minister Ariel Sharon's unilateral Israeli withdrawal from the Gaza Strip in 2005 offered a basis for a settlement. The incapacitation of Sharon in early 2006, the election of a Palestinian government dominated by Hamas, and political turmoil among Palestinians, however, provided reason for pessimism among advocates of a peace settlement.

The challenge facing the United States in the Middle East was aggravated by a perceptible level of cultural discord between the American people and Middle East Muslims. While U.S. observers noted evidence of intercommunal harmony and while government leaders stressed the universalist ideals behind American policy and their own tolerance of Islamic beliefs and values, other voices suggested that the United States was on a dangerous collision course with Middle East Muslims because of religious, ethnic, ideological, and historical differences. Small minorities on both sides, in many cases inspired by religious dogma, actually advocated such a conflict.

The Dictionary

– A –

ABBAS, MAHMOUD (1935–). Moderate Palestinian political figure who succeeded **Yasser Arafat** as leader of the **Palestine Liberation Organization (PLO)**. Born in **Palestine** in 1935, Abbas became a **Palestinian refugee** when his family fled to **Syria** during the **Arab-Israeli War of 1948–1949**. While working in **Qatar** in the 1950s, he cofounded the Palestine National Liberation Movement (al-Fatah) with Arafat. Fatah soon became the majority political faction within the PLO, and Abbas held a variety of posts close to Arafat for more than three decades. Also known as Abu Mazen, Abbas earned a reputation as a moderate by pursuing peace negotiations with Israeli peace advocates in the 1970s, participating in the **Madrid Conference** of 1991, and leading the PLO delegation in the secret talks that resulted in the **Oslo Accord** in 1993.

After Arafat rejected U.S.-brokered terms of a Palestinian–Israeli settlement in 2000, U.S. leaders eyed Abbas as a desirable alternative to the PLO chief. President **George W. Bush** publicly called for the Palestinians to empower moderates who would make peace with Israel and indicated approval when Arafat named Abbas as prime minister of the **Palestinian National Authority (PNA)** in May 2003. The next month, when Bush ventured to the Middle East to sell the **Roadmap peace plan**, he elicited from Abbas an affirmation of Israel's right to exist and a pledge to suppress terrorist attacks on Israelis. After struggling against Arafat for control of Palestinian militias, however, Abbas resigned as prime minister in September 2003.

Abbas reemerged as Palestinian leader after Arafat's death in November 2004. Abbas was named PLO chairman, and in January 2005 he won election as president of the PNA with 62 percent of the vote.

As Abbas moved in 2005 to halt **terrorism** against Israel, the Bush administration hoped that he would guide the Palestinian people into an era of peace and constitutional democracy. But the victory of the **Islamic Resistance Movement (Hamas)** in Palestinian elections of January 2006 called into question Abbas's ability to lead the Palestinian people.

ABDULLAH, KING OF SAUDI ARABIA (1924–). Became the sixth king of **Saudi Arabia** in 2005. Son of **ibn Saud**, founder of Saudi Arabia, Abdullah served as mayor of Mecca before he was made commander of the Saudi National Guard in 1963. Having been named crown prince in 1982, Abdullah essentially took control of Saudi Arabia as his brother **King Fahd** slid into bad health in the late 1990s. Abdullah became king on the death of Fahd in August 2005.

King Abdullah was expected to maintain a close relationship with the United States. Although more culturally traditional than his predecessor, Abdullah recognized the importance of battling **terrorism** and seeking stability in the Middle East. As crown prince, he visited President **George W. Bush** to present a plan for Arab–Israeli peace. Although little progress was made, the two leaders reportedly struck a good rapport.

ABDULLAH I, KING OF JORDAN (1882–1951). King of **Jordan** in 1946–1951 whose diplomatic moderation earned the respect and goodwill of the United States. Abdullah participated in the Arab revolt against the Ottoman Empire during World War I and, as a reward, was named emir of **Transjordan** by Great Britain in 1921. Abdullah declared the independence of the Hashemite Kingdom of Jordan in 1946, occupied the West Bank of the Jordan River during the **Arab-Israeli War of 1948–1949**, and annexed that territory to his kingdom in 1950. Abdullah enjoyed a close security partnership with Britain, and British officers commanded his army, the Arab Legion. With his territorial ambitions in the West Bank secured, Abdullah also proved moderate toward **Israel**. He refrained from major combat operations against Israel and, alone among Arab statesmen, indicated a willingness to consider a final peace treaty with the Jewish state.

Abdullah's pro-Western and moderate orientation gained the appreciation of the United States, which provided diplomatic recognition and political support. Yet it also earned the king the wrath of Palestinian nationalists who aimed to replace Israel with a Palestinian state. In July 1951, a Palestinian gunman assassinated Abdullah in Jerusalem.

ABDULLAH II, KING OF JORDAN (1962–). Moderate monarch of **Jordan** since 1999. Born in 1962, Abdullah was educated in Britain and the United States and served in the British army before becoming a commander of armored units in the Jordanian military. He was named crown prince of Jordan only days before his father, **King Hussein**, died in February 1999. In addition to promoting relatively liberal reforms of Jordan's political economy, King Abdullah supported statehood of **Palestine** and promoted reconciliation between **Israel** and Palestinians. He condemned the **9/11** attacks on the United States and endorsed the **U.S. invasion of Afghanistan**. Although he tried to avert the U.S. invasion that started the **Iraq War** in 2003, Abdullah offered modest tactical assistance to U.S. operations in Iraq.

ACHESON, DEAN G. (1893–1971). Undersecretary of state in 1945–1947 and secretary of state in 1949–1953 who influenced the major tenets of U.S. diplomacy in the Middle East. As undersecretary, Acheson embraced the emerging national security doctrine of anti-Soviet containment and promoted the **Truman Doctrine** policy of bolstering Greece and Turkey (as well as the more momentous Marshall Plan for Western Europe). Although he enjoyed a warm relationship with President **Harry S. Truman**, Acheson criticized the president's pro-**Zionism** policies as risky for American security interests in the Arab states.

Once appointed secretary of state in 1949, Acheson concentrated most of his attention on containment policies in Europe and East Asia. Consistent with such efforts, he favored the creation of the ill-fated **Middle East Command** in 1951, and he welcomed Greece and Turkey into the **North Atlantic Treaty Organization (NATO)** in 1952. He also confronted the delicate issue of nationalism in Middle East states such as **Iran**, where he averted a possible British military strike to unseat the nationalist premier **Mohammed Mossadegh**. While favoring in principle a permanent peace settlement after the

Arab-Israeli War of 1948–1949, Acheson made no progress advancing the belligerent states toward such a goal and instead found it necessary to resolve recurrent crises that portended another round of warfare.

AFGHANISTAN, U.S. INVASION OF (2001). An invasion undertaken in response to the **9/11** terrorist attacks and directed against Afghanistan's Taliban regime. Since the mid-1990s, the Taliban had given sanctuary to **al-Qaeda** terrorists, including **Osama bin Laden**, and the United States had launched air strikes on al-Qaeda targets in the country. On 7 October 2001, less than one month after 9/11, U.S. and allied forces launched devastating air strikes against al-Qaeda camps, airfields, and barracks. Some 500 special forces and Central Intelligence Agency paramilitary officers then attacked Taliban strongholds in partnership with fighters of the indigenous Northern Alliance, which had long resisted Taliban authority. The Taliban collapsed in November, its remnants taking refuge in the country's southeastern mountains, where they were subjected to continual air bombardment.

The **United Nations** sponsored talks among Afghan factions in Bonn, Germany, leading to the signing on 5 December of an agreement to write a new constitution for the country, appoint a transitional government, and hold elections by 2004. In June 2002, the Grand Council of Afghanistan agreed on blueprints for a new government, and Hamid Karzai was appointed interim president. The Afghan people elected Karzai president in a national election in October 2004. Yet the Karzai government remained dependent on the continued presence of U.S. military forces in the country, and remnants of the deposed Taliban regime continued military resistance against the government in Kabul through mid-2006.

AHMADINEJAD, MAHMOUD (1956–). President of **Iran** who vocalized anti-U.S. criticism and anti-Israeli extremism after taking office in August 2005. Ahmadinejad supported the Ayatollah **Ruhollah Khomeini** during the Iranian Revolution of 1979 and served in the Revolutionary Guards in the 1980s. After a stint as a university lecturer, Ahmadinejad was appointed mayor of Tehran in 2003. Shunned by the moderate president **Mohammed Khatami**, Ahmadinejad ran for president in 2005 on a platform of promoting social justice and defending **Iran's nuclear program** against foreign intervention. Gaining the support of conservative clerics such as the Ayatollah **Seyed Ali Khamenei**, Ahmadinejad defeated political veteran **Akbar Hashemi Rafsanjani** and thus became the first noncleric to sit as Iran's president in more than two decades.

Statements by Ahmadinejad in late 2005 raised alarm throughout the West. The president spoke critically of the U.S. role in the **Iraq War** and indicated reluctance to restore diplomatic relations with the United States. He defied international pressure to suspend Iran's nuclear research program. Charging that Europeans rather than Palestinians should have paid atonement for the Holocaust, Ahmadinejad also publicly declared that **Israel** should be destroyed or at least relocated to Europe.

AL-QAEDA. A shadowy network of fundamentalist Muslim warriors devoted to the use of violence and **terrorism** against the United States and certain Middle East governments. In Arabic, *al-Qaeda* literally means "the Base," in reference to a database of fighters compiled by the Saudi national **Osama bin Laden** in the 1980s. Bin Laden's database listed Muslim warriors who, motivated by a militant version of Islam, flocked to Afghanistan to resist the Soviet occupation of that country.

Although the United States encouraged the anti-Soviet resistance in Afghanistan, al-Qaeda turned against the United States in the 1990s. The decision by **King Fahd** to welcome American soldiers to **Saudi Arabia** after the August 1990 conquest of **Kuwait** by **Iraq** enraged bin Laden because it violated Muslim strictures against the presence of infidels in Muslim holy lands. Thus, bin Laden revived the al-Qaeda network and plotted to use terrorism both to oust American troops from Saudi territory and to overthrow the Saudi regime that had welcomed them. Al-Qaeda also targeted **Egypt** and **Israel** for attack. Under the protection of the Taliban regime in Afghanistan after 1996, al-Qaeda operatives trained for military action and covert operations, liaised with several Muslim terrorist groups, and planned terrorist attacks against local governments and the United States. By 2000, al-Qaeda was believed to have established loosely connected cells in some 50 countries around the world.

Al-Qaeda perpetrated numerous acts of terrorism in the 1990s. Major attacks against the United States included the bombings of the U.S. embassies in Kenya and Tanzania in August 1998 and the USS *Cole* in Aden Harbor in October 2000. The U.S. government fought back with means including defense (such as foiling a plot to attack Los Angeles International Airport in December 1999), law enforcement (such as the May 2001 conviction and life imprisonment of four al-Qaeda operatives involved in the African embassy bombings), and offensive action (such as missile strikes on al-Qaeda camps in Afghanistan in August 1998 to retaliate for the embassy bombings and to try to kill bin Laden).

The American battle against al-Qaeda reached dramatic levels in the early 2000s. Al-Qaeda conducted spectacular assaults on Washington, D.C., and New York City on **9/11**, killing some 3,000 persons and scarring the psyche of the American people. President **George W. Bush** responded by ordering the **U.S. invasion of Afghanistan**, which demolished the Taliban regime and scattered the remnants of al-Qaeda. Although al-Qaeda's military commander Muhammed Atef died in the American assault on Afghanistan, bin Laden remained at large for years after the invasion.

ALBRIGHT, MADELEINE K. (1932–). A former professor of international relations who served as ambassador to the **United Nations** (1993–1997) and secretary of state (1997–2001) under President **William J. Clinton**. Born in Czechoslovakia and naturalized as a citizen in 1957, Albright was the first woman appointed as secretary of state and thus the highest-ranking women ever to serve in the U.S. government.

Albright passionately and tirelessly implemented Clinton's policies in the Middle East. As ambassador to the United Nations, she worked hard to enforce UN resolutions designed to contain the power and influence of **Iraq**'s leader **Saddam Hussein**. As secretary of state, she became personally involved in Arab–Israeli peace negotiations, traveling repeatedly to the Middle East and participating in several major meetings in the region and elsewhere, often at Clinton's side.

ALLAWI, IYAD (1946–). Political leader in **Iraq** who served as prime minister of the government empowered after the U.S. invasion during the **Iraq War** of 2003–. Trained as a physician, Allawi belonged to Iraq's Baath Party before he fled in 1971 to exile in Great Britain, where he survived an assassination attempt perpetrated by agents of **Saddam Hussein** in 1978. In 1991, Allawi founded the Iraqi National Accord, a group of anti-Hussein dissidents who received funding from the Central Intelligence Agency and who launched a failed coup against Hussein in 1996. After the invasion ousted Hussein from power in 2003, Allawi returned to Iraq, joined the U.S.-appointed governing council, and became interim prime minister in June 2004. His popularity among Iraqis tainted by his association with Western intelligence agencies, Allawi proved unable to retain a position of power after the Iraqi democratic elections of 2005.

ALPHA PEACE PLAN. An Anglo-American plan, floated in 1955, for a permanent Arab–Israeli peace settlement. Conceived and drafted by officials of the U.S. State Department and the British Foreign Office and approved enthusiastically by President **Dwight D. Eisenhower**, the Alpha plan (named for the code name assigned to it during its formulation on a top secret basis) proposed that **Israel** and its Arab adversaries would make peace; that Israel would repatriate a fixed number of **Palestinian refugees** and that the Arab states would absorb the remainder; that the states of the region would share water resources on an equitable basis and agree to border adjustments that would establish contiguity between **Egypt** and **Jordan**; that the Arab states would terminate their economic sanctions on Israel, including the Suez Canal blockade; and that an entity of the **United Nations** would oversee Jerusalem. As an incentive to accept the plan, the United States would dispense more than $1 billion over five years, and Great Britain and the United States would guarantee the revised Arab–Israeli borders against violent changes.

American and British officials publicized the Alpha plan in 1955, but it fell flat. Neither Israel nor the Arab states showed interest in making the concessions demanded by the plan's compromise terms. Moreover, discussion of the plan was accompanied by a sharp increase in tensions within the Middle East, manifest in such episodes as the Israeli raid at Gaza in February 1955 and an ensuing wave of violence along the Egyptian–Israeli border. Egypt's criticism of **Iraq** for joining the **Baghdad Pact** and its purchase of Soviet weapons also soured the prospects for peacemaking. By the end of 1955, the plan had clearly failed.

AMERICAN-ARAB ANTI-DISCRIMINATION COMMITTEE (ADC). A civil rights organization committed to countering negative cultural stereotypes about Americans of Arab descent. Founded in 1980 by former U.S. senator James G. Abourzek, the ADC soon became the largest Arab-American organization in the United States. It earned a reputation for promoting positive images about Arab peoples in American mass media, providing legal counsel to victims of ethnic discrimination, and lobbying federal government officials on behalf of Palestinian and other Arab peoples.

AMERICAN ISRAEL PUBLIC AFFAIRS COMMITTEE (AIPAC). A powerful pro-**Israel** political lobby in the United States. Founded in 1954 by I. L. (Si) Kenen, former chair of the American Zionist Committee, AIPAC grew by the early 2000s to more than 60,000 members organized by professional staff members at a Washington, D.C., headquarters and nine regional offices. The group earned a reputation for effective political lobbying of elected officials through personal meetings, letter writing, publications, political action, and campaign contributions. In 2003, AIPAC claimed that it pushed through Congress more than 100 pro-Israel measures per year.

AMERICAN UNIVERSITY OF BEIRUT (AUB). A major institution of higher learning in **Lebanon** and an example of American progressivism and cultural expansion into the Middle East. In 1862, the American Board of Commissioners for Foreign Missions directed Dr. Daniel Bliss to establish a college and medical school in Lebanon. In 1866, after raising funds and securing a charter from the State of New York, Bliss opened the Syrian Protestant College, with 16 students. In 1920, the school was renamed the American University of Beirut. In 1926, it gained accreditation by the New York State Board of Regents.

AUB admitted women to its nursing school in 1905 and to its baccalaureate programs in 1924. By the mid-20th century, the university had achieved a worldwide reputation for excellence in the arts and sciences, medicine, agriculture, and engineering. It remained a private, nonsectarian, independent university with instruction in English. By 2002, AUB claimed more than 66,000 alumni, many of whom became political, business, and medical elites throughout the Middle East.

AUB remained in operation through the Lebanese civil war of the 1970s to 1990s. Yet violence wracked the institution: President Malcolm Kerr was assassinated on campus by assailants linked to Islamic Jihad in January 1984, and unidentified perpetrators exploded a bomb that demolished the university's landmark College Hall as well as its library in November 1991.

AMERICAN UNIVERSITY IN CAIRO (AUC). A small but significant institution of higher learning founded by Americans in the early 20th century. Dr. Charles A. Watson, born in **Egypt** to American missionaries, was appointed in 1902 to direct Middle East operations by the United Presbyterian Board of Foreign Missions. Seeking to improve Egypt through rigorous, liberal education and to deepen Americans' understanding of the Middle East, Watson founded the AUC in 1919 and served as its president until 1944. Twenty students earned diplomas in the first graduating class in 1924, and women were enrolled in 1928. The New York State Board of Regents accredited the school in 1924.

AUC remained open through World War II and the postwar political troubles in the Middle East, even though Western faculty were evacuated when German soldiers approached Cairo in 1942 and when Israeli troops invaded Egypt in 1967. AUC grew substantially in the late 20th century, from some 400 students in 1960 to more than 5,000 in 2001. Among its 13,000 alumni were many government officials, businessmen, journalists, and Suzanne Mubarak, wife of Egyptian president **Hosni Mubarak**.

ANGLO-AMERICAN COMMITTEE OF INQUIRY INTO THE PROBLEMS OF EUROPEAN JEWRY AND PALESTINE (AA-COI). A binational commission appointed by President **Harry S. Truman** and British prime minister Clement Attlee to investigate the situation in **Palestine** in 1945–1946. Attlee proposed the commission to involve the United States in Palestinian affairs after Truman, for domestic political reasons, publicly endorsed the Zionist demand that Great Britain suspend its current policy and admit 100,000 Jewish immigrants to Palestine. Formed in November 1945, the 12-member AACOI held hearings, gathered data, and toured Jewish displaced persons camps in Europe. In its final report of 20 April 1946, the AACOI recommended that Britain admit 100,000 Jews to Palestine, abolish restrictions on land purchases by Jews, and establish an international trusteeship to govern Palestine. It advised against Jewish or Palestinian statehood. Although it was soon overshadowed by the **United Nations Special Committee on Palestine**, the AACOI marked the first involvement of the U.S. government in the Arab–Zionist conflict.

ANTI-DEFAMATION LEAGUE (ADL). Founded in Chicago in 1913, the ADL combated discrimination and racism against Jews and other minorities in American law, politics, and popular culture. In the 1970s, the ADL established chapters in Europe and **Israel**, promoted Holocaust awareness programs, and advocated Israeli political interests in the aftermath of the **Arab-Israeli War of 1967** and the **Arab-Israeli War of 1973**. The ADL was affiliated with B'nai B'rith International, a worldwide Jewish organization that promoted human rights, humanitarian reform, and Israeli interests and combated anti-Semitism.

AOUN, MICHEL (1935–). Military officer and political leader of **Lebanon**. Aoun became commander of the Lebanese army in 1984 and prime minister in 1988. In 1989, he initiated hostilities against Syrian forces that had occupied his country for more than a decade. **Syria** deposed Aoun in 1990, acting with the complicity of the United States, which sought Syrian support in the **Persian Gulf War** of 1990–1991. Aoun secured asylum in France in 1991. In May 2005, he returned from exile and won a seat in the Lebanese parliament, where he presided over a substantial bloc of votes.

ARAB–ISRAELI CONFLICT. A long and tumultuous conflict between Israel and its Arab neighbors that challenged U.S. diplomats from the 1940s to the early 2000s. The conflict originated in competing claims over **Palestine** and escalated into a multinational struggle over many issues. At the beginning of the 20th century, Palestine was administered by the moribund Ottoman Empire. Arab residents of the land, beginning to embrace a sense of nationalism, aspired to achieve territorial independence as a nation-state. Imbued with **Zionism**, European Jews flocked to Palestine by the thousands both to escape manifestations of anti-Semitism in Europe and to reestablish their people's ancient claims to the land of the Jewish Bible. After Ottoman power collapsed in World War I, Great Britain assumed control of Palestine as a mandate of the League of Nations. But the British proved unable to govern effectively given the mounting tension and outbursts of violence between Jews and Arabs and the determination of both groups to challenge British influence.

The modern Arab–Israeli conflict erupted shortly after World War II. That global conflagration so weakened Britain's imperial power that it proved unable to retain the mandate, and in 1947 it notified the **United Nations** that it would withdraw from Palestine in 1948. The **United Nations Special Committee on Palestine** recommended a **partition of Palestine** into a Jewish state and an Arab state. The Jews of Palestine accepted the partition plan and declared the independence of **Israel** on 14 May 1948. The Arabs opted to resist partition, to aspire to control all of Palestine, and thus to destroy Israel with force. Five neighboring Arab states—**Egypt**, **Jordan**, **Syria**, **Lebanon**, and **Iraq**—all sent armed forces into Palestine to assist in the effort of crushing Israel. But the Israeli army performed splendidly on the battlefields while Arab forces failed to coordinate their military maneuvers or even to invest themselves fully in their common struggle. By early 1949, when a series of armistice agreements ended the **Arab-Israeli War of 1948–1949**, Israel had not only survived but also expanded its territory well beyond the original partition borders.

During this critical phase of the Arab–Israeli conflict, U.S. officials took crucial steps to assist in the creation of Israel. President **Harry S. Truman** supported immigration of Jews into British Palestine, backed the partition resolution, and recognized the state of Israel minutes after its creation. Wary of incurring any commitment to fight for Israel and resolved to protect U.S. vital interests in Arab states, by contrast, the Truman administration refrained from arming Israel or sending external forces to defend it.

The armistices of 1949 ended the hostilities but did not achieve a final peace settlement. In the following decades, in fact, Israel and its Arab neighbors squared off repeatedly: in the **Suez Crisis** of 1956, the **Arab-Israeli War of 1967**, the **War of Attrition**, the **Arab-Israeli War of 1973**, and the **Israeli invasion of Lebanon** in 1982. In addition, low-intensity warfare frequently simmered along Israel's borders, as infiltrators from Arab states committed acts of violence on Israeli territory and Israel retaliated with overwhelming force against targets on Arab land. Angry arguments erupted over a host of issues, including the political status of Jerusalem, the fate of more than 1 million **Palestinian refugees** from land that Israel occupied, Israel's right to send ships through the Suez Canal and the Straits of Tiran, and the control of territory and demarcation of borders. By the 1960s, Palestinians had organized the **Palestine Liberation Organization (PLO)**, which used diplomacy to win allies around the region and terrorism to punish Israel. During the **Persian Gulf War** of 1990–1991, Iraq fired missiles at Israel in a futile bid to shatter the international coalition arrayed against Baghdad.

American officials aspired to settle this controversy on terms consistent with their Cold War objective of containing Soviet influence and with their domestic political consensus in favor of preserving Israel. President **Dwight D. Eisenhower** formulated the **Alpha Peace Plan** in 1954–1955, but it was uniformly rejected by both sides to the dispute. President **John F. Kennedy** aimed to resolve the Palestinian refugee issue by promoting the **Joseph E. Johnson** Plan, to no avail. In the aftermath of the Arab-Israeli War of 1973, Secretary of State **Henry Kissinger** launched the so-called **shuttle diplomacy**, an initiative to disengage combatant forces from battle fronts. The resulting political process led to the **Camp David Accords**, brokered by President **Jimmy Carter** in 1978, and the Egyptian–Israeli peace treaty of 1979.

In the late 1980s, the Arab–Israeli conflict began to shift from an international dispute to a clash between Israel and the Palestinian inhabitants of Israeli-occupied land. During the first **intifada** of the late 1980s, Palestinians rebelled against Israeli occupation, and Israeli authorities responded with firm measures. Then, the end of the Cold War and the collapse of the Soviet Union neutralized aspects of the international context that had aggravated the Arab–Israeli conflict, such as Soviet support of Arab states aligned against Israel. Those developments, plus the U.S. victory in the Persian Gulf War of 1990–1991, gave birth to a renewed U.S. commitment to peacemaking and forced Arab and Israeli leaders to submit, to a degree, to American leadership.

Thus, the 1990s witnessed a concentrated burst of peacemaking led by the United States. Israel and Jordan signed a formal peace treaty in 1994. Israel withdrew its occupation forces from southern Lebanon in 2000. Israel and the PLO agreed to a variety of steps that gave the Palestinians partial autonomy over designated portions of the West Bank and the Gaza Strip and raised the prospect of Palestinian statehood.

Yet the 1990s peace process fell short of complete success. Energetic U.S. efforts to broker an Israeli–Syrian peace treaty failed to reach fruition. In 2000, the second intifada erupted across the occupied territories and within Israel itself. President **George W. Bush** formulated the **Roadmap peace plan** in 2003, but the **U.S. invasion of Iraq** distracted him from peacemaking ventures. By 2005, the intifada waned as Israel practiced firm countermeasures and as Palestinians elected new leadership following the death of **Yasser Arafat** in 2004. But the election of a **Hamas** majority in the Palestinian parliament in early 2006 raised doubts about the longevity of the truce.

ARAB-ISRAELI WAR OF 1948–1949. An armed engagement between **Israel** and five of its Arab neighbors. The war erupted in May 1948 when Israel declared its independence and **Egypt**, **Jordan**, **Syria**, **Lebanon**, and **Iraq** invaded **Palestine** to crush the new Jewish state. In the early round of fighting, which raged from 15 May to 18 July (interrupted only by a cease-fire from 8 June to 8 July), Israelis scored a series of battlefield victories that ensured the survival of their state and gained land beyond the partition lines. In a second round of fighting in mid-October, Israel secured control of Beersheba and the northern Negev, and in a third round in December 1948–January 1949, Israel occupied the southern Negev, thus gaining access to the Red Sea.

The United States became increasingly involved in international efforts to quell the fighting. The State Department endorsed the appointment on 20 May of Count **Folke Bernadotte** of Sweden as mediator for the **United Nations**, encouraged the belligerents to honor the cease-fire resolutions passed by the UN Security Council on 22 May and 15 July, and maintained an arms embargo on both sides to the conflict. In September, the State Department vigorously promoted the **Bernadotte Plan**; however, President **Harry S. Truman** scotched it under domestic political pressure. In early 1949, when an Israeli southern offensive threatened to entangle British forces stationed in Egypt, Truman pressured the Israelis to desist the attack and he authorized the State Department to secure a UN cease-fire resolution that took effect on 7 January. **Ralph Bunche**, a U.S. diplomat working on the staff of the UN secretary-general, negotiated a series of bilateral armistices between Israel and Egypt (signed on 24 February), Lebanon (23 March), Jordan (3 April), and Syria (20 July). Iraq agreed simply to withdraw its forces from the battlefield. Subsequent U.S. efforts to arbitrate a permanent peace treaty proved fruitless.

ARAB-ISRAELI WAR OF 1967. A brief but momentous Arab–Israeli war fought on 5–10 June 1967 and known in the West as the Six Day War. Festering Arab–Israeli disputes produced a sharp spike in international tensions in early 1967, and **Egypt** and **Syria** took action that presaged an attack on **Israel**. Fearful that a sudden, overwhelming assault might destroy their country, Israeli leaders launched a preemptive attack on Egypt on 5 June and in subsequent days engaged in hostilities with **Jordan** and Syria as well. By the time the **United Nations** brokered a truce that restored calm on 10 June, Israel had inflicted major defeats on all three Arab powers and occupied enormous portions of their territory (the Gaza Strip and the Sinai Peninsula, from Egypt; the West Bank, from Jordan; and the Golan Heights, from Syria).

The war dramatically recast the political dynamics of the **Arab–Israeli conflict**. Israelis became euphoric that they had survived the mortal threats arrayed against them, scored a huge victory, and captured land that they could use as bargaining chips to shape Arab behavior. Arab leaders were devastated by their enormous defeat and even blamed the United States for it by making false charges that U.S. military forces assisted the Israeli assault on Egypt. The war would prove to be a watershed event in the decline of influence among secular Arab nationalist leaders such as **Gamal Abdel Nasser** of Egypt and the rise of radical and religious forces among Arab peoples. In subsequent years, Israel's occupation of the territories would become the major point of contention between Israel and its Arab neighbors as well as between Israel and the Palestinian people.

The **Lyndon B. Johnson** administration, distracted by the Vietnam War, did little to avert the war before it started (and, according to some historians, may have subtly approved the Israeli decision to strike preemptively). Washington encouraged the cease-fire arrangements that brought the fighting to an early end and promoted passage in November 1967 of UN Security Council Resolution 242, which called for Israel to yield territories it had occupied in exchange for peace and recognition from its adversaries.

ARAB-ISRAELI WAR OF 1973. A major war of October 1973 that pitted **Egypt** and **Syria** against **Israel**. (The conflict is known as the Yom Kippur War, the Ramadan War, and the October War.) The war originated in the uneasy truces that followed the **Arab-Israeli War of 1967** and the **War of Attrition**. Egyptian president **Anwar Sadat**, who consolidated power in Cairo after the death of **Gamal Abdel Nasser** in 1970, sought to recover sovereignty over the Sinai peninsula by expelling Soviet advisers from Egypt and by seeking Western support of a diplomatic settlement. Yet the **Richard M. Nixon** administration misread Sadat's signals and bolstered Israel as the U.S. client state under the **Nixon Doctrine**. Thus, Sadat calculated that he could best serve his interests by coordinating with Syria an attack on Israel.

Warfare erupted on 6 October 1973, when Egyptian and Syrian armies launched a surprise offensive against Israeli forces in the occupied Sinai and Golan. Catching the Israelis off guard, the Arab armies made impressive advances for several days. Urgently provisioned with massive quantities of U.S. weapons, however, Israel repelled the Arab offensives, reoccupied Golan and reached within 20 miles of Damascus, and crossed to the west side of the Suez Canal, thereby isolating the entire Egyptian Third Army in the Sinai. Although Israel thus expanded its territorial reach before the cease-fire took effect on 22 October, the early Arab advances, and the relatively high Israeli casualty rates convinced the Arab world that the war was a draw, that Israel was not invincible, and that Arab states had recovered their prestige and honor so badly mauled in 1967.

Surprised by the outbreak of war, Secretary of State **Henry A. Kissinger** took action to end the fighting and to build a foundation for a lasting peace. Initially hoping that the war would end indecisively so that he could negotiate a lasting territorial settlement, he refused to arm either side, and he tried to persuade both sides to accept a cease-fire on 12 October. Flushed with success, Egypt refused. Thus, Kissinger convinced President Nixon to authorize the massive airlift of military supplies to Israel as a means of securing a U.S. diplomatic role in the conflict, ensuring an indecisive outcome to the fighting, matching the Soviet arms supply to Arab armies, pleasing domestic public opinion, and perhaps deterring Israel from resorting to nuclear weapons.

Even as he arranged to arm the Israelis, Kissinger deftly moved to end the war on terms favorable to the United States. He flew to Moscow to negotiate with the Soviets the terms of United Nations Security Council Resolution 338, passed on 22 October, which called on the belligerents to honor a cease-fire and to negotiate a permanent peace agreement on the basis of UN Resolution 242 of 1967. Then he flew to Tel Aviv to secure Israeli acceptance of the cease-fire.

American leaders also endured a superpower crisis. When Israeli forces maneuvered in Egypt in violation of the cease-fire resolution, Soviet premier Leonid Brezhnev warned on 24 October that he would send Soviet troops to defend Egypt if necessary. As Kissinger worked through diplomatic channels to rein in the Israelis and to mollify the Soviets, Nixon placed U.S. worldwide forces on alert and leaked reports of this move to the news media, in part to demonstrate U.S. firmness to the Soviets, in part to establish Washington's prestige in the eyes of Middle East leaders, and in part to deflect attention from the Watergate scandal. The Israeli troop movements ground to a halt on 25 October.

The 1973 war proved costly to the United States. Angry at U.S. rearmament of Israel, Arab oil-producing states imposed an **Arab oil embargo** on the United States and other Western powers, seriously damaging their economies. The war also eroded the appeal of Nixon's détente strategy by revealing that U.S.–Soviet rivalry remained intense on peripheral issues, such as the Arab–Israeli conflict, despite the apparent relaxation of tensions on strategic questions. The war also inflamed Arab–Israeli passions and limited the U.S. image of impartiality by encouraging the pro-Israel tendency in American public opinion.

ARAB LEAGUE. Formally known as the League of Arab States, an association of Arab countries founded in the 1940s to advance common interests of member states and promote their political and cultural unity without infringing on their national sovereignty. **Egypt, Iraq, Lebanon,** North **Yemen, Saudi Arabia,** and **Jordan** agreed to form the league at a conference in Alexandria in 1944, and in 1945 they signed the Arab League Pact, which made the partnership official. Egypt exercised leadership in forming the league, perhaps inspired by British officials who encouraged the notion of Arab unity as a bulwark against Nazi influence. The league has been based in Cairo and dominated by Egyptian officials since its inception, save for the 1979–1989 period, in which Egypt was expelled for making peace with **Israel**. By the early 2000s, the league counted 21 members (including the **Palestine Liberation Organization**). Yet its loose structure and the preservation of autonomy among member states limited the league's political influence and significance.

League officials routinely promoted various cultural and economic programs, such as educational reform, law enforcement collaboration, and free trade. The association also took official stances on several major international issues, such as opposing the establishment of Israel in 1948–1949, censuring Egypt for making peace with Israel in 1979, censuring Iraq's invasion of **Kuwait** in 1990, criticizing the **U.S. invasion of Iraq** in 2003, and offering conditional peace terms to Israel in 2002 and 2005. Disagreements among member states and the nonbinding nature of the league's resolutions, however, limited the importance of these decisions as factors in the formulation of U.S. foreign policy.

ARAB OIL EMBARGO. A move by Arab states in October 1973 to curtail oil exports as a means of shaping Western diplomatic behavior. Angered by the outcome of the **Arab-Israeli War of 1973** and the legacy of U.S. support for **Israel, Saudi Arabia** led the **Organization of Petroleum Exporting Countries (OPEC)** to declare an embargo on the sale of crude oil to Western countries and an oil production cutback of 5 percent per month until Israel withdrew from the territories it had occupied in 1967. In actuality, the embargo proved to be limited, as most OPEC members canceled the production cutbacks in early 1974 and proved unable to demonstrate effective control on worldwide oil sales.

Yet the embargo had dramatic consequences in the West. During the several weeks of the announced embargo, the price of a barrel of oil quadrupled from $2.50 to $11.00. In the United States, gasoline shortages at local filling stations—perhaps the result of internal regulatory measures that predated the Arab action—created the popular belief that the oil embargo disrupted the daily lives of Americans. President **Richard M. Nixon** decided to save energy by dimming the lights on the national Christmas tree in 1973, confirming such popular thinking.

Although short lived, the oil embargo of 1973 had important long-term consequences. Americans for a time showed interest in conservation measures (including more fuel-efficient vehicles) and in developing alternative sources of energy. In 1976–1994, the U.S. government established the Strategic Petroleum Reserve, a network of storage facilities capable of storing some 563 million barrels of crude oil, to be used to mitigate the economic shocks of future disruptions in oil supply. (Twenty-one million barrels were sold from the Reserve to arrest a price spike during the **Persian Gulf War** of 1990–1991.) Oil production was developed in Canada, Russia, Mexico, and the North Sea, leading to a decline in OPEC's share of the global market from 70 percent in 1973 to 40 percent in 2002.

ARABIAN-AMERICAN OIL COMPANY (ARAMCO). A company owned by American firms that dominated the oil industry of **Saudi Arabia** for several decades. In May 1933, the newly established Kingdom of Saudi Arabia granted an exclusive 60-year oil concession to Standard Oil of California (SOCAL, later Chevron) in exchange for 16 percent of the company's revenues. In 1936, SOCAL formed a joint venture with the Texas Company (later Texaco), alternatively known as Caltex or the California-Arabian Standard Oil Company (CASOC), and the new firm struck a major oil find at Dhahran in 1938. In 1944, CASOC was renamed the Arabian-American Oil Company (ARAMCO). In 1948, shares in ARAMCO were acquired by Standard Oil of New Jersey (later Exxon) and Socony

Vacuum (later Mobil). The company grew dramatically in the 1940s as World War II and the Cold War as well as popular consumerism generated demand for its products.

In the late 20th century, Saudi Arabia acquired a greater share of ARAMCO's oil revenues and eventually nationalized the company. Under an elaborate scheme concocted in 1950, the U.S. government conceded tax reductions to ARAMCO, enabling the company to increase Saudi Arabia's share of oil revenues from 16 to 50 percent. Officials in Washington designed the deal to stabilize the Saudi throne, affirm their emerging Cold War partnership with Saudi Arabia, and avert the prospect of nationalization of the company. The Saudi government purchased a 25 percent share of ARAMCO in 1973, a 60 percent share in 1974, and a 100 percent share in 1980. In 1984, a Saudi became president of the company for the first time, and in 1988, the Saudi government created the Saudi Arabian Oil Company, known as Saudi Aramco, to administer the country's oil industry. By the early 2000s, Saudi Aramco controlled some 25 percent of the world's proven oil reserves and operated a vast network of oilfields, pipelines, refineries, and other facilities in several countries. *See also* TARIKI, SHEIK ABDULLAH; YAMANI, AHMED ZAKI.

ARAFAT, YASSER (1929–2004). Longtime leader of the Palestinian people who made a transition from militant to aspiring statesman. Although an Egyptian birth certificate indicates that he was born in Cairo, Arafat claimed to have been born in Jerusalem, perhaps to spin a myth affirming his attachment to the city. In either case, Arafat was raised by an aunt in Jerusalem for four years and was educated as a civil engineer in **Egypt**. As a youth, he smuggled weapons to Arabs living in mandatory **Palestine**, and as a young man he fought with the Muslim Brotherhood of Egypt in the Gaza area during the **Arab-Israeli War of 1948–1949**.

American officials gradually came to know Arafat as a terrorist. While employed in **Kuwait** in 1958, Arafat cofounded al-Fatah, a militant group that called for the destruction of **Israel**, and in 1964 he moved to **Jordan** to organize terrorist strikes against Israel. Al-Fatah joined the **Palestine Liberation Organization (PLO)** in 1964, and in 1969 Arafat became chairman of the PLO executive committee. Under his leadership, the PLO conducted a long-term campaign of violence against Israel, first from bases in Jordan, until **King Hussein** expelled them in the **Black September** 1970 crackdown; then from bases in southern **Lebanon**, until Israel invaded that country in 1982; and then from Tunisia. While U.S. presidents routinely condemned the PLO's use of **terrorism** and refused to recognize or deal with the organization, Arafat became increasingly popular among Third World peoples. In 1974, he secured from the **Arab League** the recognition that the PLO rather than Arab governments represented the Palestinian people, and he was invited to address the **United Nations** General Assembly, a first for a non–head of state. By the 1990s, several dozen states granted diplomatic recognition to the PLO.

The U.S. attitude toward Arafat began to change in the 1980s. To help deescalate the **Israeli invasion of Lebanon** in 1982, the United States sent military forces to Beirut to oversee the departure of the PLO leadership to Tunisia. In 1987, Arafat skillfully took control of the **intifada**, which had begun spontaneously in the streets of Palestinian villages. The next year, under pressure from Secretary of State **George P. Shultz**, Arafat publicly pledged to renounce terrorism, to recognize Israel, and to participate in peace negotiations. Shultz responded by lifting the historic ban on U.S. officials speaking with the PLO.

Despite that breakthrough, U.S. relations with Arafat remained strained. American officials were relieved that the PLO battled to suppress its more radical rival the **Islamic Resistance Movement (Hamas)**, which vied for influence among the Palestinians in the occupied territories. Yet they were distressed that Arafat endorsed **Iraq** during the **Persian Gulf War** of 1990–1991. At Israel's insistence, the United States denied the PLO a place at the **Madrid Conference** of 1991.

Yet relations improved during the 1990s peace process. In 1993, Arafat approved the secret negotiations with Israel at Oslo, and President **William J. Clinton** welcomed Arafat, along with Israeli prime minister **Yitzhak Rabin**, to sign the **Oslo Accord** at the White House. In 1994, Arafat returned to the West Bank as head of the **Palestinian National Authority (PNA),** which governed autonomous zones of the occupied territories, and he presided over a golden era in which a Palestinian state seemed within his grasp.

But Arafat's image in the United States soured as the peace process stalled in the late 1990s. Clinton tried to resuscitate it by inviting

Arafat and Israeli prime minister **Ehud Barak** to Camp David in 2000 for the final status talks called for in the Oslo process. But Arafat rejected a compromise deal that Barak approved at Camp David and an even more generous offer advanced in December 2000 on the grounds that the deals did not adequately safeguard Palestinian interests in land, Jerusalem, and the right of refugees. Arafat made no counteroffers, and Clinton blamed him for failure of the peace process.

As the diplomacy stalled, a second and more violent intifada erupted across the occupied territories in 2000. The uprising was apparently directed mainly against the Oslo process that Arafat had embraced as well as the corruption and cronyism of PA governance, and Arafat seemed to encourage the violence to protect his own interests. Israeli authorities declared that they could no longer trust Arafat until he stopped the uprising, and they confined him for three years to his compound in Ramallah. President **George W. Bush** openly called on the Palestinian people to advance new leaders who were willing to negotiate responsibly.

In late 2004, Arafat became gravely ill, and the Israelis permitted him leave to secure medical attention in Paris, where he died in a hospital in November.

AL-ASSAD, BASHAR (1965–). Son of **Hafez Al-Assad** who became president of **Syria** in 2000. Trained in Damascus and London as an ophthalmologist, Assad returned to Syria in 1994 after his brother, who was slated to succeed their father, died in an accident. Groomed in politics and military affairs for six years, Assad assumed the presidency upon his father's death in 2000.

As president, Assad struggled to gain control of Syria's government and foreign policy in the early 2000s. He initially tolerated political dissent, targeted corruption among Syrian officials, and introduced the Internet and cell phones to his country, but counterpressure from old-guard conservatives compelled him to limit such reforms of the country's political order. Assad also found it difficult to negotiate the troubled situation in **Lebanon**, whose people rallied against Syrian occupation forces after the mysterious assassination of former prime minister **Rafik Hariri** in early 2005. Assad also dealt cautiously with the United States. He disputed charges by U.S. officials that Syria abetted the anti-American insurgency in **Iraq** even in the face of implicit threats of a U.S. incursion into his country. Reported Syrian complicity in the U.S. capture of a half brother of **Saddam Hussein** in early 2005 provided some indication of Assad's willingness to cooperate with U.S. operations in the region.

AL-ASSAD, HAFEZ (1930–2000). Dictatorial ruler of **Syria** from 1970 to his death in 2000. Assad joined the radical Baath Party in his teens, became an air force pilot in the 1950s, and emerged as Syria's minister of defense after a military coup in Damascus in 1966. In 1970, Assad consolidated control of the government and won 99 percent approval as Syria's president in a contrived referendum in 1971.

American officials considered Assad a tough and wily leader. His occupation of **Lebanon** in 1976 gave him the political position needed to deny **Israel**'s quest to neutralize that state through an Israeli–Lebanese partnership. His influence over radical militias in Lebanon enabled him to mobilize armed resistance that eventually forced Israel to end its occupation of that country. In the 1970s and 1980s, U.S. officials also suspected that Assad fomented anti-American **terrorism** and kidnappings in Lebanon and elsewhere throughout the region.

During the **Persian Gulf War** of 1990–1991, President **George H. W. Bush** nurtured an alliance of convenience with Assad against their common enemy, Iraqi dictator **Saddam Hussein**. The military partnership bore political fruit, namely, Assad's willingness to negotiate during the U.S.-led Arab–Israeli peace process of the 1990s. Despite numerous personal appeals from top American officials, however, Assad stubbornly insisted on the complete and unconditional return of the Golan Heights, which Israel had occupied in the **Arab-Israeli War of 1967** and annexed in 1982, before he would make peace. Israel refused to surrender the Golan Heights, and no Israeli–Syrian peace deal was reached during Assad's lifetime.

– B –

AL-BADR, MUHAMMED (1929–1996). Royalist leader of North **Yemen** in 1962–1970. Eight days after taking power as imam of North Yemen, al-Badr was overthrown in a coup. With the backing of

Saudi Arabia, al-Badr rallied royalist forces in a counterrevolutionary war against the new regime. Civil war ensued for eight years. When a truce was negotiated in 1970, al-Badr fled into exile in Great Britain, where he died in 1996.

BAGHDAD PACT. Informal name of a defense alliance of 1955–1979 in which the United States played a limited but influential role. The Baghdad Pact originated in a quest by the **Dwight D. Eisenhower** administration to build an anti-Soviet defense alliance in the Middle East. American officials eyed countries on the so-called Northern Tier of the region after **Egypt** scotched earlier U.S. plans to base a defense alliance in the Suez Canal area. Under American encouragement, **Iraq** and Turkey signed a "Pact of Mutual Cooperation" in Baghdad on 24 February 1955, and Great Britain, Pakistan, and **Iran** acceded to it before the end of the year. This so-called Baghdad Pact pledged the signatories to cooperate on security matters, and it invited other Middle East states to join. Because Turkey belonged to the **North Atlantic Treaty Organization (NATO)** and Pakistan belonged to the South East Asia Treaty Organization, the Baghdad Pact completed an anti-Soviet cordon from Scandinavia to East Asia.

The Baghdad Pact immediately showed weaknesses. Its member states had very limited actual ability to defend the Middle East against a Soviet invasion. The pact also drew political criticism. The Soviet Union charged that the pact was provocative. Egypt denounced Iraq for perpetuating Western imperialism in the region. **Israel** complained that the pact would bolster the military strength of its nemesis Iraq.

The United States adopted a balanced policy toward the pact. President Eisenhower declined to join formally, on the reasoning that such a move would provoke the Soviet Union, alienate Egypt, and generate Israeli demands for a reciprocal security guarantee. But he did seek to bolster the pact by assigning military officers to coordinate military planning with pact members, directing diplomats to attend pact meetings, and paying one-sixth of the pact's annual budget.

The Baghdad Pact never achieved a prominent status. After the Iraqi revolution of July 1958, the regime of General **Abdul Karim Qassim** withdrew Iraq from the pact in March 1959. The remaining members changed the pact's name to the Central Treaty Organization

(CENTO) and relocated its headquarters to Ankara. But Pakistan grew dispirited with the pact after its partners refused to back Pakistan during its wars with India in 1965 and 1971. In 1979, Iran withdrew formally from the pact after its revolution, and Pakistan quickly followed suit. With U.S. approval, Britain and Turkey formally terminated the pact in 1979.

BAHRAIN. A small, pro-Western sheikhdom comprised of 35 islands in the Persian Gulf and ruled by the al-Khalifa family. When Bahrain was a British protectorate (1861–1968), U.S. companies began developing its oil industry in the 1930s, and the U.S. military began stationing troops in the country in 1947. In 1971, Bahrain declared its independence, and the United States promptly recognized it. In 1972, the United States leased military bases in Bahrain that proved important during U.S. naval operations against **Iran** in 1987–1988 as well as during the **Persian Gulf War** of 1990–1991 and the **Iraq War** of 2003–. This security partnership survived political differences over Israeli behavior during the **Arab-Israeli War of 1967** and the **Arab-Israeli War of 1973** and over U.S. policy toward the Arab–Israeli peace process in the late 1970s.

BAKER, JAMES A. (1930–). Secretary of state in 1989–1992 under President **George H. W. Bush**. Baker personally promoted Israeli–Palestinian peace talks in 1989–1990 but made little progress overcoming basic differences or even getting the two parties to the table. After the **Persian Gulf War** of 1990–1991, Baker engaged in a vigorous diplomacy to organize the October 1991 **Madrid Conference** involving **Israel**, **Jordan**, the Palestinians, **Syria**, **Egypt**, and **Lebanon**. That conference gave birth to the 1990s Arab–Israeli peace process.

Baker also participated directly in U.S. diplomacy toward **Iraq**. In 1989, he met Iraqi foreign minister Tariq Aziz in a futile effort to improve U.S.–Iraqi relations in the aftermath of the **Iran–Iraq War**. When Iraq threatened military action against **Kuwait** in the summer of 1990, Baker formulated a stiff State Department warning against such a move. After the Iraqi conquest of Kuwait, Baker helped Bush build the international coalition arrayed against Iraq. On 9 January 1991, Baker met Aziz in Geneva in a final, unsuccessful bid to convince Iraq to withdraw from Kuwait before the start of **Operation Desert Storm**.

Baker resigned from the State Department in 1992 to manage Bush's reelection campaign. In 2003, President **George W. Bush** named Baker special emissary on the issue of Iraqi debt. In 2006, Baker cochaired the Iraq Study Group, a bipartisan panel of experts that critiqued President Bush's performance in the **Iraq War** and recomended substantial policy reforms.

BARAK, EHUD (1942–). Israeli soldier and statesman who promoted the Arab–Israeli peace process in the 1990s. Born in Palestine, Barak served 36 years (1959–1995) in the Israeli army, becoming the most decorated Israeli soldier in history and becoming chief of the general staff of the Israeli Defense Forces in 1991. As chief of staff, he implemented the **Oslo Accord** signed by Prime Minister **Yitzhak Rabin**, helped negotiate Israel's peace treaty with **Jordan** in 1994, and participated in peace talks with **Syria**. Barak won an election to the Knesset as a Labor Party candidate in May 1996, and, after a brief period of conservatism in Israeli politics, he was elected prime minister in May 1999.

As prime minister, Barak cooperated with various initiatives of the **William J. Clinton** administration to revive the peace process of the Rabin era. To fulfill a campaign pledge, Barak ordered the unilateral withdrawal of Israeli forces from south **Lebanon** in early 2000, ending an 18-year-long and increasingly costly occupation of that territory. Yet Barak achieved little progress in other areas. Under U.S. pressure, he resumed negotiations with Syrian premier **Hafez al-Asad**, and the two leaders agreed in principle that Israel would withdraw from the Golan Heights in exchange for Syrian recognition. But when Clinton brokered meetings between Barak and Syrian foreign minister Farouk Shara in Shepherdstown, West Virginia, in January 2000, deadlock emerged over the logistics of the Israeli withdrawal, and no peace treaty materialized.

Nor did Barak achieve a final settlement with Palestinian leader **Yasser Arafat**. Clinton invited Barak and Arafat to Camp David in July 2000 for two weeks of face-to-face meetings. Barak and Arafat declared a desire for a final settlement, and Barak offered to withdraw from some 90 percent of the West Bank, to provide territorial compensation for those portions that Israel retained, to recognize Palestinian sovereignty over much of Jerusalem, and to show flexibility on the refugees and security issues. Clinton endorsed these terms, but Arafat refused them. When Clinton proposed terms even more favorable to the Palestinians in late 2000, Barak approved them, but Arafat demurred, scuttling Barak's hopes for a final settlement.

Meanwhile, the eruption of the second Palestinian **intifada** in September 2000 inflamed passions on all sides and diminished Barak's popularity among Israelis. Barak resigned the prime ministry in December 2000 in the hope of regaining an electoral mandate in a February 2001 election. But his challenger, Likud Party candidate **Ariel Sharon**, soundly defeated Barak, ending his political career.

BARZANI, MASSOUD (1946–). Leader of the Kurdistan Democratic Party (KDP) that gained influence in northern **Iraq** in the 1990s. Son of legendary Kurdish nationalist **Mustapha Barzani**, Massoud Barzani joined his father's militia that fought for the autonomy of **Kurds** from Iraq in the 1960s and early 1970s. On the death of his father in 1979, Massoud Barzani assumed leadership of the KDP. In the 1980s, he vigorously but unsuccessfully pressured the **Saddam Hussein** regime in Baghdad to grant autonomy to Iraqi Kurds.

After the **Persian Gulf War** of 1990–1991, by contrast, the United States established a safe haven for Iraqi Kurds in northern Iraq and denied the Hussein regime access to the area. Barzani vied for leadership of the Kurdistan protectorate against a rival leader, **Jalal Talabani** of the Patriotic Union of Kurdistan (PUK). A civil war between the two parties was resolved in 1998 after U.S. mediation, and in 2002 a joint parliament was seated. After the **U.S. invasion of Iraq** in 2003, Barzani served on the U.S.-appointed Iraq Governing Council. He advocated continuing autonomy for Kurds under the new Iraqi government created under U.S. oversight. *See also* IRAQ WAR.

BARZANI, MUSTAPHA (1903–1979). Leader of **Kurds** and the father of modern Kurdish nationalism. Barzani emerged as leader of an armed insurrection against **Iraq** during the 1930s. He commanded the army of the Kurdish Republic, a state situated in northern **Iran** that declared its independence, under Soviet protection, in November 1945, only to be crushed by the Iranian army after the Soviets withdrew their protection, under American pressure, in May 1946. After years of exile in the Soviet Union, Barzani returned to Iraq after the 1958 revolution, and through the 1960s and early 1970s, he used violence and diplomacy in pursuit of independence of Iraqi Kurds. In 1974, a major conflict developed after Iran offered military aid to the Kurdish forces, but after Iran suddenly curtailed its support in 1975, Iraq crushed the Kurdish forces, and Barzani fled in exile to the United States. He died in Washington, D.C. *See also* BARZANI, MASSOUD.

BEGIN, MENACHEM (1913–1992). Sixth prime minister of **Israel** who developed a strained relationship with the United States. Born and educated in Poland, Begin escaped the Nazi conquest of that country and, by 1942, reached **Palestine** as a member of a Polish army-in-exile. He soon emerged as commander of the Irgun Zvei Leumi, a militant resistance group that conducted terrorist attacks against British authority in Palestine, including the bombing of the King David Hotel in Jerusalem in July 1946. On the establishment of Israeli statehood, Begin turned to politics, founding such conservative parties as Herut and the Likud coalition and sitting as a leading opposition figure in the Knesset during nearly three decades of Labor Party domination of the Israeli government. Begin became prime minister after the Likud Party won the Israeli elections of 1977.

As prime minister, Begin repeatedly interacted with the United States, increasingly on unfriendly terms. In 1977–1979, he pleased President **Jimmy Carter** by starting peace negotiations with Egyptian president **Anwar Sadat**, approving the **Camp David Accords** of 1978, and signing the Egyptian–Israeli peace treaty of 1979. Yet he earned Washington's reproach in 1981 for ordering a preemptive air strike against an Iraqi nuclear reactor under construction near Baghdad and for pushing through the Knesset a bill providing annexation of the Golan Heights in violation of UN Resolution 242, the Israeli–Syrian **Disengagement Accord** of 1974, and the Camp David Accords.

Begin drew even sharper American criticism for his policy in **Lebanon**. President **Ronald Reagan** strongly criticized the **Israeli invasion of Lebanon** in June 1982 and dispatched U.S. forces to Beirut to help end fighting between Israeli and Palestinian forces there. Yet Reagan found it necessary to return troops to Lebanon after Israeli political machinations in Beirut resulted in political instability there. The U.S. forces in Beirut found themselves in a precarious military situation, aggravated by tactical withdrawals of Israeli units from the area in defiance of U.S. wishes. Finally, when Reagan launched a major peace plan involving an Israeli departure from the West Bank and the Golan Heights, Begin dismissed it out of hand in a fervent, podium-pounding speech to the Knesset.

Under stress over the war in Lebanon, Begin resigned the prime ministry in September 1983, citing personal and health reasons.

BEN-GURION, DAVID (1886–1971). Zionist leader, a founder of **Israel**, and Israel's first prime minister. Born in Poland, Ben-Gurion became committed at a young age to the vision of **Zionism** of establishing a Jewish state in **Palestine**. He emigrated there in 1906, when the territory was a part of the Ottoman Empire, and after Palestine came under British control during World War I, Ben-Gurion organized political and economic institutions among the territory's Jewish community. In 1930, he founded Mapai, the Zionist Labor Party. Five years later, Ben-Gurion became head of the Jewish Agency for Palestine, an international political organization seeking to establish a Jewish state in Palestine.

After the **United Nations** approved a resolution in November 1947 authorizing the **partition of Palestine** into an Arab state and a Jewish state, Ben-Gurion mobilized the Jewish community to declare the statehood of Israel on the termination of the British mandate in May 1948 and to defend that new state against the anticipated invasions by the armies of neighboring Arab powers. As Israel's first and third prime minister (1948–1953 and 1955–1963), he successfully defended the state against its foreign enemies and thereby shaped the enduring political, economic, and cultural identity of Israel.

Ben-Gurion enjoyed generally warm relations with the United States. Presidents **Harry S. Truman**, **Dwight D. Eisenhower**, and **John F. Kennedy** admired him for promoting democracy in Israel and for positioning the state in the anti-Soviet Western orbit. Occasionally, disagreements arose over policy issues, most notably during the **Suez Crisis** of 1956, when Eisenhower sharply rebuked Ben-Gurion for invading Egypt. Ben-Gurion met the American presidents on official visits in 1951, 1960, and 1961, and in 1962 he secured the first-ever major sale of American weapons to Israel. Ben-Gurion also enjoyed legendary status in American public opinion as a stalwart, democratic leader.

BERNADOTTE, FOLKE (1895–1948). Swedish diplomat who, while serving as **United Nations** mediator for **Palestine** in 1948, proposed a comprehensive plan for Arab–Israeli peace. He was assassinated in Jerusalem by Israeli terrorists on 17 September 1948. With the backing of President **Harry S. Truman**, the U.S. State Department endorsed the **Bernadotte Plan**, but political pressures during the presidential election campaign of 1948 compelled Truman to retract his support. *See also* BERNADOTTE PLAN.

BERNADOTTE PLAN. An early and futile **United Nations** plan for a permanent settlement of the Arab–Israeli conflict. Formulated by UN mediator **Folke Bernadotte** in 1948, the plan sought to achieve a political settlement of vital issues on the basis of the **Partition Plan** of 1947 and the political situation that followed the hostilities of May–July 1948. Specifically, it proposed that Arab states acquiesce in the existence of **Israel**, that **Jordan** annex the portions of **Palestine** not designated to Israel, that all powers approve certain border alterations, that Israel repatriate **Palestinian refugees**, and that an international regime govern Jerusalem. Secretary of State **George C. Marshall**, with the blessing of President **Harry S. Truman**, approved the plan but made little headway against Arab and Israeli opposition before Israeli terrorists assassinated Bernadotte on 17 September.

State Department leaders sought, fruitlessly, to advance the Bernadotte Plan in late 1948. Capitalizing on the worldwide remorse and outrage against Israel that followed the assassination, Marshall publicly endorsed the plan on 20 September. But three factors stymied such peacemaking efforts. First, neither Israel nor its Arab adversaries indicated any willingness to make peace on the basis of the plan. Second, Israel's mid-October military offensive to secure the northern Negev stoked Arab animosity and eviscerated the plan's territorial provisions. Third, domestic political pressure to honor Israeli wishes compelled President Truman, engaged in a close race for reelection in November 1948, to repudiate the plan in a public statement on 24 October. By December, State Department officials concluded that Israel would not concede any territory, and thus they laid the Bernadotte Plan to rest.

BIN LADEN, OSAMA (1957–). Saudi-born militant who moved from partner with the United States in the 1980s to notorious terrorist mastermind of the 1990s and early 2000s. Bin Laden was born to Mohammed Awad bin Laden, a multibillionaire real estate developer with connections to the Saudi royal family, and a Syrian mother. In the 1980s, he gained prominence and demonstrated organizational brilliance while resisting the Soviet occupation of Afghanistan in partnership with the United States; by some accounts, he was trained by the Central Intelligence Agency (CIA) in covert warfare operations. In Afghanistan, bin Laden embraced an extreme version of Islam, networked with compatriots who flocked to the country from around the Muslim world, and compiled a database of holy warriors (jihadists) known as **al-Qaeda** ("The Base" in Arabic).

Bin Laden turned against the United States and **Saudi Arabia** during the **Persian Gulf War** of 1990–1991, when **King Fahd** decided to rely on U.S. soldiers rather than al-Qaeda warriors to defend his kingdom from **Iraq**. In 1991, bin Laden relocated to Sudan, where he renewed contacts with al-Qaeda members, and in 1996, he found his way to Afghanistan, where, under the protection of the Taliban regime, he trained legions of Islamists for holy war against Saudi Arabia and the United States. In 1996, bin Laden declared war on the United States, and in 1998, he called for his followers to kill Americans on every possible occasion.

In the late 1990s, bin Laden organized a series of attacks on the United States. The June 1996 bombing of a U.S. Air Force barracks in Saudi Arabia is believed to have been his work. In August 1998, he orchestrated simultaneous bombings of the U.S. embassies in Kenya and Tanzania that killed 257 people, including 12 Americans. In October 2000, al-Qaeda terrorists detonated a bomb adjacent to the USS *Cole* as it refueled in Aden Harbor, **Yemen**, killing 17 U.S. sailors. President **William J. Clinton** authorized the Pentagon and the CIA to capture or kill bin Laden, but he remained elusive. A U.S. missile strike on al-Qaeda camps in Afghanistan in late 1998 narrowly missed him.

The **9/11** attacks constituted bin Laden's most devastating assault on the United States. The **George W. Bush** administration responded by invading **Afghanistan** to depose the Taliban regime that had provided sanctuary to bin Laden. Although the United States occupied the country and killed hundreds of al-Qaeda warriors, bin Laden escaped the dragnet and remained at large, probably in the remote mountains along the Afghanistan–Pakistan border, in early 2006.

BLACK SEPTEMBER. A military clash in 1970–1971 between the government of **Jordan** and the **Palestine Liberation Organization (PLO)** and a Palestinian terrorist group that took shape in its aftermath. In the late 1960s, **King Hussein** of Jordan had allowed PLO militants to stage raids into **Israel** from Jordan, but his complicity had become costly in terms of both Israeli reprisals on his kingdom and the open defiance that the PLO showed for the king. In September 1970, following an incident in which the PLO landed four hijacked commercial airliners near Amman, King Hussein ordered his army to crush the PLO. Crisis loomed when **Syria** sent tanks into northern Jordan to help the Palestinians, but the Jordanian air force attacked the Syrians and forced a retreat. President **Richard M. Nixon** sent the U.S. Sixth Fleet to the eastern Mediterranean and contemplated intervention to save King Hussein from defeat, but the king secured a pledge of support from Israel that eased the pressure on Nixon to send U.S. forces. Jordanian forces effectively scattered and suppressed the PLO militants by 1971, and U.S. officials expressed relief at this outcome.

Palestinian radicals who considered the Jordanian attack on fellow Arabs a travesty coined the phrase "Black September" in reference to the month in which the fighting started. Some of them also formed a new terrorist group named Black September, which became notorious during the early 1970s for acts of terrorism, including the assassinations of Jordanian political figures; the murder of Israeli athletes at the 1972 Summer Olympic Games in Munich, Germany; and the assassination of U.S. Ambassador to Khartoum Cleo Noel and Charges D'Affaires George Curtis Moore in 1973.

BREMER, L. PAUL (1942–). American diplomat who headed the Coalition Provisional Authority (CPA) in Iraq in 2003–2004. Bremer served for 23 years as a Foreign Service officer before his retirement in 1989 and as a counterterrorism consultant thereafter. In May 2003, President **George W. Bush** appointed him administrator of the CPA with the rank of presidential envoy.

In Baghdad, Bremer managed a vast effort to rebuild Iraq's infrastructure, build a new police force, promote educational and social reform, jump-start the economy, and generate a democratic potential and sense of nationhood in Iraq. In a difficult political environment, Bremer also started a process to establish an Iraqi provisional government and a democratic constitution. Yet Bremer also made several decisions—such as purging Baath Party members from government posts and disbanding the Iraqi army—that were eventually recognized as major causes of the debilitating anti-American insurgency that erupted during Bremer's tenure in Baghdad. On 28 June 2004, Bremer transferred authority in Iraq to interim prime minister **Ayad Allawi** and departed the country.

BRZEZINSKI, ZBIGNIEW (1928–). National security advisor in 1977–1980 who advocated a hard-line policy toward Middle East adversaries. Brzezinski counseled President **Jimmy Carter**, for instance, to bolster Shah **Mohammed Reza Pahlavi** of **Iran** over the revolutionary movement of Ayatollah **Ruhollah Khomeini**. He also urged a firm response to Iranian actions during the **Iran Hostage Crisis**. Brzezinski further recommended a strong containment policy against the Soviet Union, especially after the Soviet invasion of Afghanistan in December 1979. Brzezinski frequently clashed with Secretary of State **Cyrus Vance** in giving policy advice to Carter.

BUNCHE, RALPH J. (1904–1971). Gifted academic who served both the U.S. Department of State and the **United Nations** in a variety of posts from the 1940s to the 1960s. A professor of political science at Howard University as well as an advocate of civil rights reform within the United States and of decolonization abroad, Bunche entered government service during World War II, and he became the first African American to head a division of the State Department when he became acting chief of the Division of Dependent Area Affairs in 1945. Secretary-General Trygve Lie appointed Bunche head of the UN Department of Trusteeship in 1946. Bunche then served on the staff of the **UN Special Committee on Palestine**, which formulated the plan for the **partition of Palestine** in 1947, and as head of the UN Palestine Commission, which was formed to implement the plan. When the **Arab-Israeli War of 1948–1949** rendered the partition plan obsolete, Bunche was named assistant to UN mediator **Folke Bernadotte**, and after Bernadotte's assassination in September 1948, Bunche was named acting mediator. In that capacity, Bunche conducted tireless negotiations that produced a series of armistices that ended Arab–Israeli hostilities in early 1949. Bunche remained involved in UN and academic initiatives for decades.

BUSH DOCTRINE. A national security strategy enunciated by President **George W. Bush** in the early 2000s that marked a major watershed in U.S. foreign policy. The doctrine declared that the United States would use preemptive military force against rogue states and terrorist organizations, especially those stockpiling or developing weapons of mass destruction. The doctrine further declared that the United States would act unilaterally to protect its interests and its strength and would promote the spread of democracy through the world. With roots reaching into neoconservative ideology in the 1990s, the doctrine came to life as a reaction to the **9/11** terrorist attacks. The doctrine was outlined in a series of public addresses by Bush and his top advisers in 2001–2002 and then clearly articulated in *The National Security Strategy of the United States of America*, a policy paper published in September 2002. The Bush Doctrine provided the intellectual rationale for the **U.S. invasion of Afghanistan** in 2001 and the **U.S. invasion of Iraq** in 2003.

BUSH, GEORGE H. W. (1924–). President of the United States in 1989–1993 who managed the transition of U.S. policy in the Middle East into the post–Cold War era. Bush left two important legacies in Middle East diplomacy. First, in the **Persian Gulf War** he used diplomacy and force to reverse **Iraq**'s August 1990 conquest of **Kuwait**. Under **Operation Desert Shield**, Bush rushed 100,000 U.S. soldiers to **Saudi Arabia** to protect it from Iraqi aggression, and he knitted together a broad international coalition of powers to challenge Iraq's position in Kuwait through political, legal, and economic means. Once he had secured international and domestic legal sanctions to wage war to liberate Kuwait, Bush ordered the start of offensive military action on 17 January 1991. Under **Operation Desert Storm**, U.S. and allied aircraft massively attacked Iraqi targets for several weeks, and then, in late February, coalition ground troops liberated Kuwait from Iraqi control in a 100-hour combat operation. Bush decided to end the offensive at that stage and to leave **Saddam Hussein** in power in Baghdad, thus shaping a policy of containing Hussein that was destined to last for 12 years.

Second, Bush launched an Arab–Israeli peace process that would develop favorably for several years after he left office. Exploiting U.S. prestige that grew with the end of the Cold War and the victory in the Persian Gulf War, Bush dispatched Secretary of State **James A. Baker** to organize a peace conference involving **Israel**, **Jordan**, the Palestinians, **Syria**, **Egypt**, and **Lebanon**. Such efforts led to the **Madrid Conference** of 30 October 1991, where the principals to the conflict, with Bush in attendance, agreed to reaffirm **United Nations** Resolutions 242 and 338 and to negotiate the major points of contention. Although the prescribed Israeli–Arab and Israeli–Palestinian negotiations bogged down during Bush's last year in office, the stage was set for secret meetings in Oslo in 1993 that spawned several major peace agreements.

BUSH, GEORGE W. (1946–). American president who deeply enmeshed the United States in the Middle East in the early 2000s. Taking office in January 2001 after the closest and most contested presidential election since 1876, Bush became riveted to the Middle East after the **9/11** terrorist attacks on the United States. Within months of the attacks, the United States and its military allies demolished the Taliban regime in Afghanistan, which had provided sanctuary to **Osama bin Laden**, leader of the **al-Qaeda** terrorist network and perpetrator of the 9/11 attacks. American occupation authorities built a fledgling democracy in Afghanistan, although they proved unable to achieve control over all the country or to capture or kill bin Laden.

In addition to waging war in Afghanistan, Bush also led the United States into the controversial **Iraq War**. The president took office apparently convinced that he should break the debilitating stalemate with Iraq that had evolved through the 1990s, and the 9/11 attacks—and the fear of another act of **terrorism** involving weapons of mass destruction—galvanized him to take preemptive action. In 2002, Bush steadily built a public case for war against Iraq, and in October, Congress authorized him to use force in Iraq as he saw fit. Bush also secured a **United Nations** resolution finding Iraq in breach of earlier disarmament resolutions, providing a thin legal basis for an attack, and he stressed to the world community that Iraqi leader **Saddam Hussein** possessed biological and chemical weapons and the propensity to use them. In a three-week military campaign starting on 20 March 2003, U.S., British, and Australian troops occupied Iraq, scattered its army, and dismantled its government.

In sharp contrast to the quick military victory, the U.S. occupation of Iraq presented Bush with serious problems. The administration had apparently put little thought into the task of postwar reconstruction, and Iraq experienced a wave of looting and lawlessness followed by a mounting, armed insurgency against American soldiers. Thus, Bush organized an expensive program of state building in Iraq. In May 2003, he established the Coalition Provisional Authority (CPA) to oversee an enormous effort to rebuild Iraq's infrastructure. Bush also authorized a political process leading to the establishment of a constitutional, democratic government in Iraq. The CPA transferred authority to interim prime minister **Ayad Allawi** in June 2004, and in three popular elections in 2005, the Iraqi people elected a national assembly and approved a constitution. Yet the anti-American insurgency continued; by 2005, more than 2,000 American soldiers had died in Iraq.

The Iraq War distracted Bush from other issues in the Middle East. In **Iran**, conservatives gained the upper hand in a struggle against moderates for control of Iran's sociopolitical order. Iranian president **Mahmoud Ahmadinejad**, elected in June 2005 with the backing of conservative clerics, criticized U.S. policy in the Middle East and openly called for the destruction of **Israel**.

Bush also played a passive role in the search for Israeli–Palestinian peace. The president showed deep interest in the issue after the 9/11 attacks. He called on the Palestinian people to elect new leaders and adopt a constitutional democracy that would renounce terror and live in peace, and he challenged Israel to withdraw from occupied territories and support the creation of a state of **Palestine**. Together with Russia, the European Union, and the United Nations, the United States promoted the **Roadmap peace plan**. Yet Bush's efforts to sell the peace plan, including a personal visit to Middle East leaders in June 2003, proved insufficient to achieve its goals. *See also* AFGHANISTAN, U.S. INVASION OF.

– C –

CAMP DAVID ACCORDS. Peace accords between **Egypt** and **Israel** negotiated with the assistance of President **Jimmy Carter** in September 1978. Carter took office in 1977 determined to promote Arab–Israeli peace. When Egyptian–Israeli talks bogged down, therefore, he invited Israeli prime minister **Menachem Begin** and Egyptian premier **Anwar Sadat** to a summit meeting at Camp David, the presidential retreat in Maryland.

Through days of hard bargaining, Carter diligently persuaded the two parties to sign two accords that provided a blueprint for a peace agreement between them. The first agreement, "A Framework for Peace in the Middle East," sketched a three-year plan for a transition of the West Bank and Gaza from occupied territories to self-governing districts under Palestinian autonomy with Israeli security interests guaranteed. The second accord, "A Framework for the Conclusion of a Peace Treaty between Egypt and Israel," provided for Israeli withdrawal from the Sinai, demilitarization of the Sinai under **United Nations** oversight and opening of diplomatic relations between the two powers.

After the summit meeting, Carter remained involved in the negotiations that led to the signing of the Egyptian–Israeli peace treaty of March 1979, the first such agreement between Israel and one of its Arab adversaries and one modeled on the second Camp David accord. The president's hopes of implementing the first accord or of building a regional peace agreement proved fleeting, however, as the Arab community ostracized Egypt because it made peace, as Palestinians continued to resist Israel with violence, and as Israel used assertive diplomacy and military force to secure its interests in the West Bank, Gaza, **Syria**, and **Lebanon**. By 1982, such events as the **Israeli invasion of Lebanon** embroiled the region in tension and animosity.

CARTER DOCTRINE. A statement issued in January 1980 by President **Jimmy Carter** declaring that the United States would fight to defend its interests in the Persian Gulf region from capture by the Soviet Union or any other power. Inaugurated as president in 1977, Carter initially hoped to develop a stable and amicable relationship with Moscow, but tensions mounted steadily over several issues. Shortly after the Iranian revolution of 1979, the Soviet army invaded and occupied Afghanistan. As a result, Carter came to fear that the Soviets might exploit the internal disarray of **Iran** to expand into the Persian Gulf, the oil of which was vital to the economic prosperity and security of the Western world. Thus, he contested the Soviet action in Afghanistan through a variety of economic and political sanctions, ordered development of U.S. capabilities for military and covert operations in the Middle East and South Asia, and declared, in his January 1980 State of the Union Address, that "an attempt by any outside force to gain control of the Persian Gulf region will be regarded as an assault on the vital interests of the United States of America, and such an assault will be repelled by any means necessary, including military force."

Dubbed the Carter Doctrine by the press, the president's statement repudiated the **Nixon Doctrine**, which had declared American reliance on local powers to police the Middle East, as well as Carter's own initial hope of achieving amicable relations with Moscow. The Carter Doctrine reaffirmed the older U.S. policy of containment of Soviet power, and it signaled an end of the post–Vietnam War retraction of American security commitments.

CARTER, JIMMY (1924–). President in 1977–1981 who faced enormous challenges in the Middle East. Motivated in part by his personal Christian faith, Carter took office intent on achieving a comprehensive Arab–Israeli peace agreement. He tried to organize an international peace conference at Geneva that would involve all parties to the dispute including the Palestinians as well as the United States and the Soviet Union. Yet **Egypt** and **Israel**, fearing American pressure to make concessions, instead started their own bilateral peace process in late 1977. Although upstaged by this dramatic initiative, Carter devoted himself to nurturing the Egyptian–Israeli peace process to fruition. When the bilateral talks deadlocked, he carefully brokered the **Camp David Accords** during a summit meeting with Egyptian premier **Anwar Sadat** and Israeli prime minister **Menachem Begin** in September 1978. When Egyptian–Israeli talks again bogged down in early 1979, Carter visited Cairo and Jerusalem to forge compromises on several issues, and he presided over the signing of the Egyptian–Israeli peace treaty on 26 March. While Egyptian and Israeli willingness to make peace was a crucial factor in this outcome, Carter exercised substantial influence in clinching the settlement. While imperfect, the 1979 treaty permanently ended three decades of war between Israel and Egypt and laid the foundation for the peace process of the 1990s.

In contrast to his peacemaking achievements, Carter also experienced enormous setbacks in the Middle East. He faced a special burden in **Iran**, where a revolutionary movement led by the Ayatollah **Ruhollah Khomeini** ousted Shah **Mohammed Reza Pahlavi** in early 1979. The revolution took an anti-American direction in part because of the long-term legacy of U.S. support for the autocratic shah and in part because Carter tried belatedly to curb the revolution. Carter faced a difficult relationship with Khomeini's new, theocratic government, which routinely attacked the United States in blunt propaganda and fomented mass anti-American demonstrations near the U.S. embassy in Tehran. After Carter decided, on humanitarian grounds, to admit the fallen shah to the United States in October 1979 for medical treatment, a mob overran the U.S. embassy, provoking the infamous **Iran Hostage Crisis**. That ordeal remained a major challenge for Carter to the end of his presidency and proved to be one major factor causing his loss in the presidential election of 1980.

Carter also faced trouble in Afghanistan. Fearing the spread of Islamic fundamentalism along its southern border in the aftermath of the Iranian revolution, the Soviet Union invaded Afghanistan in December 1979. The operation, involving the largest Soviet military movement outside Eastern Europe since World War II, profoundly disturbed Carter. He strongly condemned the assault and implemented a series of countermeasures, including the suspension of official diplomatic contacts with the Soviets, various trade embargoes, increased military preparations and covert operations, selective service registration of young men, and a boycott of the 1980 summer Olympic Games in Moscow. Suspecting that the Soviets had territorial aspirations on the oil-rich region south of Afghanistan, the president also issued the **Carter Doctrine** in January 1980. American–Soviet tensions and the prospect for armed hostilities in the Middle East remained elevated at the end of the Carter presidency.

CASEY, WILLIAM J. (1913–1987). Attorney and longtime government official who served as a powerful and controversial director of the Central Intelligence Agency under President **Ronald Reagan** in 1981–1987. Casey was appointed director after earning Reagan's confidence by directing his 1980 campaign for the White House.

As director, Casey was reportedly involved in several major events in Middle East diplomacy. He was believed to have authorized the initiatives to supply weapons and aid to the partisans who resisted the Soviet occupation of Afghanistan and to **Iraq** during the **Iran–Iraq War**. By some accounts, Casey conspired with Saudi intelligence officers in an assassination attempt against Sheikh Mohammed Hussein Fadlallah, head of **Hizballah** in **Lebanon**, in 1985; the attempt killed 80 persons but missed Fadlallah. It was also widely rumored that Casey was involved deeply in the **Iran-Contra scandal**. Shortly before Casey was scheduled to testify before a committee of Congress on the scandal in December 1986, he fell ill with brain cancer; he died five months later without ever publicly revealing his role.

CHALABI, AHMAD (1945–). An Iraqi political figure with whom the United States has had a complicated relationship. Born in 1945, Chalabi left **Iraq** in 1956, was educated in U.S. universities, and established Petra Bank in Jordan in 1977. In 1992, two years after the bank collapsed, a Jordanian court sentenced Chalabi in absentia to prison for bank fraud.

In 1992, Chalabi founded the Iraqi National Congress (INC), an opposition-in-exile to Iraqi dictator **Saddam Hussein**. In 1995, the INC provoked an uprising in **Kurdish**-controlled northern Iraq. Hundreds of persons died as Hussein's army crushed the revolt, although Chalabi escaped the country. After Hussein halted international inspections of Iraqi weapons sites in 1998, President **William J. Clinton** allocated $100 million to such groups as the INC devoted to ousting Saddam Hussein. Chalabi reportedly received some $300,000 per month from the U.S. government.

Chalabi became a central figure in the plans of the **George W. Bush** administration to liberate Iraq from Hussein's control. Chalabi reportedly provided much of the information about Hussein's program of weapons of mass destruction that formed the basis of the Bush administration's decision to invade Iraq in 2003. He returned to

Iraq in the immediate aftermath of the invasion and reportedly advised the Pentagon to dismantle the Iraqi army and the Baath political party. Despite State Department and Central Intelligence Agency (CIA) skepticism about his credibility, Chalabi emerged under Pentagon sponsorship as Iraq's first postwar governor. He sat in a place of honor near First Lady Laura Bush during the president's January 2004 State of the Union Address. Shiite, secular, and pro-Western, Chalabi appeared to certain U.S. officials as the ideal replacement for Hussein.

Yet Chalabi's political tenure in Baghdad proved to be tumultuous. In early 2004, U.S. forces helped Iraqi police raid Chalabi's office to search for evidence of criminal wrongdoing. State Department and CIA officials fed the media a portrait of Chalabi as a master con artist who had misled Pentagon neoconservatives with false intelligence about Hussein and became wealthy in the process. In August 2004, an Iraqi court issued a warrant for the arrest of Chalabi on charges of counterfeiting, and reports circulated that Chalabi had leaked U.S. intelligence secrets to **Iran**. The counterfeiting charges were dropped in September 2004, however, and in early 2005 Chalabi became a deputy prime minister in the interim government of **Ibrahim Jaafari**.

CHAMOUN, CAMILLE (1900–1987). Maronite Christian president of **Lebanon** (1952–1958) who aligned his government with the United States. Chamoun's effort to amend the constitution of Lebanon to allow himself to run for a second six-year term as president provoked a rebellion among the country's nationalists and disaffected Muslims. Even after Chamoun abandoned his reelection quest, unrest persisted and eventually contributed to the U.S. decision to intervene militarily in the country in July 1958. Chamoun returned to the Lebanese parliament in 1960, and he held a variety of ministerial posts during 1975–1985, when he emerged as a leading opponent of intervention by **Syria** in Lebanon.

CHEHAB, FUAD (1902–1973). Lebanese army general who emerged as president of **Lebanon** during a wave of political turmoil in 1958. Named commander of Lebanon's army in 1945, Chehab earned a reputation for refraining from intervention in domestic politics. As Lebanese nationalists engaged in violent resistance to the pro-Western government of **Camille Chamoun** from 1957 to early 1958, Chehab refrained from using military force to crush the rebellion. Once Chamoun ended his bid to extend his hold on the presidency, Chehab ordered his soldiers to defend the government against the unrest. In July 1958, shortly after the U.S. military intervention in Lebanon, Chehab was elected president of Lebanon and governed to 1964. Recognizing the popular will, Chehab indicated that Lebanon would aim for a nonaligned foreign policy, although he continued to accept aid and assistance from the United States.

CHENEY, RICHARD B. (1941–). Longtime government official and five-term congressman from Wyoming who served as secretary of defense in 1989–1993 and who was elected vice president of the United States in 2000 and 2004. As secretary of defense, Cheney became directly involved in Middle East policy after the Iraqi invasion of **Kuwait** in August 1990. He implemented the orders of President **George H. W. Bush** to protect **Saudi Arabia** from Iraqi attack and, eventually, to liberate Kuwait through air strikes and ground combat operations. Cheney devoted close personal attention to the late 1990 preparation for war against **Iraq** and virtually exclusive attention to the combat phase of January–February 1991. Cheney supported Bush's decision to halt operations after the liberation of Kuwait rather than invade Iraq and depose **Saddam Hussein**.

Returning to office as vice president in 2001, Cheney modified his earlier position on Iraq. In the late 1990s, he had apparently come to favor the view that military action to remove Hussein from power in Baghdad would advance U.S. interests. After the **9/11** attacks, Cheney emerged within the **George W. Bush** administration as a leading advocate of a preemptive invasion of Iraq. He justified such a move by suggesting that Iraq might supply weapons of mass destruction, which it was believed (erroneously) to possess, to terrorist groups intent on inflicting massive harm on the American people. Cheney also favored a firm counter**terrorism** policy, strongly endorsing the **U.S. invasion of Afghanistan** in 2001 and other counterterrorist policies around the globe.

CHRISTIAN ZIONISM. Support by Christians for the fulfillment of the Zionist vision of the return of Jewish people to **Palestine**, the independence of the state of **Israel**, and the promotion of Israel's interests in its conflict with Arab states and people. With roots reaching into antiquity, modern Christian Zionism emerged in mid-19th-century Great Britain and spread to the Protestant community of the United States by 1900. In the 20th century, it proved to be an important factor in shaping key diplomatic decisions, including the recognition of Israel in 1948 by President **Harry S. Truman** and the negotiation by President **Ronald Reagan** of a strategic partnership with Israel. In the 1970s, Christian Zionism was expressed in eschatological visions, popularized by best-selling authors such as Hal Lindsay, that linked the state of Israel with Bible prophecies predicting the end of time and the Second Coming of Jesus Christ. By the 1990s, Christian Zionism took deep roots in the evangelical community, which proved decisive in the electoral victories of President **George W. Bush** in 2000 and 2004. Such evangelicals tended to oppose the peace process of the 1990s and early 2000s and instead advocated a policy of strengthening Israel through security assistance.

CHRISTOPHER, WARREN (1925–). Lawyer and civil servant who twice became active in U.S. policy in the Middle East. While serving as deputy secretary of state in 1977–1981, Christopher conducted the sensitive negotiations leading to the release of the 52 Americans held hostage by **Iran**. President **Jimmy Carter** awarded him the Presidential Medal of Freedom in recognition of his accomplishment.

As secretary of state in 1993–1997, Christopher expended much time and effort promoting Arab–Israeli peace. He assisted President **William J. Clinton** in brokering the peace treaty signed by **Israel** and **Jordan** in 1994. Christopher shuttled repeatedly between Jerusalem and Damascus in 1993–1996 trying to arrange an Israeli–Syrian peace treaty featuring Israeli withdrawal from the Golan Heights. But he could not bridge the gap between Israel, which offered a gradual withdrawal after **Syria** made peace, and Syria, which insisted on an unconditional Israeli withdrawal in advance of a peace treaty.

CLIFFORD, CLARK M. (1906–1998). Attorney and government official who served several Democratic presidents in the Cold War era and directly shaped President **Harry S. Truman**'s policy toward **Israel**. As special assistant to the president in 1946–1950, Clifford masterminded Truman's stunning reelection campaign of 1948. Clifford was seminal in convincing Truman to endorse the 1947 plan of the **United Nations** for the **partition of Palestine**, to resist State Department efforts to reverse the plan in 1948, to recognize Israel on its declaration of independence in May 1948, and to block the **Bernadotte Plan** of the United Nations, which would have forced Israel to cede territory as a condition of peace. Although Clifford later claimed that these policies were based on moral and humanitarian considerations, domestic political calculations about winning the votes of pro-Zionists in the election of 1948 were probably paramount in his mind.

Clifford later served as foreign policy adviser to President **John F. Kennedy** and briefly as secretary of defense under President **Lyndon B. Johnson**. As chairman of a private bank in 1982–1991, Clifford became enmeshed in a scandal involving illegal arrangements with foreign banks, a scandal in which intelligence officials of the United States and **Saudi Arabia** were implicated. Clifford was indicted by a grand jury in 1992, although the charges were dropped the next year in light of his failing health.

CLINTON, WILLIAM JEFFERSON (1946–). American president in 1993–2001 who took an active interest in U.S. policy in the Middle East. Although he claimed little foreign policy experience when elected president in 1992, Clinton paid close attention to the **Arab–Israeli conflict**, security issues in the Persian Gulf, and **terrorism**.

Early in his presidency, Clinton significantly contributed to the Arab–Israeli peace process. He endorsed the **Oslo Accord** announced in August 1993 and he invited Israeli prime minister **Yitzhak Rabin** and **Palestinian Liberation Organization** leader **Yasser Arafat** formally to sign the Oslo Accord on the lawn of the White House the following month. In 1994, Clinton invited Rabin and **King Hussein** of **Jordan** to visit Washington jointly to declare the termination of hostilities between their two states, and he cosigned a formal Israeli–Jordanian peace treaty in October. Clinton also encouraged the signing of the Israeli-Palestinian Interim Agreement on the West Bank and Gaza of 1995, and he endorsed efforts of the **Palestinian National Authority (PNA)** to establish a stable political system in West Bank and Gaza Strip territory that came under Palestinian control.

Yet Clinton's peacemaking met clear limits. The president failed to achieve an Israeli–Syrian peace treaty even though he visited Damascus in October 1994 to encourage **Syria**'s Premier **Hafiz al-Asad** to accept a compromise on the terms of Israeli withdrawal from the Golan Heights. Terrorist attacks by extremists inflamed passions on both sides of the Israeli–Palestinian dispute. An Israeli extremist who opposed Israeli withdrawal from the West Bank on religious grounds assassinated Rabin in November 1995, and the political climate in **Israel** shifted away from peace making as voters elected the security-minded prime minister **Benjamin Netanyahu** in May 1996.

Clinton took great personal initiatives to resuscitate the peace process in the late 1990s. In October 1998, he personally and energetically arbitrated the **Wye River Memorandum**, a deal between Arafat and Netanyahu to resume the final status talks prescribed by the Oslo peace process. In December 1998, Clinton visited Gaza to witness the Palestine National Council's vote to remove from its charter those passages calling for the destruction of Israel, and in March 1999, he welcomed Arafat to the White House to encourage him to practice moderation. After the election of the moderate **Ehud Barak** as Israeli prime minister in May 1999, Clinton convinced both Israel and the Palestinians to pledge to seek a final settlement by September 2000.

Yet Clinton's second-term efforts fell far short of their targets. He personally brokered negotiations between Israel and Syria at Shepherdstown, West Virginia, in January 2000 and in Geneva, Switzerland, two months later, but no agreement materialized. The president also invited Barak and Arafat to Camp David in July 2000, but despite his intense arbitration over two weeks, he could not convince Arafat to accept a deal that would have established a state of **Palestine** over most of the West Bank and Gaza. Nor could Clinton convince Arafat to accept an even more generous deal approved by Barak in December 2000. Worse, the second Palestinian **intifada**, which exceeded the first uprising in terms of its violence, erupted in September 2000 and raged long after Clinton left office.

In the Persian Gulf, Clinton continued President **George H. W. Bush**'s strategy of containing **Saddam Hussein**. He embraced the major features of Bush's post–Gulf War apparatus for containing Iraq, including restrictions on its military mobility, international financial sanctions enforced by a multinational naval presence in the Persian Gulf, and a rigorous system of **United Nations** inspections to ensure **Iraq**'s compliance with the disarmament provisions of UN resolutions. Clinton extended the Bush administration's enforcement of so-called no-fly restrictions in two zones of Iraq, and he ordered military strikes on Iraq in 1993, 1996, and 1998 in retaliation for various Iraqi transgressions. Yet that policy faltered when Hussein interfered with the UN inspections in 1997 and ended them in 1998. Clinton adopted a policy of "containment plus," bolstering the U.S. military presence in the region, toughening its patrols in the no-fly zones, and funding Iraqi opposition forces committed to ousting Hussein. This show of strength, however, did little to ensure that Iraq was not building proscribed weapons systems.

Clinton also faced a mounting threat of Islamic terrorism against the United States. Muslim terrorists connected to **Osama bin Laden**'s **al-Qaeda** organization bombed the World Trade Center in New York City in February 1993; the Khobar Towers complex (home to U.S. Air Force personnel) in Dhahran, **Saudi Arabia**, in June 1996; the U.S. embassies in Kenya and Tanzania, in August 1998; and the USS *Cole* in Aden Harbor, **Yemen**, in October 2000. In response, Clinton pursued various counterterrorism policies at home and abroad, ranging from more vigorous law enforcement and intelligence gathering to military strikes and covert operations against al-Qaeda facilities in Sudan and Afghanistan. He claimed some successes, such as foiling a December 1999 attack on Los Angeles International Airport. But bin Laden remained at large, and al-Qaeda launched its dramatic **9/11** strike against the United States shortly after the end of Clinton's presidency.

– D –

DAYAN, MOSHE (1915–1981). Legendary Israeli soldier and politician. Born in **Palestine**, Dayan joined the Haganah, a prestate Jewish army, and fought against Vichy French forces in **Lebanon**, losing an eye in a battle. Sporting an eye patch that came to symbolize Israel's military resolve, Dayan commanded soldiers in battles near Jerusalem during the **Arab-Israeli War of 1948–1949**. As chief of staff of the Israeli Defense Forces in 1953–1957, he commanded the successful Israeli invasion of the Sinai in 1956, and, named minister of defense in 1967, he planned and executed Israel's dramatic victory in the **Arab-Israeli War of 1967**. Dayan's role in consolidating Israel's control of the territories occupied in 1967—via land purchases, settlement construction, and annexation—made him a darling of Israeli public opinion and an enemy of Palestinians. He also advocated a strong partnership with the United States.

The surprise Egyptian–Syrian attack on Israel during the **Arab-Israeli War of 1973** diminished Dayan's legendary reputation and forced him to resign as minister of defense. He then embraced the conservative Likud Party and served as foreign minister under Prime Minister **Menachem Begin**. Dayan attended the Camp David summit meeting of September 1978 that produced the **Camp David Accords** between **Israel** and **Egypt**, and he negotiated terms of the Egyptian–Israeli peace treaty of 1979.

DEMOCRATIZATION. A major political initiative in the Middle East announced by President **George W. Bush** during a series of speeches, notably his second inaugural address, in the early 2000s. Bush declared that democracy was essential to construct political stability and avert extremism and **terrorism** in the region. He asserted that democracy was compatible with Islam and that the United States would welcome the practice of democracy on terms consistent with the cultures of local states.

Bush contextualized the **U.S. invasion of Afghanistan** and the **U.S. invasion of Iraq** as efforts to advance democracy. He also celebrated the liberalization of politics in **Bahrein** and Morocco, and he pressured **Egypt** and **Saudi Arabia** to hold free elections. He called on the Palestinian people to practice democracy in choosing their leaders, and he envisioned a friendly relationship between the United States and a democratic **Iran**.

Critics of Bush argued that the ongoing insurgencies in Iraq and Afghanistan, the resistance of Egypt and Saudi Arabia to reform, and the election of a **Hamas** government in the Palestinian territories were evidence that his quest lacked realism.

DISENGAGEMENT ACCORDS. Three agreements between **Israel** and its adversaries **Egypt** and **Syria** negotiated in 1974–1975 by Secretary of State **Henry Kissinger**. Aiming to bolster the cease-fire that ended the **Arab-Israeli War of 1973**, Kissinger traveled extensively, in an exhaustive initiative known as **shuttle diplomacy**, to foster the disengagement of enemy troops from the battlefronts and the insertion of **United Nations** peacekeepers between them. Kissinger achieved such aims in Egyptian–Israeli agreements (also known as the Sinai I and **Sinai II accords**) signed in January 1974 and September 1975 and in a Syrian–Israeli accord signed in May 1974. Kissinger's diplomacy eased tensions along the frontiers, improved U.S. relations with the local powers, and generated some momentum that led to the Egyptian–Israeli peace treaty of 1979.

DULLES, ALLEN W. (1893–1969). Director of the Central Intelligence Agency (CIA) in 1953–1961 who used the CIA to implement U.S. policies in the Middle East. Trained as a lawyer and experienced in spycraft during World War II, Dulles was named deputy director of the CIA in 1951 and promoted to director by President **Dwight D. Eisenhower** in 1953. Dulles and his brother, Secretary of State **John Foster Dulles**, consulted frequently as they assisted Eisenhower in making foreign policy. Allen Dulles orchestrated CIA covert operations through the Eisenhower era, perhaps most famously in planning and executing the coup against Premier **Mohammed Mossadegh** of **Iran** in August 1953.

DULLES, JOHN FOSTER (1888–1959). American secretary of state in 1953–1959 who helped shape and implement President **Dwight D. Eisenhower**'s policies in the Middle East. Taking the helm of the State Department after decades of government service in a variety of posts, Dulles assisted Eisenhower in conceiving such initiatives as the covert operation in **Iran** in 1953, the **Baghdad Pact**, the **Alpha peace plan**, and the **Eisenhower Doctrine**, showing special determination to promote U.S. security interests and to advance Arab–Israeli peace. Dulles also promoted other State Department initiatives, such as the brokering of the Anglo–Egyptian treaty of 1954, which provided for the withdrawal of British forces from **Egypt** in early 1956, and a series of steps to ensure freedom of passage through the Suez Canal and the Straits of Tiran.

Dulles also played a central role in the development of American relations with Egypt. His efforts to nurture close relations with the regime of **Gamal Abdel Nasser** foundered over policy differences toward **Israel** and Western interests in the region. Dulles tried to revive friendliness in 1955 by offering Egypt a major aid package for construction of the Aswan Dam, but continuing disagreements convinced him that he must withdraw that aid offer in 1956, a step that triggered the **Suez Crisis**.

– E –

ECONOMIC SURVEY MISSION (ESM). A U.S. initiative in 1949–1951 to settle the **Palestinian refugees** controversy through economic development. After the **Arab-Israeli War of 1948–1949**, nearly 1 million Palestinians who had fled **Israel** and Israeli-occupied territory during the war languished in squalid refugee camps, seemingly ripe for communist propaganda, while Israel and surrounding Arab states categorically refused U.S. requests to absorb the refugees into their societies. Thus, the State Department launched the ESM to promote major economic development schemes—such as river dams and irrigation works—that would create jobs and residual benefits for the refugees and integrate them into the societies of the region. The ESM reflected the optimism among Western officials in the mid-20th century that technical assistance would stabilize the Third World. The United States secured **United Nations** approval of this scheme, but Israel and the Arab states showed no interest in participating and continued to assert that the other side must accept responsibility for the refugee problem.

EGYPT. A populous and significant Middle East state with which the United States nurtured a close relationship in the late 20th century. Prior to 1945, U.S. interests in Egypt were limited to cultural institutions such as the **American University in Cairo (AUC)** and certain commercial ventures, but the U.S. government passively tolerated the British imperial administration of the country. During World War II, the **Franklin D. Roosevelt** administration endorsed British domination of Egypt on behalf of the common Anglo-American goal of defeating Axis armies in North Africa.

In the late 1940s, U.S.–Egyptian relations were strained by several issues. The United States backed Great Britain's efforts to retain military base rights in Egypt, deemed necessary during the early Cold War, rather than endorse Egypt's independence. American backing of the creation of **Israel** also generated resentment in Cairo, aggravated by Egypt's disastrous military defeats during the **Arab-Israeli War of 1948–1949**. In 1950–1951, Egypt rejected a Western bid to create a **Middle East Command** defense arrangement, based in Cairo, to secure the Middle East from Soviet threats.

Relations between the United States and Egypt were tumultuous in the 1950s. As **Gamal Abdel Nasser** took control of the Egyptian government after the revolution of 1952, American officials welcomed him as a progressive alternative to the deposed **King Farouk**, they helped Britain and Egypt negotiate a treaty that ended the British occupation of Egypt, and they offered Egypt economic and military aid. Yet the U.S.–Egyptian relationship soured after 1954. The United States hoped that Egypt would cooperate with Western anti-Soviet defense planning and build regional stability by making peace with Israel. Nasser, however, decided to seek prestige among African and Arab states by challenging the Western presence in the Middle East and confronting Israel. Hence, Nasser refused to join U.S.-backed defense schemes such as the **Middle East Defense Organization** and the **Baghdad Pact**, he purchased Soviet arms, and he rejected American plans for peace with Israel. The **Dwight D. Eisenhower** administration aimed to undermine Nasser's prestige by cutting off economic aid, but that step only provoked Nasser to nationalize the Suez Canal Company, in turn triggering the **Suez Crisis** of 1956. Although the United States stopped an Anglo–French–Israeli attack on Egypt in that conflict, the U.S.–Egyptian relationship remained tense. American officials remained concerned by evidence that Nasser fomented anti-Western nationalism across the region and by the expansionism manifest in the merger of Egypt, **Syria**, and **Yemen** into the United Arab Republic in 1958–1961.

The relationship experienced trouble through the end of the Nasser era in 1970. Presidents Eisenhower and **John F. Kennedy** nurtured a rapprochement with Nasser that featured the resumption of U.S. economic aid, an agreement not to discuss the Israel issue, and friendly political gestures. But the rapprochement ended in the early 1960s when Nasser intervened in a civil war in **Yemen** in opposition to America's friend **Saudi Arabia**. After a series of incidents—such as a mob burning down a United States Information Service Library in

Cairo in 1964—Nasser and President **Lyndon B. Johnson** traded insults, and Johnson suspended economic aid to Egypt. Nasser severed diplomatic relations with the United States during the **Arab-Israeli War of 1967** after he accused the United States of directly assisting in Israel's devastating air attacks on his country. During the **War of Attrition** in 1967–1970, Egypt became dependent on Soviet military support, and the United States tended to back Israel.

In contrast to the unsteadiness of the Nasser years, U.S.–Egyptian relations improved dramatically after **Anwar Sadat** replaced Nasser as premier in 1970. Sadat expelled Soviet military advisers from Egypt in 1972, and, in the aftermath of the **Arab-Israeli War of 1973**, he proved receptive to various peacemaking schemes concocted by Secretary of State **Henry Kissinger**. Sadat restored formal relations with Washington in 1974 and soon became the recipient of substantial U.S. economic aid. When President **Jimmy Carter** promoted Arab–Israeli peace in 1977, Sadat launched a diplomatic initiative that led, eventually and with much American nurturing, to the Egyptian–Israeli peace treaty of 1979. The United States rewarded Egypt's willingness to make peace with massive financial aid.

The U.S.–Egyptian relationship continued to improve after **Hosni Mubarak** became prime minister in 1981. Mubarak cooperated with plans of President **Ronald Reagan** for anti-Soviet security planning, provided the United States certain military base rights, fully cooperated with U.S. prosecution of the **Persian Gulf War** of 1990–1991, and promoted the Arab–Israeli peace process of the 1990s. The United States endorsed Mubarak's effort to defeat radical Islamic fundamentalists who sought to seize control of Egypt. Despite President **George W. Bush**'s zeal in promoting democracy elsewhere in the Middle East, Washington did not press the matter in Egypt. *See also* FOREIGN AID.

EGYPTIAN ISLAMIC JIHAD (EIJ). A loosely organized terrorist group based in **Egypt** that targeted the United States in the 1990s and after. Also known as Islamic Jihad, Jihad Group, Al-Jihad, and Al-Jihad al-Islami, EIJ sought to replace the secular government of Egypt with a theocratic state. It conspired to assassinate Premier **Anwar Sadat** in 1981, and it launched other attacks on the Egyptian government in the 1990s and early 2000s.

EIJ also targeted the United States because it backed the Egyptian government. It organized the 1993 bombing of the World Trade Center in New York and reportedly assisted in the 1998 bombings of the U.S. embassies in Tanzania and Kenya, and it plotted a 1998 attack (that was thwarted) on the U.S. embassy in Albania. After merging with the **al-Qaeda** network, EIJ contributed to the planning of the **9/11** attacks on the United States. The United States prosecuted and imprisoned Sheikh Omar Abdel Rahman, spiritual leader of EIJ, for involvement in the 1993 World Trade Center attack, and it sought to arrest or kill **Ayman al-Zawahiri**, who apparently took control of the group in the late 1990s.

EISENHOWER DOCTRINE. A U.S. security policy in the Middle East issued in 1957. The doctrine declared that the United States would distribute economic and military aid and, if necessary, use military force to stop the spread of communism in the Middle East. President **Dwight D. Eisenhower** proposed the doctrine in an address to Congress in January 1957, and Congress reluctantly approved it two months later.

The **Suez Crisis** of 1956 prompted Eisenhower to issue the doctrine. That crisis had undermined British and French prestige in the region, elevated the stature of Egyptian president **Gamal Abdel Nasser**, and seemingly raised the prospect of Soviet intervention in the Middle East. Eisenhower calculated that the United States must take a dominant position in the region to shore up its remaining pro-Western governments before revolutionary movements backed by the Soviet Union or **Egypt** swept the Middle East to the detriment of U.S. interests.

Although Eisenhower never formally invoked the doctrine, he intervened in three situations under the doctrine's provisions. In the spring of 1957, the president dispensed economic aid to **Jordan** and sent U.S. naval ships into the eastern Mediterranean to help **King Hussein** suppress a rebellion among pro-Egyptian army officers. Late in 1957, Eisenhower encouraged Turkey and other friendly states to consider an incursion into **Syria** to stop a radical regime from consolidating power there. When a violent revolution in **Iraq** in July 1958 threatened to spark similar uprisings in **Lebanon** and Jordan, finally, Eisenhower ordered U.S. soldiers to occupy Beirut and to transport supplies to British forces occupying Jordan.

In late 1958, the Eisenhower administration realized that the policy of resisting Arab nationalism seemed counterproductive, and it downplayed the Eisenhower Doctrine in favor of a new policy of accommodating Arab nationalism. *See also* FOREIGN AID.

EISENHOWER, DWIGHT D. (1890–1969). Career army officer and World War II hero who, as president of the United States in 1953–1961, shaped bold, new U.S. policies in the Middle East. On taking office in 1953, Eisenhower moved quickly to resolve a showdown in **Iran** that had originated in 1951 when Prime Minister **Mohammed Mossadegh** nationalized the British-owned Anglo-Iranian Oil Company and challenged the authority of pro-Western Shah **Mohammed Reza Pahlavi**. Eisenhower declined a request from Mossadegh for financial assistance and instead authorized U.S. and British intelligence officers covertly to overthrow the Iranian premier in August 1953. Eisenhower acted because Mossadegh seemed to be leading his oil-rich state from the Western orbit to the Soviet orbit, to the detriment of U.S. interests in the Cold War. The U.S.–U.K. action bolstered the shah as Iran's leader and secured the country's oil for a generation, but it also planted the seeds of the Iranian revolution of 1979.

Eisenhower took steps to establish a security system among friendly powers in the Middle East in order to prevent the spread of Soviet influence into the region and to ensure the defeat of the Soviet Union in the event of war. In 1954–1955, his administration used political persuasion and military aid to induce Turkey, Pakistan, Iran, **Iraq**, and Great Britain to sign the **Baghdad Pact** mutual defense agreement. The United States did not formally join the pact, citing a likely backlash from the Soviet Union and from Israel, although it funded the pact and participated in its meetings. The Baghdad Pact lost credibility after the Iraqi revolution of 1958, although it marked a milestone in the growing U.S. commitment to Middle East security.

In 1955–1956, Eisenhower briefly promoted a comprehensive plan for Arab–Israeli peace. The **Alpha peace plan** proposed a permanent Arab–Israeli peace settlement featuring compromises on specific points of controversy, such as borders, the status of **Palestinian refugees**, and the control of Jerusalem. Working with British leaders, Eisenhower encouraged **Egypt** and **Israel** to accept the Alpha plan as a first step toward a regionwide settlement. But neither of those states complied, and violent incidents occurred along their common border, leading to the **Suez Crisis** of 1956.

Eisenhower made momentous decisions during the Suez Crisis, in which his British and French allies secretly colluded with Israel to launch an attack on Egypt designed to oust its premier, **Gamal Abdel Nasser**. In mid-1956, Eisenhower encouraged Britain, France, and Israel to rely on diplomacy rather than force to resolve their mounting grievances against Egypt. When the three states attacked Egypt over his objections, Eisenhower used a variety of political and economic levers to compel them to halt their offensives and to withdraw from Egyptian territory. His policy helped to mark the end of Anglo–French primacy in the Middle East and the dawn of American dominance there.

As a consequence of the Suez Crisis, Eisenhower declared a major new security policy in the Middle East in early 1957. With Anglo–French influence in the Middle East vanquished and Soviet interest in the region rising, the president secured congressional approval of the **Eisenhower Doctrine**, a statement that the United States would distribute economic and military aid and, if necessary, use military force to contain communism in the Middle East. Although never formally invoked, the Eisenhower Doctrine guided U.S. policy in three controversies. Under it, Eisenhower bolstered **King Hussein** of Jordan against a simmering revolution by discontented army officers, encouraged local states to resist political radicalism in **Syria**, and ordered U.S. Marines to occupy Beirut in July 1958 to stabilize its government against revolutionary forces. *See also* FOREIGN AID.

ESHKOL, LEVI (1895–1969). Prime minister who led **Israel** through a crucial era in U.S.–Israeli relations. Born in Ukraine, Eshkol migrated to **Palestine** in 1914 and became involved in Zionist politics. He held a variety of posts in the early Israeli government, most notably minister of finance (1952–1963). Eshkol succeeded **David Ben-Gurion** as prime minister in 1963 and held that office until a heart attack claimed his life in February 1969.

As prime minister, Eshkol laid the foundations for a close relationship with the United States. He visited the United States in 1964, the first Israeli prime minister to do so in an official capacity, and he enjoyed a friendly reception by President **Lyndon B. Johnson**. In 1965–1966, Eshkol secured tanks and advanced military aircraft by signing the first U.S.–Israeli major arms deals that provided weapons with offensive capabilities. During the Egyptian–Israeli crisis of the spring of 1967, Eshkol deftly deflected pressure from Johnson to show restraint, and he ordered the invasion of **Egypt** that marked the start of the **Arab-Israeli War of 1967**. During that war, Eshkol delicately handled the political fallout of the USS *Liberty* incident, which had the potential to undermine U.S.–Israeli amity, and after the war he worked assiduously to secure U.S. endorsement of Israel's determination to use the land Israel had occupied as bargaining chips to secure peace with and recognition by Arab adversaries. The United States embodied the principle of land-for-peace in **United Nations Security Council Resolution 242** of November 1967.

– F –

FAHD, KING, OF SAUDI ARABIA (1923–2005). The fifth king of **Saudi Arabia** who developed a close relationship with the United States. Fahd was born to **ibn Saud**, who would declare the kingdom of **Saudi Arabia** in 1932, and ibn Saud's favorite wife, Hassa Bint Ahmad al-Sudayri. Fahd served in Saudi Arabia's foreign ministry and as minister of education and minister of interior before he became crown prince in 1975. He became king of Saudi Arabia on the death of his brother, **King Khalid**, in June 1982.

King Fahd endeared himself to the United States with his diplomatic activism. In 1981–1982, he proposed an Arab–Israeli peace plan calling for establishment of a state of **Palestine** in exchange for Arab acceptance of Israel, although he could not convince fellow Arab leaders to endorse it. Fahd assisted in the U.S. effort to organize armed resistance to the Soviet occupation of Afghanistan, and he facilitated secret U.S. arms sales to **Iran**. In 1988, he attempted to broker an end to the **Iran–Iraq War**, and in 1989 he hosted the entire National Assembly of **Lebanon** at a conference at the Saudi resort city of al-Taif, where, removed from the instability in Beirut, they were able to adopt a plan for ending the civil war in Lebanon.

Fahd also used his country's immense oil wealth to fund Islamic schools throughout the Middle East and to benefit the Palestinian people. To burnish his Islamist credentials, Fahd took on the title of Custodian of the Two Holy Mosques in 1986.

Most important to the United States, Fahd welcomed American military forces to his kingdom during the **Persian Gulf War** of 1990–1991. The ability to use Saudi military bases was vital to the success of the United States in liberating **Kuwait** in 1991, containing **Iraq** in 1991–2003, and invading and overthrowing Iraqi dictator **Saddam Hussein** in 2003. Yet the presence of American forces also stimulated resistance, including **terrorism**, by Saudi nationalists. American forces departed Saudi Arabia in 2003, shortly after the occupation of Iraq.

King Fahd suffered a stroke in 1995 and thereafter became progressively incapacitated by a series of medical problems. Crown Prince **Abdullah** increasingly exercised power as Fahd descended into figurehead status. King Fahd died in August 2005.

FAISAL, KING, OF SAUDI ARABIA (1905–1975). Third king of **Saudi Arabia** who fashioned a foreign policy at odds with the United States. Son of Saudi Arabian founder **ibn Saud**, Faisal led an internal struggle against his brother **King Saud**, serving as premier and foreign minister in 1958–1960, returning as premier in 1962, and organizing a coup that ousted Saud in 1964. On becoming king in 1964, Faisal quickly stabilized Saudi Arabia's financial situation and introduced a series of domestic reforms ranging from free health care and education to the abolition of slavery and the introduction of television. Faisal practiced an austere and religious lifestyle that earned him the respect of his subjects. He was assassinated in November 1975 by a disgruntled nephew.

During his 11-year reign, Faisal used diplomacy to protect the vital interests of the Saudi monarchy. Before and after his coronation, he organized Saudi resistance to the influence of **Egypt** in the civil war in **Yemen**. He funded the **Palestine Liberation Organization (PLO)** and, after the **Arab-Israeli War of 1967**, underscored the need for Arab unity against **Israel** by sending aid to Egypt, **Jordan**, and **Syria**. After the United States assisted Israel during the **Arab-Israeli War of 1973**, Faisal organized the **Arab oil embargo** that had a harsh effect on the U.S. economy.

FAISAL I, KING, OF IRAQ (1885–1933). First king of modern **Iraq** (1921–1933). The third son of Sharif Husayn of Mecca, Faisal led the Arab revolt in partnership with Great Britain and against the Ottoman Empire during World War I. Arab forces under Faisal's command occupied Damascus in 1918. After Faisal's attempt to become king of postwar **Syria** was frustrated by France, the British arranged for Faisal to become king of Iraq in 1921 after they secured a mandate over that territory. Under Faisal's leadership, Iraq achieved nominal independence and membership in the League of Nations in 1932.

FAISAL II, KING, OF IRAQ (1935–1958). A pro-Western monarch of the Hashimite family, overthrown in a violent coup in July 1958. The grandson of King **Faisal I**, Faisal II became king at age three in 1939 when his father Ghazi died in an automobile accident; an uncle ruled as regent for 15 years. Educated in Great Britain, Faisal II showed friendship toward the West, and in early 1958 he federated his country with the Hashimite Kingdom of **Jordan**, ruled by his cousin **King Hussein**, as a counterweight to the recent merger of **Egypt**, **Syria**, and **Yemen** in the United Arab Republic. In July 1958, nationalistic army officers staged a coup and murdered Faisal II and his family. Faisal II was the last monarch of Iraq.

FAROUK, KING, OF EGYPT (1920–1965). The last monarch of **Egypt** and the first Egyptian leader with whom the United States developed a political relationship. Farouk took power in Cairo in 1936, at age 16, on the death of his father, King Fuad. Seeking to shore up its Middle East presence in the World War II era, Great Britain pressed Farouk's government to sign a 20-year military alliance in 1936. Using a show of military force in February 1942, the British bullied the king into appointing a government favored by London. That episode deeply humiliated Farouk, whose political reputation among Egyptians never recovered, and it encouraged nationalists to conspire to overthrow him. Farouk's image was further damaged by Egypt's setbacks in the **Arab-Israeli War of 1948–1949** and by widespread reports of his incompetence, corruption, and debauched lifestyle. As U.S. officials identified interests in Egypt during the early Cold War, they regretted the instability of Farouk's regime and the mounting tension between Egypt and Britain. American officials were surprised but also a bit relieved when nationalistic army officers overthrew Farouk in July 1952. Exiled to Italy, Farouk died in 1965.

FORD, GERALD R. (1913–2006). President in 1974–1977 who largely continued the Middle East policies inherited from President **Richard M. Nixon**. Ford authorized Secretary of State **Henry Kissinger** to continue his **shuttle diplomacy**, which culminated in September 1975 with the so-called **Sinai II agreement** between **Egypt** and **Israel**. To overcome Israeli reluctance to sign anything short of a full peace treaty, Ford and Kissinger issued incentives, such as economic aid and a secret pledge not to negotiate with the **Palestine Liberation Organization (PLO)** or launch any diplomatic initiatives in the region without first consulting Israel, as well as warnings that Ford would reassess his policy toward Israel if it remained stubborn. Ford secured Egyptian cooperation with Sinai II by pledging to seek a follow-up accord between Israel and **Syria** and to seek a settlement of the **Palestinian refugees** problem.

FOREIGN AID, U.S. Monetary assistance distributed by the U.S. government to foreign states and institutions for the purpose of serving U.S. foreign policy aims. The U.S. government spent lavishly on foreign aid in the late 1940s and early 1950s, mostly on the Marshall Plan, which sparked the economic recovery of war-torn Europe. Over subsequent decades, foreign aid (when adjusted for inflation and as a percentage of federal spending) declined steadily despite occasional spikes, such as the Alliance for Progress of the early 1960s and the Egyptian–Israeli peace initiative of the late 1970s. Foreign aid hit bottom in the mid-1990s but then surged in the early 2000s to the highest levels since the Marshall Plan era.

During the Cold War, foreign aid was dispensed for the broad purpose of containing communism. After the Cold War, foreign aid officials identified a variety of political, economic, and humanitarian objectives. In the early 2000s, officials divided foreign aid programs into five different categories: bilateral development assistance ($6.2 billion in 2004), economic aid in support of U.S. policies ($5.4 billion), humanitarian aid ($2.6 billion), aid to multilateral institutions including the **United Nations** ($1.7 billion), and military assistance ($4.6 billion).

Before 1970, U.S. foreign aid to the Middle East was modest compared to that to other regions. In 1950–1970, aid to the Middle East totaled $7.8 billion, with **Iran** ($2.1 billion) and **Israel** ($1.3 billion) the top recipients. Aid to the region was curtailed sharply in the late 1960s as Arab states severed relations with the United States during the **Arab-Israeli War of 1967** and as the Vietnam War consumed U.S. resources.

The United States took new interest in the Middle East in the 1970s after Egypt shunned Soviet assistance and made peace with Israel. To encourage peace making, the United States offered Israel and **Egypt** aid in the range of some $3 billion and $2 billion per year, respectively, making those states the top two recipients worldwide. The United States also extended special incentives to Middle East states, such as forgiving $6.7 billion in Egypt's debts to reward that state's support of American objectives in the **Persian Gulf War**, subsidizing Israel's absorption of immigrants from former Soviet territory to the tune of $9.2 billion, and allocating several hundreds of millions of dollars to various states as incentives to make peace. In 1971–2001, the United States dispensed some $145 billion in the Middle East (measured in constant dollars), including $79 billion to Israel and $53 billion to Egypt. As a region, the Middle East absorbed 58 percent of U.S. foreign aid in 1994 and 73 percent in 2004. In the post–World War II era, Israel ranked as the largest recipient of U.S. aid in the world.

After the **U.S. invasion of Iraq** in 2003, that country became the recipient of the largest annual foreign aid allotment, garnering some $18.5 billion in reconstruction aid in 2004. In reaction to **9/11**, the United States also increased aid to such countries as Pakistan, Afghanistan, Turkey, and **Jordan** for the purpose of advancing counterterrorism objectives.

FORRESTAL, JAMES (1892–1949). Lawyer and U.S. government official who served as the first secretary of defense (1947–1949) after the creation of the National Military Establishment (later the Department of Defense) in 1947. Forrestal strongly objected to President **Harry S. Truman**'s support of **Israel**, which he suspected was motivated by domestic political considerations, arguing that support of Israel would alienate Arab states whose friendship was vital to U.S. national security interests in the Cold War.

FRANKS, TOMMY (1945–). American army general who commanded U.S. forces during the **U.S. invasion of Afghanistan** in 2001 and the early portion of the **Iraq War** in 2003. Franks became a career soldier and served in **Operation Desert Storm** in 1991. In 2000, he was promoted to general and named commander of Central Command, with responsibility for U.S. military operations in the Middle East, Africa, and South Asia. After the **9/11** attacks, Franks quickly conceived a war plan for the destruction of the Taliban regime in Afghanistan and implemented that plan when President **George W. Bush** gave the order in October 2001. In March–April 2003, Franks commanded the **U.S. invasion of Iraq** that ousted the **Saddam Hussein** regime. Franks retired from the army in July 2003.

– G –

GARNER, JAY (1938–). A retired U.S. Army lieutenant general who initially headed the U.S. occupation of **Iraq** during the **Iraq War**. Garner served for 34 years as a soldier, including a command post in Iraq after the **Persian Gulf War** of 1990–1991, before retiring in 1997. In January 2003, Secretary of Defense **Donald Rumsfeld** recruited Garner to serve as the director of the Office of Reconstruction and Humanitarian Assistance, an office established to govern Iraq after the impending American invasion. Garner arrived in Iraq soon after the conquest of the country but quickly realized the futility of his goal of arranging an orderly transfer of sovereignty to Iraqis within 90 days. Garner's authority diminished when President **George W. Bush** created the Coalition Provisional Authority in May 2003.

GEMAYEL, AMIN. *See* GEMAYEL, BASHIR.

GEMAYEL, BASHIR (1947–1982). Lebanese Maronite Christian who sought to govern **Lebanon** in 1982. The son of Pierre Gemayel, who founded Lebanon's conservative Phalange Party, Bashir Gemayel became leader of the Phalange militia in the 1970s as it battled Muslim and Druze forces in the Lebanese civil war. Gemayel cooperated with Israeli forces during the **Israeli invasion of Lebanon** in June 1982 because they targeted his domestic adversaries. After winning a presidential election in August, Gemayel met with Israeli leaders to discuss a possible peace treaty, but before he was inaugurated, he was assassinated by one of his enemy factions, probably backed by **Syria**. Bashir Gemayel's brother and successor, Amin Gemayel, who officially led the country through the depth of its civil war in 1982–1988, indicated no desire to make peace with Israel.

– H –

HABIB, PHILIP C. (1920–1992). A career U.S. foreign service officer who implemented American policy in the Middle East in the late 1970s and early 1980s. The son of an immigrant Lebanese grocer in New York City, Habib served in the State Department from 1949 to 1980. Late in his career, he helped arrange talks between **Israeli** prime minster **Menachem Begin** and **Egyptian** premier **Anwar Sadat** that set the stage for negotiation of the **Camp David Accords**.

In 1981–1983, Habib returned from retirement to serve as President **Ronald Reagan**'s special emissary to the Middle East. In that capacity, he brokered a 1981 cease-fire between Israel and **Lebanon**, destined to collapse in the **Israeli invasion of Lebanon** in June 1982. By August 1982, the Israeli army had besieged Beirut, trapping **Palestine Liberation Organization (PLO)** leader **Yasser Arafat** and some 11,000 PLO combatants there. Habib returned to the region to broker a deal in which PLO units evacuated Beirut under the watchful eyes of American and French soldiers and Israel pledged not to attack the city. For his achievement, Habib was awarded the Presidential Medal of Freedom in September 1982.

HAIG, ALEXANDER M. (1924–). American army general and White House chief of staff under President **Richard M. Nixon** who served briefly as President **Ronald Reagan**'s first secretary of state. Haig played a central role in U.S. policy toward **Israel's invasion of Lebanon** in June 1982. As tensions mounted in early 1982 over Palestinian **terrorism** against Israel, Israeli defense minister **Ariel Sharon** discussed with Haig the prospects of attacking **Palestine Liberation Organization (PLO)** forces in **Lebanon** and warned that Israel would retaliate forcefully against the next provocation. Given

Israel's propensity for action, Haig's ambiguous response—in which he set conditions on which an invasion would be justified rather than warning starkly against one—probably encouraged the Israeli attack. Reagan's anger over the Israeli invasion and Haig's apparent support of it aggravated the other policy differences between the two men. On 25 June, Reagan dismissed Haig from office.

HAMAS. *See* ISLAMIC RESISTANCE MOVEMENT.

HARIRI, RAFIK (1944–2005). Lebanese businessman who led **Lebanon** through its post–civil war reconstruction in the 1990s. Born in modest circumstances, Hariri became a multibillionaire businessman in the construction industry in **Saudi Arabia** and Lebanon. He spearheaded the effort to negotiate the Taif Accord of 1989, which ended his country's brutal civil war, and as prime minister of Lebanon in 1992–1998 and 2000–2004, he restored Lebanon's political stability and rebuilt its war-torn infrastructure. In October 2004, Hariri resigned the prime ministry to protest political machinations by Lebanon's pro-Syrian president **Emile Lahoud**. He apparently planned to contest Lahoud's government in the May 2005 elections, but he was assassinated by a car bomb in February 2005, widely reported to have been perpetrated by **Syria**. Hariri's murder sparked massive popular protests that forced the resignation of pro-Syrian prime minister **Omar Karami** and generated pressure that led to Syria's withdrawal of its military forces from Lebanon in April 2005.

HEIKAL, MOHAMMED HASSANEIN (1923–). Egyptian official and public commentator. A journalist for more than 60 years, Heikal was longtime editor of the influential Cairo newspaper *Al-Ahram*. He also served as confidante to President **Gamal Abdel Nasser** and as foreign minister of **Egypt** in 1970. Heikal was jailed briefly in 1980 by President **Anwar al-Sadat** for opposing the **Camp David Accords**. Although he thereafter eschewed politics, he remained a prolific author and vocal commentator on Middle East diplomacy.

HENDERSON, LOY (1892–1986). Career Foreign Service officer who shaped U.S. diplomacy in the Middle East during the early Cold War era. Henderson first became involved in the Middle East during

World War II, when his intense mistrust of the Soviet Union, formed during service in Moscow during the 1930s, proved a liability to President **Franklin D. Roosevelt**'s aims of building a wartime Grand Alliance with the Soviet Union. In November 1943, Roosevelt appointed Henderson minister to **Iraq**, in which post he monitored U.S. interests in the British-dominated Persian Gulf region.

In 1945, President **Harry S. Truman** named Henderson to head the State Department's Office of Near Eastern and African Affairs, in which post Henderson vigorously promoted anti-Soviet policies, such as the **Truman Doctrine**. Yet Henderson also stringently resisted the White House's pro-**Zionism** policies, such as support for the plan for the **partition of Palestine** and the recognition of **Israel**, on the grounds that anti-Soviet containment policy demanded the loyalty and friendship of the Arab states. Intense criticism of Henderson by American Zionists during a close presidential election campaign convinced Truman to reassign Henderson as ambassador to India in July 1948.

Henderson returned to Middle East affairs as ambassador to **Iran** in 1951–1955. Appointed to that post by Secretary of State **Dean G. Acheson** to monitor the emerging crisis between Premier **Mohammed Mossadegh** and Shah **Mohammed Reza Pahlavi**, Henderson carefully averted a British military strike against Iran but eventually concluded that the United States needed to remove Mossadegh from office in order to prevent the spread of Soviet communism into the country. In Tehran, Henderson also facilitated the delicate U.S. policy of supporting while not officially joining the **Baghdad Pact** military alliance.

In the late 1950s, Henderson acted as a Middle East troubleshooter. He served on the **United Nations** Suez Committee, which visited Cairo in September 1956 on a quest (that proved futile) to find a peaceful solution to the **Suez Crisis**. In 1957, he mobilized leaders in Turkey, Iraq, and **Jordan** to counter communist inroads in **Syria**. By the time of his retirement from the State Department in 1961, Henderson had become one of its highest-ranking officers and had earned the nickname "Mr. Foreign Service."

HERTER, CHRISTIAN A. (1895–1966). U.S. secretary of state in 1959–1961 who showed limited interest in Middle East policies.

President **Dwight D. Eisenhower** appointed Herter after **John Foster Dulles** resigned from the State Department only weeks before his death, and Herter essentially served as a caretaker. Distracted by crises in other regions, he reasoned that he lacked the time or political mandate to launch bold new initiatives in the Middle East, and he declined the advice of his departmental advisers that he promote Arab–Israeli peacemaking.

HIZBALLAH. A militant group in **Lebanon** that used violence and **terrorism** against the United States, **Israel**, and other powers. Founded in 1982 in response to the **Israeli invasion of Lebanon**, Hizballah fielded fighters who violently resisted the Israeli occupation of south Lebanon. With financial and political backing from **Iran** and logistical support from **Syria**, Hizballah developed the tactic of suicide bombing, such as organizing the October 1983 attack on a barracks in Beirut that caused the deaths of 241 U.S. soldiers and that convinced President **Ronald Reagan** to withdraw U.S troops from Lebanon. Hizballah also kidnapped Americans and other Westerners in Lebanon during the 1980s, holding captives until the end of the Lebanese civil war in 1992. The group conducted terrorist attacks in several countries around the world and reportedly colluded with **al-Qaeda** and Palestinian resistance groups in the 1990s and after. Hizballah resistance helped convince the Israeli government to end its occupation of south Lebanon in 2000.

Hizballah also provided various social welfare benefits to the people of south Lebanon and organized a political arm that won seats in Lebanon's elected legislature in the 1990s and early 2000s. Its name meaning "Party of God" in Arabic, Hizbollah aimed to establish a fundamentalist Shiite state in Lebanon, to destroy Israel, and to purge Western influence from the Middle East. Although the United States branded Hizbollah an outlaw terrorist group, it remained very popular among the Shiite minority of Lebanon.

HUSSEIN, KING, OF JORDAN (1935–1999). Long-term Jordanian monarch who developed a warm and friendly relationship with the United States. Hussein ascended to the throne of **Jordan** on his 18th birthday in 1953, succeeding his grandfather **King Abdullah I**, who was assassinated in 1951, and his father, Talal, who was found mentally incompetent to rule in 1952. The early years of Hussein's reign were marked by frequent attempted assassinations and coups, notably by disaffected Palestinians who made up some two-thirds of his subjects. Yet Hussein became a master at survival, and by the time of his death from cancer in 1999, he claimed the title of the world's longest-serving head of state.

Hussein's relationship with the United States was generally friendly although occasionally uneven. American leaders tended to value the king's support on Cold War–era security issues and came to see him as a barrier against the spread of Palestinian radicalism and as a buffer against expansionism by **Israel** or **Egypt**. Thus, the United States bolstered Hussein with generous financial aid and political encouragement. Under the **Eisenhower Doctrine**, most notably, the United States backed Hussein's suppression of an internal revolt in April 1957, and it endorsed and logistically supported a British military occupation of Jordan to save the king in July 1958. Hussein enjoyed American political support during the so-called **Black September** episode of 1970–1971, when he cracked down on Palestinians who had challenged his authority and whose violence against Israel had drawn reprisals against his kingdom. In 1978, Hussein married the American-born Lisa Najeeb Halaby, who took the royal name **Queen Noor**.

On two occasions, regional dynamics threatened the accord between the United States and King Hussein. In May 1967, King Hussein joined a military alliance with Egypt and **Syria**, to the chagrin of U.S. officials who aimed to ease mounting tensions in the Middle East. Hussein's action backfired during the **Arab-Israeli War of 1967**, during which conflict he lost control of the West Bank to Israel. Decades later, Hussein briefly alienated the **George H. W. Bush** administration by embracing neutrality during the **Persian Gulf War** of 1990–1991.

During the remainder of the 1990s, by contrast, Hussein consolidated a close relationship with the United States. The king was instrumental in organizing the **Madrid Conference** of 1991, and he formed a joint delegation with Palestinian delegates that enabled Palestinian and Israeli officials to meet face-to-face. Consistent with larger American peacemaking ambitions, Hussein signed a formal peace treaty with Israel in 1994. When U.S.-arbitrated Israeli–Palestinian talks stalemated in 1998, King Hussein, despite his own serious illness, attended a crucial meeting and assisted in clinching the **Wye River Memorandum**.

HUSSEIN, SADDAM (1937–2006). Ruthless tyrant who governed **Iraq** from 1979 to 2003. A masterful political strategist, Hussein gained influence during Iraq's political instability of the 1960s and 1970s, and in 1979 he became head of the Baath Party and President of Iraq and named himself field marshal in Iraq's army. Hussein provoked the **Iran–Iraq War** of 1980–1988, during which he gained American backing as a bulwark against revolutionary **Iran**. In 1990, he provoked the **Persian Gulf War**, this time becoming the target of a U.S.-organized international counteroffensive that forced him to relinquish his occupation of **Kuwait**. Through the 1980s and 1990s, Hussein consolidated his hold on power in Iraq by brutally suppressing all domestic rivals, and in the 1990s, he became a nuisance to the United States by resisting **United Nations**–backed arms inspections of his country.

In the **Iraq War** of 2003–, President **George W. Bush** ordered an invasion of Iraq to depose Saddam Hussein and install a democratic government. The capture of Baghdad in April 2003 and the toppling of towering statues of Hussein signaled the end of his regime. Hussein remained a fugitive until 13 December 2003, when a U.S. Army patrol discovered him hiding in a crude cellar on a farm near Tikrit. He was tried and convicted in an Iraqi court for crimes against humanity and crimes against the Iraqi people, and hanged on 30 December 2006.

– I –

IBN SAUD, KING, OF SAUDI ARABIA (ca. 1880–1953). Founder and first king of **Saudi Arabia** and an important partner of the United States. Ibn Saud, a desert chieftain imbued with a conservative form of Sunni Islam known as Wahhabism, took control of most of Arabia through a series of tribal wars starting in 1902. He declared the Kingdom of Saudi Arabia in 1932 and ruled it absolutely for 21 years.

In the 1930s, Ibn Saud granted oil concessions to American firms whose discovery and marketing of Saudi Arabia's vast oil resources brought great wealth to the kingdom. He also indicated a willingness to partner with the U.S. government by accepting American military aid and by permitting the United States to use military facilities in his kingdom. He affirmed his friendship with President **Franklin D. Roosevelt** during a meeting aboard the USS *Quincy* on the Suez Canal in 1945. Ibn Saud criticized President **Harry S. Truman** for supporting **Israel** as a violation of a pledge from Roosevelt that the United States would not change its policy on **Palestine** without consulting Arab leaders. But he did not allow disagreements about Israel to spoil Saudi–U.S. relations.

"ICEBOX AGREEMENT." An unofficial deal between President **John F. Kennedy** and Egyptian premier **Gamal Abdel Nasser** to suspend consideration of the contentious issue of **Israel** and move on to other matters where accord might be achieved. The agreement to place the Israel issue "in the icebox" was part of a larger rapprochement that Kennedy inherited from President **Dwight D. Eisenhower** and that Kennedy built on with such gestures as trading personal letters with Nasser and extending U.S. economic aid to Egypt. Within a few years, the rapprochement ended after U.S.–Egyptian differences on Israel resurfaced.

IDRIS, KING, OF LIBYA (1890–1983). King of **Libya** in 1951–1969 and friend of the West. In 1917, Idris was named emir of Cyrenaica, one of Italy's North African colonies; in 1922, he took refuge in Cairo after a political fight with Italy's fascist regime. Idris returned to Cyrenaica in 1943 after British forces occupied it. When Cyrenaica merged with Tripolitania and Fezzan in 1951 as the independent state of Libya, Idris became king. King Idris governed his country on terms friendly to the West, allowing American and British forces to enjoy military base rights on his territory and welcoming Western oil firms to develop Libya's nascent oil industry. In 1969, Idris was overthrown in a nonviolent coup led by Colonel **Muammar al-Qaddafi**. He died in exile in Cairo in 1983.

INTIFADA. An Arabic word for "shaking off" used to denote two popular, violent uprisings by Palestinians against Israeli forces in occupation of the West Bank and Gaza. The first intifada erupted spontaneously in December 1987. Having languished for 40 years without a state and for 20 years under Israeli occupation, the Palestinians had become dispirited by their poverty, disillusioned with the **Palestine Liberation Organization (PLO)** and the Arab states, humiliated by Israeli curfews and restrictions, and frustrated by the construction of Israeli settlements in the West Bank and Gaza. A simple motor vehicle accident in Gaza triggered street protests that grew quickly into a widespread uprising across the territories as thousands of Palestinians took to the streets to demonstrate, throw rocks and incendiaries, and burn tires. Israeli security forces responded with economic sanctions, curfews, closures of universities, mass arrests, and crowd control techniques ranging from water cannons to live ammunition. By mid-1990, more than 1,000 Palestinians and about 50 Israelis had died in the uprising. The PLO under **Yasser Arafat** gradually took control of resistance activities, gaining sufficient political stature to declare statehood of **Palestine** as well as implicitly affirm the legitimacy of **Israel** in November 1988. But the intifada also empowered the more radical **Islamic Resistance Movement** (**Hamas**), which contested the PLO for control of the Palestinian people.

The prospect of the intifada fomenting extremism prompted U.S. officials to promote peace talks between Israel and the Palestinians. In March 1988, Secretary of State **George P. Shultz** called for negotiations between Israel and a joint **Jordan**–PLO delegation, arbitrated by the United States and aiming to reach a final agreement on the occupied territories within one year and to complete a transitional settlement within three years. In December 1988, when Arafat publicly renounced **terrorism**, Shultz declared that the United States would speak to the PLO. The administration of **George H. W. Bush** continued to promote such peace plans and ultimately convened the **Madrid Conference** in October 1991.

The second intifada began after the peace process of the 1990s stalemated. In September 2000, Israeli Likud party leader **Ariel Sharon**, in a political gimmick designed to affirm his hard-line credentials, marched across the Temple Mount in Jerusalem under a heavy police guard and vowed in a speech that Israel would never surrender the land that held the Al-Aqsa Mosque. Within 24 hours, Palestinians rioted across the West Bank in protest. The rioting quickly spread into a second intifada that proved to be more intense and deadly than the first. The second uprising featured Palestinian terrorist attacks during religious holiday celebrations, the grisly murder of two Israeli soldiers after they sought refuge in a Palestinian police station, the fatal shootings of Palestinian children by Israeli soldiers, and countless Israeli air strikes and tank barrages. More than 90 suicide bombers attacked Israeli targets between September 2000 and June 2003, including seven who struck in seven days during the Israeli Passover holiday of 2002. Suspicious that Arafat fomented the violence, Sharon, elected Israeli prime minister in 2001, dispatched tanks to besiege Arafat's headquarters in Ramallah, where the Palestinian leader remained in virtual house arrest until days before his death of natural causes in November 2004. By January 2005, the violence had claimed the lives of some 3,500 Palestinians and 1,000 Israelis. More than a dozen proposed cease-fires failed to stop the carnage.

American officials tried, with little success, to stem the bloodletting. Presidents **William J. Clinton** and **George W. Bush** promoted various cease-fire deals, to no avail. Ultimately, Bush called on the Palestinian people to replace Arafat with a moderate leader and to embrace a democratic peace process that would lead to Palestinian statehood. Tensions abated slightly in 2004–2006 as Arafat's death brought moderates into control of the PLO, Hamas suspended suicide attacks on Israel, and Israel withdrew from Gaza.

IRAN. An oil-rich country on the Persian Gulf with which the United States has had a long and complicated relationship. Predominantly Shiite Muslims, Iranians are not Arabs. Prior to 1945, the United States enjoyed a limited but friendly relationship with Iran. The United States recognized the country—still known as Persia—in 1856, and it generally gained a favorable reputation in Tehran as an honest broker standing in contrast to the British and Russians who had long competed for imperial preferences there. The U.S. reputation was further enhanced by the widespread charitable work conducted by American missionaries starting in the mid-19th century and the technical advice offered by Arthur Millspaugh during two missions in the early 1920s and the early 1940s. After Great Britain and the Soviet Union invaded Iran and forced the abdication of **Shah Reza** in 1941, the United States sent some 30,000 soldiers to the country to guard supply lines to the Soviet Union, provided Iran with its own lend-lease aid, and sent military missions to train Iranian soldiers and police officers.

In the years following World War II, the United States and Iran nurtured a Cold War partnership. In 1946, Soviet forces, in violation of agreements with Western powers, remained in occupation of northern Iran, where they propped up a secessionist movement. American leaders pressured the Soviets to withdraw, however, enabling Shah **Mohammed Reza Pahlavi** to restore sovereignty over his territory and winning his enduring gratitude. The United States also rescued the shah from a domestic political resistance movement led by **Mohammed Mossadegh**, who became prime minister and nationalized the country's British-owned oil industry in 1951. President **Dwight D. Eisenhower** authorized the Central Intelligence Agency to oust Mossadegh in a covert operation in July–August 1953. Thereafter, the United States bolstered the shah with extensive economic aid, military and police training, intelligence collaboration, and membership in the **Baghdad Pact**. The shah restored full power in Tehran and emerged as a close dependent of the United States. In 1964, the shah granted U.S. personnel in Iran the legal right of extraterritoriality (essentially, diplomatic immunity from Iranian law). Under the **Nixon Doctrine**, the United States identified Iran as its major partner in the Middle East and sold it vast quantities of military arms.

American–Iranian relations changed vastly during and after the Iranian revolution of 1979, in which the anti-American and intensely nationalistic cleric Ayatollah **Ruhollah Khomeini** overthrew the shah. After President **Jimmy Carter** admitted the deposed shah to the United States for medical treatment, Khomeini provoked the infamous **Iran hostage crisis**, in which a mob, with the ayatollah's blessing, stormed the U.S. embassy in Tehran and took captive 52 Americans. Carter's inability to win the release of the hostages through diplomacy and an ill-fated military rescue mission in April 1980 contributed to his defeat in the presidential election of 1980. The crisis, unresolved until January 1981, generated enormous tension in the U.S.–Iranian relationship at all levels.

American–Iranian relations remained tense after 1981. President **Ronald Reagan** deplored Iran's sponsorship of **Hizballah** in **Lebanon** but also saw Iran as a potential barrier to Soviet influence that had recently swept through Afghanistan. Briefly, Reagan provided arms to

Iran in the hope of winning the release of Americans taken hostage by Iranian-backed captors in Lebanon, but the revelation of that policy caused Reagan considerable embarrassment. Thereafter, Reagan intervened modestly on **Iraq**'s side in the **Iran–Iraq War**, compelling Iran to accept terms ending that conflict in 1988. Iran further antagonized the West by calling for the death of British author Salman Rushdie, whose novel *Satanic Verses* reputedly insulted Muslims.

American–Iranian relations grew more ambivalent after Khomeini's death in June 1989. On the one hand, the United States tried to accommodate moderate Iranian politicians who sought to limit the power of the clerics and integrate Iran into the international community. Yet officials in Washington continued to decry Iran's nuclear weapons development programs and its alleged sponsorship of international **terrorism**. Efforts to modify Iranian policy through economic sanctions failed because of the refusal of European powers to honor such sanctions. The designation of Iran by President **George W. Bush** as one sphere in an "axis of evil," U.S. policy in the **Iraq War**, and the foreign policy of Iranian president **Mahmoud Ahmadinejad** in 2005–2006 strained the U.S.–Iranian relationship. *See also* FOREIGN AID; IRAN-CONTRA SCANDAL; IRAN'S NUCLEAR PROGRAM.

IRAN-CONTRA SCANDAL. A diplomatic quagmire that badly tarnished the reputation of the **Ronald Reagan** administration. In the aftermath of the **Iran hostage crisis** of 1979–1981, U.S. leaders had organized an international embargo on arms sales to **Iran** and publicly vowed not to deal with regimes backing **terrorism** or hostage taking. Yet in a series of deals executed in 1985–1986, White House staff members secretly supplied Iran with hundreds of anti-tank and anti-aircraft missiles. Reagan later claimed that these arms shipments were intended to improve the badly strained U.S. relationship with Iran, an oil-rich state of critical importance to the West, as well as to win the release of several Americans held hostage by radical Islamic groups in **Lebanon**. When disclosed by the media, however, public criticism mounted against the president for violating his stated refusal to deal with terrorists and his embargo against arms sales to Iran. While the arms supply seemed to win the release of several captives in Lebanon, moreover, it also seemed to stimulate the taking of additional hostages. Revelations that Reagan aides had illegally diverted proceeds of the Iran arms sales to the Contra rebels in Nicaragua damaged Reagan's reputation in American public opinion.

IRAN HOSTAGE CRISIS. A major conflict between the United States and **Iran** that deeply soured their official relationship and contributed to the defeat of President **Jimmy Carter** in the U.S. presidential election of 1980. The conflict developed in the aftermath of the Iranian revolution of 1979, in which the Ayatollah **Ruhollah Khomeini** overthrew the pro-Western Shah **Mohammed Reza Pahlavi**. As U.S. officials debated policy toward the new regime, President Carter decided, on humanitarian grounds, to admit the ousted shah to the United States in October 1979 so that he could secure advanced medical care for a grave illness.

Khomeini responded by provoking the hostage crisis. Perhaps the ayatollah sought vengeance against his hated nemesis; perhaps he feared that the United States might try to restore the shah or his son to power in Tehran. For whatever motive, he urged his followers to take to the streets of Tehran to protest Carter's decision; on 1 November, a throng of 3 million persons gathered in Tehran to march past the U.S. embassy and condemn the United States as the "Great Satan." Three days later, hundreds of militants stormed the embassy and seized the Foreign Service officers and marines on duty there. Khomeini applauded the mob action and indicated that he would release the captives in exchange for the shah. Fifty-two of the hostages were destined to remain in captivity for 444 days.

Carter's policy toward the crisis developed in stages. Initially, Carter implemented a series of diplomatic options: he froze Iranian assets (worth about $10 billion) in U.S. banks, expelled Iranian diplomats and students from the United States, isolated Iran diplomatically and organized international financial sanctions, secured a censure of Iran's actions by the International Court of Justice, sought to secure the release of the hostages through back-channel negotiations, and, in April 1980, broke diplomatic relations with Tehran. Because the crisis remained deadlocked, however, Carter shifted gears in April 1980 when he ordered a military rescue mission. But the mission ended in calamity when mechanical problems forced Carter to abort the operation after U.S. soldiers reached Iranian territory, and in the haste to evacuate, a helicopter and an airplane collided and exploded, killing eight U.S. soldiers. The botched rescue mission comprised a severe setback for the United States. The hostage ordeal diminished Carter's prospect of winning reelection on 4 November 1980.

In late 1980, Carter intensified his efforts to resolve the hostage crisis on the hope that a so-called October surprise—a release of the hostages on the eve of the election—might save his embattled presidency. The death of the shah in July raised hopes that a settlement was possible, and the eruption of the **Iran-Iraq War** in September gave Khomeini reason to secure the release of frozen financial assets. Through back-channel negotiations arbitrated by Algeria, U.S. and Iranian officials negotiated a deal in which the hostages would be released in exchange for the unfreezing of Iranian financial assets. But agreement came only in January 1981, after U.S. voters elected **Ronald Reagan** president. As a final snub to Carter, Khomeini delayed the release of the captives until moments after Reagan's inauguration on 20 January.

IRAN–IRAQ WAR. A destabilizing regional war that spanned the 1980s. In September 1980, Iraqi forces invaded **Iran** along a broad battlefront and occupied 10,000 square miles of the country. Iraqi dictator **Saddam Hussein** aimed to extend his territorial domain and oil assets as well as counter threats from the Ayatollah **Ruhollah Khomeini** to export Islamic fundamentalism to **Iraq**. By 1982, Iran launched a counteroffensive, liberated its own territory, and moved into Iraq. In 1984, Hussein widened the war by attacking Iranian oil tankers in hopes of cutting off Iran's oil revenues, while Iran retaliated by attacking tankers registered in **Kuwait** and **Saudi Arabia**, Iraq's material supporters. This "war of the tankers" was followed in 1985 by a "war of the cities," in which both sides bombed or fired missiles against civilian population centers. In addition, a series of major offensives by ground troops proved generally ineffective at breaking the stalemate. By 1988, the two powers suffered more than 1 million casualties.

While officially neutral, the **Ronald Reagan** administration essentially sided with Iraq in this war. Although Hussein was a ruthless dictator, officials in Washington came to fear an Iranian military triumph after Khomeini's armies gained momentum in 1982, and they monitored evidence that Khomeini promoted revolutionary activity in Saudi Arabia, Kuwait, **Bahrain**, and North **Yemen** in 1981–1982 and backed radical groups that attacked U.S. forces and kidnapped U.S. nationals in **Lebanon**. In this context, Reagan bolstered Baghdad by providing Iraq economic aid and military supplies and by restoring diplomatic relations in November 1984. The State Department also organized an international embargo on arms supply to Iran. In 1987, Reagan arranged the reflagging of Kuwaiti oil tankers as U.S. flagships and ordered the navy to escort them through the Persian Gulf. After Iran contested the U.S. flag tankers with speedboat assaults and marine mines, U.S. naval forces militarily engaged Iranian vessels from July 1987 to July 1988.

As the naval warfare escalated, Reagan also practiced diplomacy to end the war. In July 1987, the United States secured a unanimous resolution of the **United Nations** Security Council calling for a cease-fire under the terms of the UN Charter and imposing sanctions against noncompliers. Although initially defiant, Iran accepted the resolution in July 1988. The financial and human costs of the war had exceeded Khomeini's tolerance, and Iranian public morale had waned as Iraq regained the military initiative, fired missiles at Iranian cities, and used poison gas on Iranian soldiers. The war ended when a cease-fire took effect on 20 August. *See also* FOREIGN AID.

IRAN'S NUCLEAR PROGRAM. The subject of a major international controversy that emerged in the early 2000s. **Iran** first developed nuclear capabilities under **Shah Mohammed Reza Pahlavi** by participating in the U.S. Atoms for Peace Program in the 1950s. The shah advanced his country's nuclear power program by ratifying the Nuclear Non-Proliferation Treaty in 1970, a step that enabled him to contract with Western firms to build nuclear facilities designed for nonmilitary purposes. Through the 1970s the shah's government launched an ambitious nuclear program, but the Iranian Revolution of 1979, the anti-nuclear position of the **Ayatollah Ruhollah Khomeini**, and the **Iran–Iraq War** curtailed Iran's nuclear program through the 1980s. In the 1990s, Iran reconstituted a viable nuclear research program with the technical assistance of Pakistan, China, and Russia.

By the early 2000s, Western observers monitored evidence that Iran was secretly developing the capability to produce weapons-grade plutonium and nuclear-capable military weapons. Iran responded alternatively by submitting to additional inspections by officials of the International Atomic Energy Authority and signing agreements not to produce weapons-grade enriched uranium and by continuing such work clandestinely and defending its right to develop nuclear capability. American officials called for imposing international sanctions on Tehran, but Iranian president **Mahmoud Ahmadinejad**, inaugurated in August 2005, assertively declared that Iran's nuclear programs would continue. In April 2006, Ahmadinejad announced that his government had enriched uranium at a facility at Natanz. The American media reported that President **George W. Bush** contemplated military strikes against facilities at Natanz and elsewhere. Bush denied those reports, although he continued firmly to press Iran to accept strict limitations to its nuclear program.

IRAQ. An influential power with a checkered history with which the United States has had a tumultuous relationship. Established of remnants of the Ottoman Empire in 1920, Iraq was governed as a League of Nations mandate by Great Britain until 1932. Established with Britain's blessing in 1921, the Iraqi monarchy ruled with a generally pro-Western orientation and became a signatory member of the U.S.-organized **Baghdad Pact** in 1955. American officials saw Iraq's moderate government as a political counterweight to the more radical regimes in **Egypt** and **Syria**.

In 1958, the pro-Western monarchy fell in a violent coup led by General **Abdul Karim Qassim**, who withdrew Iraq from the Baghdad Pact and sought accord with the Soviet Union. As Iraq tumbled through a period of political instability in the 1960s and 1970s, U.S.–Iraqi relations remained cool and detached. Iraq severed diplomatic relations with Washington during the **Arab-Israeli War of 1967**, and in the 1970s, the United States bolstered Shah **Mohammed Reza Pahlavi** of **Iran** as a counterweight to the Soviet-leaning Iraqi regime.

A limited U.S.–Iraqi rapprochement developed in the 1980s. In 1979, Ayatollah **Ruhollah Khomeini** took power in Tehran and **Sad-**

dam Hussein took power in Baghdad, and in 1980 Iraq invaded Iran. These dynamics raised the strategic value of Iraq in U.S. eyes. The **Ronald Reagan** administration provided Iraq economic aid, intelligence sharing, and covert military aid to bolster its military prospects in the **Iran–Iraq War**. Formal diplomatic relations were restored in 1984. To advance Iraq's interests, the United States protected oil shipments on the Persian Gulf and used vigorous diplomacy to pressure Iran to accept a cease-fire in 1988.

Although the United States helped to end the Iran–Iraq War on terms favorable to Baghdad, U.S.–Iraqi relations worsened after the war. Saddam Hussein rejected overtures from President **George H. W. Bush** for improved relations and instead invaded **Kuwait** in August 1990, triggering the **Persian Gulf War**. Bush knitted together a widespread international coalition of powers that militarily liberated Kuwait in early 1991. But Bush stopped short of invading Iraq, calculating that Hussein's military defeat would undermine his hold on power in Baghdad. Yet Hussein was able to crush uprisings among the Shiites and **Kurds** of his country and to consolidate his rule.

Through the 1990s, the United States used a variety of means—including **United Nations** sanctions, arms inspections, military aerial patrols over northern and southern Iraq, and occasional military strikes—to contain Hussein's military and political power. By the early 2000s, the policy of containment, although working, suffered serious setbacks, such as Hussein's expulsion of UN arms inspectors who had monitored Iraq's compliance with UN resolutions limiting the country's military arsenal.

When he took office in 2001, President **George W. Bush** contemplated an invasion of Iraq to replace the containment policy. In the aftermath of the **9/11** attacks on the United States, Bush decided to order such an invasion despite the absence of evidence that Iraq had perpetrated the assault. Bush justified the invasion on the grounds that Hussein had denied access to arms inspectors and that he might develop weapons of mass destruction and provide them to terrorists intent on harming the United States. The United States and a small number of allied powers invaded Iraq in March 2003 and rather quickly deposed the Hussein government. Yet the task of occupying Iraq, building a stable government in Baghdad, and otherwise restoring the stability of the state proved more challenging than

Bush had anticipated. The United States organized an interim Iraqi government, held popular elections in early 2005, and encouraged Iraqis to write a democratic constitution, which was approved by referendum in late 2005. But a violent insurgency bitterly contested the American occupation and the U.S.-backed Iraqi government. *See also* IRAQ WAR.

IRAQ PETROLEUM COMPANY (IPC). A consortium comprised of large, Western oil companies that dominated the petroleum production industry of the former Ottoman Empire in the early 20th century. Incorporated in 1911 as African and Eastern Concessions, Limited, the firm was renamed the Turkish Petroleum Company in 1912 and the IPC in 1929. Ownership of the IPC was distributed among such giant oil companies as Anglo-Persian Oil Company (later Anglo-Iranian Oil Company), Shell, Compagnie Française des Petroles, and Standard Oil, with exact percentages of shares held changing over time under various negotiated business agreements. The IPC secured a concession from **Iraq** in 1925 and struck oil near Kirkuk in 1927. It secured or built oil assets, including pipelines and refineries, across the Middle East and for several decades turned enormous profits. Iraq nationalized most of the IPC's concession in 1961 and the remainder in 1971.

IRAQ, U.S. INVASION OF (2003). *See* IRAQ WAR.

IRAQ WAR (2003–). A major and controversial military conflict initiated by the United States under the leadership of President **George W. Bush**. The president and several of his top aides took office apparently determined to overthrow Iraqi dictator **Saddam Hussein**, who had openly flouted the restrictions imposed on him as conditions for ending the **Persian Gulf War** of 1990–1991. In the aftermath of **9/11**, Bush openly contemplated a preemptive invasion of **Iraq**, expressing the fear that Hussein might provide weapons of mass destruction to anti-American terrorists. Shell-shocked by 9/11, the American people generally endorsed such action, and in October 2002 Congress authorized the president to use necessary and appropriate force against Iraq. Bush also secured a **United Nations** resolution that provided a modicum of international sanction for a preemptive strike. On 18 March 2003, the president issued an ultimatum to Hussein that he must leave Iraq within 48 hours or face the wrath of the U.S. military. Hussein defied the ultimatum. In a brief campaign that started on 20 March 2003, U.S., British, and Australian forces conquered Iraq, scattered its army, and drove Hussein into hiding. On 1 May, Bush declared an end to major combat operations. The U.S. Army captured Hussein on 13 December.

In sharp contrast to the successful invasion, the U.S. occupation of Iraq encountered serious problems. Looting and lawlessness swept the country, spoiling its infrastructure as well as the euphoria surrounding Hussein's departure from power. American efforts to base a new government on Iraqi exile **Ahmad Chalabi** foundered when it became clear that Chalabi was corrupt and unpopular. The absence of evidence that Hussein had stockpiled weapons of mass destruction undermined the credibility of the Bush administration's justification for the attack. A crescendo of anti-Americanism swept Iraq in the spring of 2004 when photographs depicting the inhumane abuse of detainees by U.S. soldiers at Abu Ghraib Prison near Baghdad circulated around the world via television and the Internet. An insurgency rose against U.S. occupation soldiers, UN officials, and other foreigners in Iraq, and the country's Shiite majority and Sunni minority battled each other in violent clashes. By 2006, more than 2,200 American soldiers had died in Iraq, the vast majority during the occupation period.

President Bush adopted a long-term strategy to build a stable democracy in Iraq. He established the Coalition Provisional Authority (CPA), under **L. Paul Bremer**, to rebuild Iraq's infrastructure, form an Iraqi police force, and jump-start the nation's economy. In July 2003, the United States appointed the Iraq Governing Council, which signed an interim constitution in March 2004. In June, the CPA passed control of the country to a regime headed by **Ayad Allawi**. In January 2005, 8 million Iraqi voters elected the membership of a 275-member Transitional National Assembly, which drafted a constitution that was approved in a popular referendum in late 2005. **Ibrahim Jaafari** became prime minister of Iraq in late 2005.

ISLAMIC RESISTANCE MOVEMENT (HAMAS). A Palestinian Islamic fundamentalist group dedicated to the establishment of an

Islamic state in **Palestine**. (In Arabic, *Hamas*, an acronym for Islamic Resistance Movement, literally means "zeal.") Hamas was formed in 1987–1988 by Palestinian members of the Muslim Brotherhood who engaged in resistance activities during the first **intifada**.

During its first decade, Hamas emerged as a major factor in Palestinian politics. Fervently religious, it contested the secular leadership of **Yasser Arafat** and the **Palestine Liberation Organization (PLO)**. Hamas also developed a network of mosques, medical clinics, schools, and social welfare agencies that earned the popularity of the Palestinian people and accentuated the PLO's corruption and ineffectiveness. Arafat responded with a blend of repression and cooptation but could not arrest the spread of the popularity of Hamas, especially among Palestinians in the Gaza Strip.

Hamas also strongly opposed the peace process of the 1990s. It declared that Palestinian resistance must continue until **Israel** unconditionally withdrew from the West Bank, Gaza, and Jerusalem (and it perhaps secretly aimed to destroy Israel in its entirety). By the mid-1990s, the Izzedine al-Qassam Brigades, a secret military wing of Hamas, organized a wave of **terrorism**, notably suicide bombings, on Israeli civilians and soldiers, intended to derail the peace process. A series of attacks in 1995–1996 achieved that goal by so angering the Israeli people that they elected more conservative leaders who suspended peace negotiations. During the second intifada, Hamas gained popularity among the Palestinian people by organizing resistance activities. Israel retaliated for attacks by Hamas with military counterstrikes, including the killing of Hamas spiritual leader Sheikh Ahmad Yassin in a targeted missile strike in 2004.

The United States avoided direct confrontation with Hamas, which refrained from attacking American targets. However, U.S. officials identified Hamas as a major impediment to their peacemaking objectives and thus encouraged the PLO to suppress it. While promoting the **Roadmap peace plan** in 2003, President **George W. Bush** publicly called for the dismantling of Hamas as a necessary step toward progress.

In 2005, Hamas leaders began transitioning the organization into a political party and declared a moratorium on suicide bombings against Israel. Hamas candidates won the Palestinian elections of January 2006, securing control of the Legislative Council of the **Palestinian National Authority (PNA)**.

ISRAEL. A largely Jewish democracy with a close and unique relationship with the United States. The establishment of Israel as an independent state in May 1948 fulfilled the Zionist dream of restoring the Jewish people to their ancient homeland in **Palestine**. Under the sway of Zionism, thousands of European Jews had arrived in Palestine while it was part of the Ottoman Empire (through World War I) and the British Empire (from the end of World War I to 1948). They overcame the resistance of the local Palestinian Arab people, built a sociopolitical infrastructure, and thus were poised to declare statehood on the exhaustion of British resolve to govern the land.

The United States long viewed Zionism with sympathy. President **Woodrow Wilson** indicated support for the Balfour Declaration of 1917, in which the British government pledged to support establishment of a "Jewish national home" in Palestine, and succeeding presidents reaffirmed their support for Zionism. President **Franklin D. Roosevelt** downplayed Zionist demands during World War II when they conflicted with U.S. national security aims in the Middle East, but Zionism became widely popular in Congress and public opinion for a variety of reasons, including sympathy for the victims of the Nazi Holocaust in Europe, political activism among American Jews, and a favorable disposition toward Zionism among American evangelical Christians. President **Harry S. Truman** took several steps—ranging from political endorsements to support of the **United Nations partition** plan of 1947—that facilitated the independence of Israel. Truman also recognized Israel minutes after its declaration of independence, bolstering the morale of the Israeli people and earning the wrath of the Arab world.

After 1948, the United States and Israel experienced several points of serious contention. Israel's initial neutralist orientation in the Cold War bothered American strategists intent on containing the Soviet Union. President **Dwight D. Eisenhower** opposed Israel's attack on **Egypt** during the **Suez Crisis** of 1956 and used various pressures to compel an Israeli withdrawal. Periodic U.S. decisions to sell military equipment or negotiate military partnerships with Arab powers left Israelis bitter and fearful for their own security. The **Ronald Reagan** administration sharply disapproved of **Israel's invasion of Lebanon** in 1982. During the **Persian Gulf War** of 1990–1991, Israel chafed when the United States refused to allow Israeli retaliation on **Iraq** for its missile attacks on Israel.

On balance, however, the two states developed a close and friendly relationship. The United States provided Israel with massive material and military aid, and it embraced Israel as a partner in strategic initiatives, military planning, and intelligence operations, especially from the 1970s to the early 2000s. For a generation after 1967, the United States tended to identify Israel as a partner in the Cold War and the Arab states as clients of the Soviet Union. Such dynamics solidified America's traditional determination that Israel had a right to exist and made U.S. leaders reluctant to force Israel to make concessions to its adversaries. Israel remained widely popular across a broad cross section of the American electorate, creating pressure on officials in Washington to support the Jewish state. Trade and tourism between the two countries strengthened the bonds between the American and Israeli peoples.

The Arab–Israeli conflict generated the potential for controversy in U.S.–Israeli relations. While grateful for U.S. endorsement of their statehood, Israelis criticized U.S. passivity during the **Arab-Israeli War of 1948–1949**, when they fought desperately to defeat invading Arab armies intent on their destruction. Differences of judgment on the best solutions to lingering problems about territorial borders, the status of Jerusalem, and the treatment of **Palestinian refugees** raised tensions after that war, and Israel's decision to attack Egypt during the Suez Crisis created perhaps the deepest divide ever in the relationship. Moreover, Israel's occupation of the Sinai, Gaza, the West Bank, and the Golan Heights during the **Arab-Israeli War of 1967** set the stage for controversy over the terms of Israeli withdrawal from such lands.

After 1967, U.S. leaders generally favored a policy of "land for peace," meaning that Israel would be expected to relinquish the occupied territories as its Arab adversaries accepted and recognized it as a legitimate nation state. Such a philosophy informed efforts by Secretary of State **Henry Kissinger** to extricate hostile forces from the battlefronts at the end of the **Arab-Israeli War of 1973**, and it drove the U.S. quest to negotiate the Egyptian–Israeli peace treaty of 1979 that led to Israeli withdrawal from the Sinai. It also fueled American efforts in the 1990s and early 2000s to broker Israeli–Syrian and Israeli–Palestinian deals that would return the Golan Heights to **Syria** and establish a state of **Palestine** in the West Bank and Gaza. *See also* FOREIGN AID.

– J –

JAAFARI, IBRAHIM (1947–). Political leader who served as prime minister of **Iraq** in 2005–2006. Born in Iraq in 1947 and trained as a physician, Jaafari joined the Dawaa Party, a Shiite Islamist group that resisted President **Saddam Hussein** in the 1970s. After the resistance movement failed, Jaafari fled to exile in **Iran** and Great Britain. He returned to Iraq in the wake of the U.S. invasion of 2003. He served in various posts in U.S.-appointed interim governments. On the basis of the results of the Iraqi elections of January 2005, Jaafari was named prime minister in April. Yet Jaafari faced a massive challenge of governing Iraq, averting civil war, and finding terms on which U.S. occupation forces could be withdrawn. Because Jaafari alienated the Sunni and Kurdish factions of Iraq's parliament, the legislature replaced him with **Nuri al-Maliki** in May 2006.

JOHNSON, JOSEPH E. (1906–1990). Emissary of President **John F. Kennedy** who promoted a scheme to settle the **Palestinian refugees** dispute in 1961–1962. Educated at Harvard University, Johnson taught history at Williams College in 1936–1950 and thereafter became trustee and eventually president of the Carnegie Endowment for International Peace. Under pressure from Arab leaders to address the refugees controversy, Kennedy arranged to have the **Palestine Conciliation Commission**, a **United Nations** agency, appoint Johnson as special representative in August 1961. With an endorsement from the UN General Assembly, Johnson visited the Middle East in the summer of 1961 and the spring of 1962 to study the status of the 1.1 million Palestinian refugees, and he filed an action plan in the summer of 1962.

The Johnson plan proposed a process of confidential surveys and interviews to ascertain the refugees' preferences for repatriation to **Israel** or resettlement with compensation in other countries. Subsequent multilateral negotiations would effect a permanent settlement of the dispute in which Israel would be expected to absorb 100,000 to 150,000 refugees and Western states to accept large numbers and to finance the settlement.

Israel, which had only reluctantly allowed the mission to begin, indicated its resistance to the prospect of repatriating a substantial number of refugees. Under pressure from Israel and pro-Israeli Americans, Kennedy refrained from taking any action on the Johnson plan, which consequently died of neglect.

JOHNSON, LYNDON B. (1908–1973). American president in 1963–1969 who faced substantial challenges in the Middle East. Johnson initially aimed to practice anti-Soviet containment in the Middle East, to maintain sound relations with all countries in the region, and to avert Arab–Israeli war. Distracted by the war in Vietnam, however, the president found it difficult to remain friendly to both sides in the **Arab–Israeli conflict**. While he held profound respect and admiration for **Israel**, he also regretted Israel's refusal to embrace U.S. goals regarding nuclear nonproliferation and its vigorous policy of conducting reprisals against its neighbors for cross-border attacks originating on their soil. Johnson also found it difficult to maintain friendship with **Egypt** after Premier **Gamal Abdel Nasser** issued anti-U.S. propaganda, intervened in the civil war in **Yemen**, accepted Soviet arms supply, stirred unrest in Congo, encouraged the **Palestine Liberation Organization (PLO)** to attack Israel, expressed sympathy for the Vietcong, and criticized the pro-U.S. monarchies in **Iran** and **Saudi Arabia**.

Nor was Johnson able to avert the **Arab-Israeli War of 1967**. Nasser provoked a crisis in May 1967 by imposing a blockade of Israel's southern coast and threatening offensive operations against the Jewish state. At first, Johnson attempted to resolve the crisis through diplomatic initiatives including appeals to Nasser to rescind his moves against Israel, appeals to Israel to rely on peaceful means to ensure its interests, and efforts to organize a multilateral initiative among Western states to break the Egyptian blockade through assertive means, including the threat of naval intervention. Yet these diplomatic maneuvers faced numerous political and tactical obstacles, and they failed to dissuade Nasser from his confrontational approach or to deter Israel from escalating to hostilities. On 5 June, Israel triggered a brief war in which it soundly defeated Egypt, **Jordan**, and **Syria** and occupied enormous portions of their territory. Scholars continue to debate whether Johnson, in the days preceding hostilities, secretly authorized or continued to discourage the Israelis' offensive action.

President Harry S. Truman greets Iranian prime minister Mohammed Mossadegh, 23 October 1951. Despite the amicable pose, Truman and Mossadegh experienced a strained relationship, and President Dwight D. Eisenhower overthrew Mossadegh in a coup in 1953. Photo by Abbie Rowe, National Park Service, courtesy of the Harry S. Truman Presidential Library.

Prince Faisal Al-Saud of Saudi Arabia and his entourage pose near the Washington Monument during a visit to Washington, 16 July 1952. Openly critical of U.S. policy in Palestine, Faisal was destined to become the third king of Saudi Arabia in 1964. Photo by Abbie Rowe, National Park Service, courtesy of the Harry S. Truman Presidential Library.

President John F. Kennedy and Secretary of Defense Robert McNamara meet Shah Mohammad Reza Pahlavi of Iran in the White House Cabinet Room, 13 April 1962. Restored to power by U.S. covert action in 1953, the shah ruled his country as a friend of the United States until he was ousted in a revolution in early 1979. Photo by Robert Knudsen, courtesy of the John F. Kennedy Presidential Library and Museum.

President Richard M. Nixon and Secretary of State Henry Kissinger meet Israeli prime minister Golda Meir in the Oval Office, 1 March 1973. Nixon and Kissinger faced the daunting challenge of balancing their commitments to Israeli security, containment of Soviet communism away from the Middle East, and regional stability. Courtesy of the National Archives and Records Administration of the United States.

President Jimmy Carter and Egyptian president Anwar Sadat, 4 April 1977. The two statesmen shared a common goal of Egyptian–Israeli peace, a goal eventually reached in the Camp David Accords of 1978. Courtesy of the Jimmy Carter Library.

President Jimmy Carter greets Israeli prime minister Menachem Begin during a state visit, 1 May 1978. Under Carter's leadership, Begin would agree to make peace with Egypt in 1979, but other Israeli–Arab conflicts would persist. Courtesy of the Jimmy Carter Library.

President and Mrs. Ronald Reagan honor the victims of the terrorist bombing of the U.S. embassy in Beirut, 23 April 1983, at Andrews Air Force Base. An even more devastating terrorist attack on a U.S. Marines compound in Beirut in October 1983 would force the president to reevaluate his interventionist policy in Lebanon. Courtesy of the Ronald Reagan Library.

President George H. W. Bush and General H. Norman Schwarzkopf Jr. review U.S. troops in Saudi Arabia on Thanksgiving Day, 22 November 1990. The soldiers, initially deployed under Operation Desert Shield, would participate in the liberation of Kuwait in early 1991. Courtesy of the George Bush Presidential Library.

President George H.W. Bush meets King Hussein of Jordan in the Oval Office, 12 March 1992. King Hussein would play an active role in the U.S.-led peace process of the 1990s. Courtesy of the George Bush Presidential Library.

President George W. Bush, Afghanistan president Hamid Karzai, First Lady Laura Bush, and Secretary of State Condoleezza Rice pose at the ceremony dedicating the new U.S. embassy building in Kabul, Afghanistan, 1 March 2006. Despite the festive air, deep problems continued to beset U.S. officials seeking to transform Afghanistan into a stable democracy. Photo by Eric Draper, reprinted with permission of the White House Photo Office.

Once the war erupted, the Johnson administration adopted a three-track policy toward it. First, to end the fighting as soon as possible, U.S. officials quickly secured a **United Nations** Security Council cease-fire resolution and pressured the belligerents to accept it. Second, Johnson sought to prevent any Soviet political gain by pressuring Moscow to accept U.S. cease-fire terms and by moving U.S. Navy ships into the eastern Mediterranean after the Soviets vaguely threatened to intervene militarily on behalf of the Arab states.

Third, Johnson sought to build a permanent peace settlement in the months following the war. Bitter anger among Arab leaders and an attitude of superiority among Israeli leaders, however, created poor conditions for peacemaking. In November 1967, the Johnson administration achieved UN Security Council Resolution 242, which called for a peace settlement including Israeli withdrawal from territories occupied in June and Arab recognition of Israel's right to exist as a state. That resolution, however, included two crucial ambiguities: it provided that Israel would withdraw from "territories" rather than "the territories," a loophole that gave Israel legal footing to claim permanent retention of some of the land it had occupied in June, and the resolution failed to specify whether Israeli withdrawal should precede or follow Arab recognition. The resolution proved ineffective at advancing Johnson's peacemaking goals.

The Arab-Israeli War also strained Washington's relations with the belligerents in the Middle East. Various Arab leaders charged that U.S. warplanes had participated in Israeli attacks against them. Although U.S. officials rejected these charges as specious, anti-U.S. passions soared in Arab countries, mobs threatened the safety of U.S. nationals, and Arab governments severed diplomatic relations with the United States. American–Israeli relations also experienced strain. Many U.S. officials were incensed after Israeli warplanes attacked the **USS *Liberty***, a U.S. Navy intelligence-gathering ship sailing off the coast of Egypt, killing 34 U.S. sailors, on 8 June. Israeli resistance to postwar U.S. efforts to achieve a permanent peace agreement also irritated U.S. officials.

JORDAN. A constitutional monarchy whose political orientation and geographical location made it strategically important to the United States in the post–World War II period. At the end of World War I,

Great Britain acquired a League of Nations mandate over **Palestine**, and in 1922 it designated the portion east of the Jordan River as the separate mandate of Transjordan under Emir **Abdullah ibn-Hussein**. In May 1946, Abdullah gained conditional independence from Britain and declared the Hashemite Kingdom of Jordan. In 1948, Jordan occupied the so-called West Bank—certain portions of mandatory Palestine that did not fall under control of **Israel**—and in 1950 it formally annexed that territory. Israel captured the West Bank in the process of defeating Jordan during the **Arab-Israeli War of 1967**, and Jordan formally relinquished territorial claims to the West Bank in 1988, although it continued to seek administrative privileges through agreements with Israel.

The United States enjoyed a relatively stable relationship with Jordan since the independence of the kingdom. The **Harry S. Truman** administration endorsed the efforts by King Abdullah to show moderation toward Israel, and it rewarded Jordan with political recognition and economic aid. After Abdullah was assassinated in July 1951, the United States nurtured a friendly relationship with **King Hussein**, who ruled from 1953 to his death in 1999. Hussein's hold on power seemed tenuous during the early decades of his reign, and the United States, in an act of dual containment, provided economic aid and political assistance to sustain the kingdom as a bulwark against expansionism by **Egypt** or Israel. In 1958, when a radical revolution in **Iraq** raised fears in the West of a similar development in Jordan, President **Dwight D. Eisenhower** endorsed and logistically supported a British military occupation of Jordan that shored up King Hussein. The United States provided Jordan some $9 billion in economic aid between 1952 and 2005.

The presence and political activities of **Palestinian refugees** in Jordan complicated U.S. policy toward the kingdom. About 700,000 Palestinians took refuge in Jordan during the **Arab-Israeli War of 1948–1949**, and another 300,000 arrived during the **Arab-Israeli War of 1967**. A Palestinian enraged by King Abdullah's moderate stance toward Israel assassinated the king in 1951. In the 1950s and 1960s, Palestinian militants conducted raids and terrorist strikes against Israel that frequently triggered Israeli reprisals on Jordan. In the so-called **Black September** episode of 1970–1971, King Hussein forcibly expelled leaders of the **Palestine Liberation Organization**

(**PLO**) from his country. The United States encouraged that step, which contributed immensely to Jordan's long-term stability. Yet King Hussein remained sensitive to the demands of the Palestinian expatriates, such as by refusing to join the anti-Iraq coalition during the **Persian Gulf War** of 1990–1991. By the early 2000s, 1.7 million registered Palestinian refugees made up nearly one-third of Jordan's population.

American–Jordanian relations grew especially friendly during the 1990s. In part to appease Western resentment of his Gulf War policy, King Hussein endorsed U.S. objectives in the Arab–Israeli peace process and signed a formal peace treaty with Israel in October 1994 in the presence of President **William J. Clinton**. Jordan also cooperated in enforcing **United Nations** sanctions against **Iraq**. **Trade** and tourism between the United States and Jordan began to take root, and U.S. officials encouraged Jordan's modest democratic reforms, which included free parliamentary elections and the legalization of political parties.

American relations with Jordan remained strong after **King Abdullah II** claimed the throne in 1999. Abdullah II reaffirmed Jordan's commitment to peace with Israel, promoted Israeli–Palestinian reconciliation after the eruption of the second **intifada** in 2000, and endorsed the U.S.-backed **Roadmap peace plan**. In 2001, he approved a free trade agreement that provided for the removal of trade barriers and duties between the United States and Jordan by 2010.

King Abdullah II immediately condemned the **9/11** terrorist attacks on the United States and dispatched medical and mine-clearing military personnel to support the **U.S. invasion of Afghanistan**. After the start of the **Iraq War** in 2003, Jordan allowed U.S. forces to station in Jordan, trained some 30,000 Iraqi police officers, and opened a field hospital in Iraq to provide care to civilians. Jordan's support of Washington's policy in Iraq left it vulnerable to terrorist counterstrikes, including the bombings of hotels in November 2005 in which dozens of persons died. *See also* DEMOCRATIZATION; FOREIGN AID.

JORDAN VALLEY PLAN (JVP). A plan promoted by the **Dwight D. Eisenhower** administration in 1953–1955 to settle **Arab–Israeli conflict** over control of the freshwater of the Jordan River valley and thereby to build a foundation for a general peace agreement in the region. Aware that competition for precious freshwater might trigger regional strife, President Eisenhower and Secretary of State **John Foster Dulles** aimed to achieve a regional plan for the conservation, storage, and distribution of the region's water on terms that would avert conflict, spawn economic development for the benefit of **Palestinian refugees**, and encourage Arab–Israeli cooperation in other matters. American officials based their initiative on the JVP, an impartial, technical study composed by engineers of the Tennessee Valley Authority.

Eisenhower appointed Eric Johnston, chairman of the Advisory Board for International Development, as his personal representative to sell the plan to Middle East states through a series of missions to the Middle East in 1953–1955. Johnston's efforts were hindered by the deep reservoir of mistrust between the Arab states and **Israel** and by the tension that spiked after Israel's brutal raid of the town of Qibya in October 1953.

Despite such obstacles, Johnston made some progress in advancing the JVP. By November 1953, he had elicited pledges from **Lebanon, Jordan, Syria, Egypt**, and Israel not to reject the plan out of hand. In 1954, Arab and Israeli leaders affirmed the principle of unified water development under international supervision and agreed in principle that shared water would be stored in Lake Tiberias. In early 1955, Johnston persuaded Lebanon, Syria, and Jordan to approve a tentative memorandum of agreement that allocated one-third of the available water to the Arab states and the balance to Israel.

Despite Johnston's achievements, the JVP faded in 1955. Israeli leaders refused to approve the memorandum because they doubted it would safeguard their water or security interests. Furious at Israel's Gaza raid in February, Jordan, Syria, and Lebanon retracted their approvals of the JVP. Johnston persuaded Israel to approve the plan in July, but this agreement came too late to assuage the Arab states, especially as Egyptian–Israeli border clashes in August inflamed passions across the region. In October, the **Arab League** voted to postpone discussion of the JVP. As American officials had feared, conflicts over water continued to brew in the years that followed.

– K –

KENNEDY, JOHN F. (1917–1963). President in 1961–1963 who contributed to a transition in U.S. diplomacy in the Middle East. Although distracted by momentous diplomatic challenges in Germany, Cuba, and Vietnam, Kennedy aimed to improve U.S. interests in the Middle East by balancing between **Israel** and **Egypt**.

Kennedy sought to nurture a rapprochement with Egyptian premier **Gamal Abdel Nasser** on the calculation that he would better serve U.S. interests by accommodating rather than confronting the Egyptian leader. The rapprochement rested on several foundations, including a U.S. food aid package to Egypt; a series of long, personal letters between Kennedy and Nasser that established a sense of trust and mutual respect; and the **"icebox agreement"** between the two leaders to downplay the **Arab–Israeli conflict** and move on to other matters. Yet the rapprochement crumbled over the situation in **Yemen**, where Egyptian- and Saudi-backed factions fought a civil war for control of the country.

Kennedy also facilitated the emergence of a close security partnership between the United States and Israel. To achieve stability in the Middle East, he initially sought to promote a settlement of the **Palestinian refugees** issue and to dissuade Israel from developing its nuclear weapons capability. As relations with Egypt cooled, however, the president gradually abandoned both initiatives in the face of Israeli resistance and approved a sale of advanced weapons (HAWK anti-aircraft missiles) to Israel. The HAWK deal set the stage for massive U.S. arms supply to Israel over the next decade.

KERR, MALCOLM (1931–1984). An American academic and expert on the Arab world. Born in Beirut, where his parents taught at the **American University of Beirut (AUB)**, Kerr divided his childhood between **Lebanon** and the United States, graduated from Princeton University, and earned a doctorate from Johns Hopkins University in 1958. He taught at AUB in 1958–1961 and then taught political science at the University of California, Los Angeles, for 20 years, publishing along the way several milestone books on the politics and diplomacy of Arab states. Kerr was named president of AUB in 1982.

On 18 January 1984, he was shot to death on the campus by two gunmen linked to the terrorist group Islamic Jihad.

KHALID, KING, OF SAUDI ARABIA (1913–1982). Son of **Saudi Arabia** founder **King ibn Saud** and fourth king of the country. Suffering from a heart condition when chosen to succeed **King Faisal** in 1975, Khalid ruled with the close support of Crown Prince **Fahd**, who succeeded him after his death in 1982.

To the chagrin of U.S. officials, King Khalid took a hard-line stance on the **Arab–Israeli conflict**. During a meeting with President **Jimmy Carter** in Riyadh in January 1978, Khalid insisted that **Israel** withdraw unconditionally from the territories it had occupied in 1967. He disapproved of the **Camp David Accords** of 1978 and the Egyptian–Israeli peace treaty of 1979 because they broke Arab unity, and in response he severed relations with **Egypt** and organized Arab economic sanctions against it.

Worried by domestic unrest, the revolution in **Iran** in 1979, and the Soviet invasion of Afghanistan in 1979, and the eruption of the **Iran–Iraq War** in 1980, however, Khalid strengthened his relationship with the United States. He secured agreements with the Carter and **Ronald Reagan** administrations to purchase military hardware, including fighter planes and advanced surveillance aircraft, purportedly to stop the spread of communism and Iranian influence in the region. *See also* FOREIGN AID.

KHALILZAD, ZALMAY (1951–). American diplomat who implemented the policy of President **George W. Bush** in Afghanistan and **Iraq**. Born in Afghanistan, Khalilzad was educated at the **American University of Beirut (AUB)** and the University of Chicago and served as an assistant professor of political science at Columbia University in 1979–1986. In 1985–1999, Khalilzad held a variety of State and Defense Department and nongovernmental assignments related to the Middle East and South Asia. In the 1990s, he joined a group of conservative American elites who called for the overthrow of **Saddam Hussein** of Iraq, and in 2000–2001, he headed the Pentagon's Bush transition team. As ambassador to Afghanistan in 2003–2005, Khalilzad shored up the government of **Hamid Karzai**. In June 2005, President Bush appointed Khalilzad as ambassador to

Iraq, where he sought to form a unified national government and avert civil war.

KHAMENEI, AYATOLLAH SEYED ALI (1939–). An anti-American Iranian religious cleric who emerged as supreme leader of **Iran** in 1989. Khamenei devoted his early life to religious training and in the 1960s joined a clerics' opposition movement to Shah **Mohammed Reza Pahlavi**. In 1975, Khameini was arrested and jailed briefly by the shah's government. Shortly after the Iranian revolution of 1979 ousted the Shah, Khamenei assisted Ayatollah **Ruhollah Khomeini** in organizing the new government, founding the Islamic Republic Party, and deposing the government of moderate president Abolhassan Bani-Sadr in 1981, a move that consolidated clerical control of the country. Khameini served as president of Iran in 1981–1989, earned the title ayatollah in 1989, and, on the death of Ayatollah Khomeini in 1989, won election as supreme leader of the Islamic Republic. In that capacity, Khamenei resisted efforts by Iranian moderates to reform the country's civil codes, political practices, and cultural customs, suggesting that the United States stirred the dissidents to action. He also remained outspokenly critical of U.S. policies in the Middle East, especially after President **George W. Bush** branded Iran as one dimension of an "axis of evil" and ordered the invasion of **Iraq** in 2003. As head of Iran's security apparatus, Khamenei was also believed to organize anti-Western **terrorism** across the Middle East and to abet the anti-U.S. insurgency in Iraq.

KHATAMI, MOHAMMED (1943–). Moderate president of **Iran** in 1997–2005 who challenged the influence of the conservative, anti-American clerical establishment. Educated in Islamic schools in Iran, Khatami assisted Ayatollah **Ruhollah Khomeini** in the revolutionary movement that captured control of Iran in 1979, and he served in a variety of government posts in subsequent years. Khatami was overwhelmingly elected by the Iranian people as the fifth president of the Islamic Republic in 1997 and resoundingly reelected in 2001. As president, Khatami was known as a moderate who promoted reform of Iran's conservative theocratic order and improved relations with the West. But his progress at gaining political power against the entrenched clerical establishment was inhibited by the renewal of tensions in U.S.–Iranian relations in the early 2000s.

KHOMEINI, AYATOLLAH RUHOLLAH (1902–1989). Anti-American religious cleric who led the 1979 revolution against Shah **Mohammed Reza Pahlavi** and dominated **Iran** for a decade after. Khomeini earned the title ayatollah in the 1950s and soon thereafter organized an opposition movement against the shah, whom he portrayed in angry rhetoric as a lackey of American imperialism and a secularist who desecrated Islam. Arrested by the shah's government in 1963 and exiled in 1964, Khomeini settled in **Iraq** and continued to conspire against the shah through a network of sympathetic clerics. When Iraq, under pressure from Iran, expelled Khomeini in 1978, he relocated to Paris, where he gained access to the Western media and modern communications links that enabled him to take control of the Iranian revolution only months before unrest in Iran forced the abdication of the shah in early 1979. Khomeini returned triumphantly to Tehran and quickly declared an Islamic Republic, crushed political rivals, and imposed a conservative theocratic order on the country.

In November 1979, Khomeini provoked the infamous **Iran Hostage Crisis** by taking captive American diplomats and soldiers on duty at the U.S. embassy in Tehran, demanding as their ransom his own custody over the deposed shah, who had taken refuge in the United States. As the hostages languished in captivity for 444 days, the American people formed a visceral dislike of the ayatollah and his government. American officials were also alarmed that Khomeini's regime openly promoted religious extremism and revolutionary political activity in neighboring Muslim states. The United States backed Iraq after it invaded Iran in 1980 because Iraq seemed to contain Iran's influence and deplete its political energy. Before the **Iran–Iraq War** of 1980–1988 was settled, U.S. Navy ships engaged in hostilities against Iranian ships in the Persian Gulf. After accepting an American-brokered cease-fire, Khomeini antagonized the West by calling for the death of British author Salman Rushdie on the grounds that his book *Satanic Verses* committed heresy against Islam. Khomeini remained a passionate anti-American nationalist at the time of his death in June 1989.

KING-CRANE COMMISSION. A presidential commission that advised President **Woodrow Wilson** on post–World War I policy in the Middle East. In March 1919, the United States, Great Britain, and France agreed to appoint a commission impartially to study the political conditions and public opinions in Middle East territories stripped from the Ottoman Empire during World War I. President Wilson appointed Henry Churchill King, president of Oberlin College, and Charles R. Crane, a Chicago businessman and a trustee of Robert College in Constantinople, as the American commissioners. After the French and British refused to appoint delegates, King and Crane toured the Middle East in June–August 1919 and filed a report on their own authority.

The King-Crane Commission report recommended that the Western powers establish temporary mandates, under League of Nations authority, over **Syria** (including **Lebanon**) and **Iraq**. It advised that the peoples of those territories would most welcome American authority under such mandates and, barring that, would prefer British over French control. The commission also advised that fulfillment of the Zionists' ambitions to purchase land and establish a state in **Palestine** would trigger an enduring conflict with Palestinian Arabs.

The King-Crane Commission marked the U.S. government's first-ever, high-level official inquiry into political conditions in the Middle East. It had virtually no impact on diplomacy, however, as Great Britain and France proceeded with bilateral plans to assign Palestine and Iraq as British mandates and Syria (including Lebanon) as a French mandate. By the time the commission finished its report, President Wilson was too distracted by other matters to consider seriously its recommendations.

KISSINGER, HENRY A. (1923–). National security advisor (1969–1975) and secretary of state (1973–1977) who dramatically shaped Arab–Israeli relations through personal diplomacy. Under the administration of President **Richard M. Nixon** (1969–1974), Kissinger persuaded the president to centralize foreign policy authority in the Oval Office and the National Security Council and to insulate it from the State Department. Kissinger also convinced Nixon to rely on **Israel** as a security partner to balance Soviet influence among Arab leaders. Under Kissinger's influence, Nixon resisted the efforts of

Secretary of State **William P. Rogers** and the **United Nations** to promote an Arab–Israeli settlement on compromise terms. He also formulated the **Nixon Doctrine** and designated **Iran** as a U.S. client state in the Middle East.

Previously distracted by the war in Vietnam and the détente policy toward China and the Soviet Union, Kissinger became very active in Middle East diplomacy during and after the **Arab-Israeli War of 1973**. Surprised by the outbreak of fighting, Kissinger immediately took action to end the war and to build a foundation for a lasting peace. He convinced Nixon to authorize a massive airlift of military supplies to Israel to stave off an Israeli defeat, to secure a UN cease-fire resolution, and to warn the Soviets from intervening militarily to assist **Egypt** or **Syria**. As Nixon's political integrity collapsed because of the Watergate scandal in 1973–1974, Kissinger transformed the Arab–Israeli cease-fire into a full-fledged peace process through an exhaustive initiative known as **shuttle diplomacy**. Under President **Gerald R. Ford** (1974–1977), Kissinger also secured the so-called **Sinai II agreement** between Egypt and Israel in September 1975.

KOMER, ROBERT W. (1922–2000). Intelligence officer and diplomat who guided U.S. policy in the Middle East in the early 1960s. Born in Chicago and educated at Harvard University, Komer served in the Central Intelligence Agency in 1947–1961 before becoming a staff member of the National Security Council under President **John F. Kennedy**. Concentrating on Middle East affairs, Komer promoted a policy of disengaging the forces of **Egypt** and **Saudi Arabia** involved in indirect war in **Yemen**. In 1965, Komer spearheaded a deal under which the United States supplied **Israel** with sophisticated weapons in exchange for an Israeli pledge not to be the first power to introduce nuclear weapons into the Middle East. In 1966, President Lyndon B. Johnson appointed Komer as his special assistant in charge of pacification policy in Vietnam.

KURDS. An ethnic group of some 20 million people who inhabit a region astride the borders of **Turkey**, **Syria**, **Iraq**, **Iran**, and Armenia. Predominantly Sunni Muslims, Kurds are ethnically and linguistically close to Iranians and are not Arabs. In the 20th century, development forced the Kurds to abandon their traditional lifestyle of nomadic herding and adopt a more sedentary lifestyle. Kurdish nationalism took root during the era of World War I, when Kurds began pressing for the independence of their territory as Kurdistan. The Treaty of Sèvres (1920), which established the modern states of Iraq, Syria, and **Kuwait**, also proposed the creation of Kurdistan, but Turkey, Iran, and Iraq blocked its emergence. Through the 20th century, Kurds used political activity and violence to promote independence, but those aspirations remained unfulfilled in the face of resistance from Turkey, Iraq, and Iran.

The Kurds of northern Iraq gained limited autonomy under U.S. protection in the 1990s. Iraqi dictator **Saddam Hussein** had used brutal means, including poison gas, against those Kurds when they supported Iran during the **Iran–Iraq War** of 1980–1988 and when they rebelled at the end of the **Persian Gulf War** in 1991. In the aftermath of the latter war, the United States delineated a safe haven in northern Iraq and used air power to prevent the Iraqi army from entering the area. Under such protection, the Kurds developed a limited form of self-rule.

Iraqi Kurds cooperated with the U.S. invasion of Iraq in 2003. Kurdish troops fought with American soldiers in the conquest of several cities in northern Iraq. Kurdish political parties cooperated with U.S. efforts to compose a new constitution and hold democratic elections. As a result, Kurds were also targeted by the anti-U.S. insurgency that erupted after the capture of Saddam Hussein. *See also* BARZANI, MASSOUD; BARZANI, MUSTAPHA; IRAQ WAR; TALABANI, JALAL.

KUWAIT. An oil-rich emirate, ruled by the al-Sabah dynasty, at the northern edge of the Persian Gulf for which the United States went to war in 1990–1991. As a British protectorate in 1899–1961, Kuwait had only cultural and commercial ties with the United States. The Kuwait Oil Company, comprised of U.S. and British companies, gained a concession in 1934 to market Kuwait's oil. In 1961–1963, the United States supported Kuwait's independence over the opposition of **Iraq**, although U.S.–Kuwaiti relations remained distant in the 1960s and 1970s because of Kuwaiti anger at U.S. support of **Israel**. Consistent with trends in other states across the region, Kuwait nationalized the Kuwait Oil Company in 1976.

American–Kuwaiti relations grew closer during the **Iran–Iraq War** of 1980–1988, when **Iran** attacked Kuwaiti tankers that carried Iraqi oil across the Persian Gulf. Kuwait requested and received U.S. Navy protection of its tankers, which, at the insistence of President **Ronald Reagan**, were reflagged as U.S. vessels. The escorting of reflagged Kuwaiti ships brought the U.S. Navy into armed conflict with Iranian naval forces in 1987–1988.

Kuwait loomed even larger in American strategic calculations when Iraq invaded and conquered it in August 1990, sparking the **Persian Gulf War**. President **George H. W. Bush** formed an international coalition to contest this conquest, thus setting the stage for **Operation Desert Storm** in 1991, which resulted in the liberation of Kuwait from Iraqi control. At the end of the war, the United States and Kuwait signed a 10-year security pact, the text of which remains classified by the U.S. government, and in 2001 the two powers renewed the pact for an additional 10 years. Kuwait supported Washington's policy of containing Iraq in 1991–2003 by allowing the stationing of American forces on its territory and bearing some of the financial costs of U.S. operations. Kuwait also hosted American forces deployed for the **U.S. invasion of Afghanistan** in 2001. Although Kuwait publicly opposed the **U.S. invasion of Iraq** in 2003, it offered both staging grounds for tens of thousands of U.S. troops and substantial financial assistance to U.S. operations.

– L –

LEAGUE OF ARAB STATES. *See* ARAB LEAGUE.

LEBANON. A small republic on the eastern shore of the Mediterranean Sea that emerged as a major challenge to U.S. policymakers in the late 20th century. Although Lebanon lacked any interests deemed vital to the United States, commercial and cultural connections between the two countries led officials in Washington to value Lebanon's political stability and friendship.

American missionaries blazed trails into Lebanon in the 19th century at a time when the territory remained a part of the Ottoman Empire. Among other projects, they established Syrian Protestant College (later **American University of Beirut [AUB]**) in 1866. During World War I, U.S. philanthropists sent humanitarian relief to the people of Lebanon who suffered deprivation under Ottoman rule. Yet the U.S. government took little official interest in the country before World War II. President **Woodrow Wilson** declined the suggestion by the **King-Crane Commission** of a U.S. mandate in the area, and the government in Washington said little when France secured a mandate over Lebanon and **Syria** jointly in 1920 and established Lebanon as a distinct mandate in 1922.

In the 1940s, by contrast, President **Franklin D. Roosevelt** facilitated Lebanon's independence. British and Free French forces liberated Lebanon from Vichy control in 1941. The Free French, under Charles De Gaulle, attempted to reimpose political control, but Roosevelt pressured them to recognize Lebanese sovereignty. France relinquished practical authority to Lebanese leaders in 1943, and the United States recognized Lebanon as an independent state in September 1944. In 1943, Lebanese leaders ratified the "National Pact," a power-sharing arrangement between the country's Christian and Muslim communities.

The United States enjoyed relatively sound relations with Lebanon during the early Cold War. Despite popular anger over the American recognition of **Israel** in 1948, Lebanese leaders indicated support for U.S. anti-Soviet containment policies, received U.S. economic aid, and downplayed Arab–Israeli animosity. **Camille Chamoun**, elected to a six-year term as president in 1952, was openly friendly toward the United States.

Trouble developed, however, in the late 1950s. Lebanese nationalists under the political sway of **Gamal Abdel Nasser** of **Egypt** protested Chamoun's pro-Western orientation, and Lebanese Muslims, citing changes in the country's demographics, demanded revisions to the National Pact. In such a context, Chamoun's efforts to amend the constitution to enable himself to run for reelection in 1958 provoked a wave of political protest and low-intensity violence against his government. The **Dwight D. Eisenhower** administration refused pleas from Chamoun to intervene to save his beleaguered presidency, and in June 1958, Chamoun abandoned his reelection quest. However, after a bloody coup toppled the pro-West regime in **Iraq** the next month, Eisenhower ordered U.S. Marines to occupy

Lebanon to prevent a copycat strike against the government in Beirut. Under the marines' watchful eyes, General **Fuad Chehab**, who displayed a more neutral diplomatic disposition, was elected president.

In subsequent decades, mounting political volatility and instability in Lebanon caused severe problems for U.S. officials. Hundreds of thousands of **Palestinian refugees** who had taken up residence in Lebanon since 1948 became politically active, joining Lebanese Muslims to contest the political authority of the country's Christian leadership. The Palestinians also conducted low-intensity warfare against Israel, provoking Israeli reprisals against Lebanon. Passions soared during the **Arab-Israeli War of 1967**, when anti-American mobs damaged American property, and in the early 1970s, when Palestinians expelled from **Jordan** during the **Black September** episode in 1970 settled in Lebanon and radicalized its politics. By 1975, Lebanon was decimated by full-scale civil war between the Lebanese Front, a coalition of Christian Phalangist militias, and the Lebanese National Movement, composed of Muslim, Druze, and Palestinian factions. American efforts in 1975–1977 to mediate a truce failed, and in 1976 a Palestinian militia assassinated U.S. Ambassador Francis E. Meloy Jr. and embassy counselor Robert O. Waring.

American officials strove with limited success to contain Arab–Israeli violence in Lebanon. When Israel occupied south Lebanon in 1978, U.S. officials helped organize the deployment of the **United Nations** Interim Force in Lebanon to pacify the area and thereby facilitate Israeli withdrawal. In the summer of 1981, U.S. presidential envoy **Philip C. Habib** brokered a resolution of an Israeli–Syrian showdown in the Bekaa Valley of Lebanon. Over U.S. opposition, Israel launched a full-scale **invasion of Lebanon** in June 1982 for the purposes of eradicating Palestinian influence, limiting Syrian power, and empowering Christian Phalangists. Together with France and Italy, the United States deployed military forces to facilitate the evacuation of Palestinians from Beirut and the withdrawal of the Israeli invasion force to the southern border regions.

Although this multilateral Western intervention achieved its objectives, President **Ronald Reagan** sent U.S. forces back into Beirut in late 1982 after Christian Phlangists, acting with Israeli complicity, massacred Palestinian refugees in two camps at Sabra and Shatila.

The marines faced the difficult political challenge of facilitating Israeli and Syrian withdrawals from the Beirut area and propping up the Christian government there. Yet those troops came under attack by Syrian-backed fighters. In April 1983, a car bomb demolished the U.S. embassy in Beirut, killing 63 persons, and in October, a truck bomb at a barracks killed 241 marines. Even as Reagan refrained from additional political involvement in Lebanon, terrorist groups in 1982–1988 took hostage 18 Americans (three of whom died in captivity). Given such dangers, the United States banned travel by Americans to Lebanon in 1987–1997 and closed its embassy in Beirut in 1989.

The United States remained generally uninvolved as Lebanon achieved a modicum of stability in the 1990s. In late 1989, **Arab League** officials brokered the so-called Taif Accord, which established a government with powers balanced among confessional groups. When Christian general **Michel Aoun** resisted the accord, Syrian forces deposed him, acting with the complicity of the United States given in exchange for Syrian cooperation with American actions in the **Persian Gulf War**. In the 1990s, Lebanon held elections through which moderates gained positions of authority and Prime Minister **Rafiq Hariri** energized the country and rebuilt its infrastructure. The United States included Lebanon in the **Madrid Conference** of 1991 and officially endorsed an Israeli–Lebanese peace treaty, and Israeli military forces departed their occupation zone in south Lebanon in 2000. In 2005, the assassination of former prime minister Hariri, an act widely attributed to Syria, led to popular protests that triggered the withdrawal of Syrian forces from Lebanon. In 2006, however, Lebanon remained in the throes of political rivalries.

LEBANON, ISRAELI INVASION OF. A military attack that caused grave consequences for the United States. **Israel** became concerned about **Lebanon** after civil war erupted there in 1975, **Syria** occupied central Lebanon in 1976, and Palestinian fighters based in southern Lebanon launched attacks against northern Israel. Following a major terrorist strike in March 1978, Israel occupied southern Lebanon for three months. After a series of additional border clashes, Israeli prime minister **Menachem Begin** planned a major invasion of Lebanon that would eradicate Palestinian forces, neutralize Syrian forces, and empower Maronite leader **Bashir Gemayel** in the hope that he would sign a peace treaty with Israel. Some evidence suggests that Secretary of State **Alexander Haig** indirectly if unintentionally encouraged Israeli belligerence. In June 1982, Israel launched the invasion and besieged Palestinian leaders in Beirut.

Bothered by Israel's action, President **Ronald Reagan** dispatched veteran envoy **Philip Habib** to broker a settlement. Under a deal signed on 12 August, U.S., French, and Italian troops arrived in Beirut to supervise the relocation of some 11,000 Palestinian fighters to various Arab states distant from Israel. The evacuation was completed by 1 September, and the Western soldiers departed Lebanon. Violence and instability continued to reign in Beirut, however, prompting U.S. forces to reoccupy the city in late 1982.

Secretary of State **George P. Schultz** brokered a deal, signed on 17 May 1983, that formally terminated the war between Israel and Lebanon, provided for a retreat of Israeli units to a security zone in southern Lebanon, and introduced **United Nations** troops as peacekeepers to the north of Israeli forces. In the wake of Israel's departure from central Lebanon, internecine fighting erupted on several fronts, vastly complicating the Lebanese civil war. The U.S. forces in Beirut gradually became the targets of attacks and acts of terrorism, including a suicide truck bomber who killed 241 marines in October 1983.

LIBYA. An oil-rich, Arab state in North Africa whose relationship with the United States deteriorated in the late 20th century. Long the object of foreign conquerors, Libya was seized by the Ottoman Empire in the 16th century and colonized by Italy in 1911. After the defeat of Axis forces in North Africa in 1943, Great Britain occupied the provinces of Tripolitania and Cyrenaica while France occupied Fezzan. Italy renounced all claims to these territories in a 1947 peace treaty, and the **United Nations** resolved in 1949 that Tripolitania, Cyrenaica, and Fezzan should be merged into an independent state within three years. In December 1951, Libya declared its independence as a constitutional, hereditary monarchy under **King Idris**.

American–Libyan relations were friendly and strong under King Idris. Libya gave the United States rights at Wheelus Field, an air base from which the United States projected power through the

Mediterranean world. American oil firms discovered vast oil reserves in Libya in 1959 and thereafter integrated that oil into Western markets, earning vast wealth for the royal regime and for themselves but also earning the resentment of the country's impoverished masses.

American–Libyan relations declined sharply after **Muammar al-Qaddafi** seized power in a coup in 1969. Inspired by **Gamal Abdel Nasser** of **Egypt**, Qaddafi aspired to assume a position of leadership in the Arab and African worlds, in part by confronting the West and **Israel**. He expelled U.S. forces from Wheelus Field in 1970, participated in the anti-American **Arab oil embargo of 1973**, gradually seized the assets of Western oil firms operating in his country, purchased vast quantities of Soviet weapons, and sponsored **terrorism** throughout the Mediterranean area. The United States recalled its ambassador from Tripoli in 1972, closed its embassy after a mob set fire to it in 1979, and declared Libya a state sponsor of terrorism in December 1979. In 1977, Qaddafi renamed his state the Great Socialist People's Libyan Arab Jamahiriya (State of the Masses), and in 1980 he invaded Chad in a quest to project his influence into central Africa.

The United States and Libya engaged in indirect war during the 1980s. In 1981, President **Ronald Reagan** expelled Libyan officials from the United States and sent the U.S. Sixth Fleet into the disputed Gulf of Sidra off Libya's coast. In August, navy jets downed two Libyan fighters that fired on them. In 1982, the United States embargoed the importation of Libyan oil, and in 1986, it embargoed all trade with Libya. Qaddafi redoubled his covert support of anti-American terrorists and 1984 and 1985 witnessed a series of attacks on Western airports, airliners, and cruise ships. The U.S. Navy returned to the Gulf of Sidra in March 1986 and, when challenged, destroyed several Libyan patrol boats and radar sites. Within weeks, a bomb devastated a West Berlin discotheque popular among U.S. soldiers, killing two people and wounding dozens. Citing evidence linking Qaddafi to the deed, Reagan ordered U.S. warplanes to bomb Tripoli and other military sites in Libya; the air strikes killed Qaddafi's daughter and narrowly missed the dictator himself. Libya retaliated in December 1988 when agents of Qaddafi's intelligence service placed a bomb aboard Pan Am Flight 103, which exploded over Lockerbie, Scotland, killing 270 people, including 189 Americans.

American–Libyan relations settled down after 1990. In 1992, the United States organized **United Nations**–backed international sanctions on Libya to pressure Qaddafi to extradite conspirators in the Lockerbie bombing. Isolated internationally, Qaddafi relented in 1999 by surrendering two intelligence officers implicated in the Lockerbie bombing. In September 2003, sanctions were lifted after a Scottish court convicted and imprisoned for life one of the intelligence officers. In December 2003, Libya renounced its programs to develop weapons of mass destruction. In 2004–2006, Qaddafi renewed diplomatic representation with European states and paid financial compensation to victims of various terrorist strikes in which his country was implicated. In 2004, President **George W. Bush** lifted economic sanctions against Libya, and the United States and Libya reopened diplomatic liaison offices in each other's capitals.

– M –

MADRID CONFERENCE. An international gathering in October 1991 that launched the Arab–Israeli peace process of the 1990s. Secretary of State **James Baker** engaged in vigorous diplomacy to organize a peace conference involving **Israel**, **Jordan**, the Palestinians, **Syria**, **Egypt**, and **Lebanon**. His efforts were boosted by two dramatic developments of 1991. First, the collapse of the Soviet Union eliminated the traditional Soviet patronage of Arab radicals and created unprecedented potential for Russian–American cooperation in Middle East diplomacy. Second, the outcome of the **Persian Gulf War** earned the United States the goodwill of moderate Arab states such as **Saudi Arabia** and Egypt and even the begrudging appreciation of Syria, and it gained President **George H. W. Bush** worldwide respect as a leader with a mandate for action. It also made **King Hussein** of Jordan and Palestinian leader **Yasser Arafat**, who had expressed sympathy for **Iraq**, anxious to make amends. Iraqi missile attacks during the war awakened Israeli leaders to the dangers of perpetual conflict, even as the end of the Cold War raised their fear that the United States, its containment objectives reached, might retreat from the region.

Baker's diplomacy culminated on 30 October 1991, when Bush and Soviet leader Mikhail Gorbachev presided over the Madrid Conference, a face-to-face meeting of the principals to the **Arab–Israeli conflict**. Although the conferees achieved nothing concrete beyond the reaffirmation of **United Nations** Resolutions 242 and 338, the conference qualified as a watershed event by shattering the popular Arab taboo against negotiating with Israel and by giving Palestinian diplomats a place at the table. Although serious conflicts persisted through 1992, the Madrid Conference laid one important foundation for the negotiation of the **Oslo Accord** in 1993.

AL-MALIKI, NURI (JAWAD) (1950–). Iraqi Shiite political figure named prime minister in May 2006. Al-Maliki was trained in Arabic literature, and he worked as an educator before fleeing **Iraq** in 1979, reportedly to escape execution by the **Saddam Hussein** regime. During 23 years of exile, al-Maliki directed the Damascus office of the Shiite Dawa political party, adopting Jawad as a name of resistance. Al-Maliki secretly returned to his native land in 2002, and following the **U.S. invasion of Iraq** in 2003, he helped draft the country's new constitution. Al-Maliki was selected as prime minister to replace **Ibrahim al-Jaafari**, who had alienated the Sunni and Kurdish wings of the Iraqi parliament. President **George W. Bush** welcomed al-Maliki's selection as a sign of political stability in Baghdad. But al-Maliki's reputation as a nationalist Shiite who had sharply criticized U.S. diplomacy left doubt about the type of relationship the two leaders would develop.

MCFARLANE, ROBERT C. (1937–). Major figure in the **Iran-Contra scandal**. As national security advisor to President **Ronald Reagan** in 1983–1985, McFarlane and his aide **Oliver North** arranged the sale of weapons to **Iran** and diversion of funds to Nicaragua. McFarlane traveled to Iran in May 1986 to negotiate an arms-for-hostages deal. In 1989, he pleaded guilty to withholding information from Congress and was fined and placed on probation.

MCGHEE, GEORGE (1912–2005). An oilman who shaped U.S. policy in the Middle East after World War II. After receiving a doctorate at Oxford University in 1937, McGhee became a successful and wealthy oil prospector at a young age. After military service in World

War II, he entered the State Department, accepting a post in which he oversaw the expenditure of $400 million in aid to Greece and Turkey under the **Truman Doctrine**. As assistant secretary of state for Near Eastern affairs, McGhee advocated strengthening the U.S. commitment to anticommunist containment in the Middle East, promoted the **Tripartite Declaration** of 1950 and the **Middle East Command** concept of 1951, and argued for accommodation with Arab nationalism. McGhee served as ambassador to **Turkey** in 1951–1953, overseeing that country's entrance into the **North Atlantic Treaty Organization (NATO)**. In the 1960s, McGhee served in other diplomatic missions in Africa, Latin America, and Europe.

MEIR, GOLDA (1898–1978). Prime minister of **Israel** who led her country through turbulent times. Born Golda Mabovitch in Kiev, Meir was raised and educated in Milwaukee, Wisconsin, before migrating to **Palestine** in 1921. In the years preceding Israeli statehood, Meir promoted **Zionism** and raised funds among Americans, served as acting head of the political department of the Jewish Agency for Palestine in 1946–1948 and in early 1948 met secretly with **King Abdullah I** of **Jordan** in an unsuccessful bid to head off an Arab invasion of Palestine. Meir served as Israeli ambassador to Moscow in 1948–1949 and as foreign minister in 1956–1965. She returned from retirement in 1969 to serve as prime minister after **Levi Eshkol** died in office.

Meir governed Israel at a crucial moment in its relationship with the United States. Exploiting the strength Israel earned in its victory in the **Arab-Israeli War of 1967**, Meir resisted the **Rogers Plan** for Arab–Israeli peace negotiations until President **Richard M. Nixon** assured her that Israel would not be forced to absorb **Palestinian refugees** or to relinquish territory in the absence of a final peace treaty. On that condition, she accepted the Rogers Plan and thereby achieved an end of the **War of Attrition** in August 1970.

Meir also earned American goodwill during a crisis in September 1970 by pledging to back **King Hussein** if **Syria** attacked Jordan, relieving Nixon from the burden of having to consider sending U.S. forces to rescue the king. Under the influence of Secretary of State **Henry Kissinger**, Nixon came to view Meir as a partner who could help contain both Soviet communism and Arab radicalism. He met

Meir in December 1971 and suspended the Rogers Plan in exchange for the prime minister's pledge merely to consider a partial withdrawal of Israeli forces from the Suez Canal area.

Meir's firmness toward her Arab adversaries set the stage for the **Arab-Israeli War of 1973**, which began when **Egypt** and Syria, frustrated by the diplomatic deadlock, attacked Israeli forces that occupied the Sinai and the Golan Heights. Although she secured an emergency shipment of American arms and commanded the Israeli counteroffensives that neutralized the initial Arab gains on the battlefields, Meir's political stature among Israelis was tarnished by her government's failure to have anticipated the Egyptian–Syrian assault. Meir won reelection as prime minister in December 1973, but lingering criticism of her lack of preparedness convinced her to resign from office in 1974.

MIDDLE EAST COMMAND (MEC). A Middle East security scheme proposed by the **Harry S. Truman** administration but never established. In 1950, U.S. planners conceived of MEC as a means to safeguard the Middle East against a Soviet onslaught expected in the shadow of the outbreak of the Korean War. Inspired by the **North Atlantic Treaty Organization (NATO)**, they aimed to establish an integrated command structure that would enlist Arab states as partners of the West in the Cold War. By basing MEC in **Egypt**, they hoped to solve an Anglo–Egyptian dispute over military bases in the Suez Canal Zone, to attract other Arab states to join the pact, and to settle an Anglo–U.S. disagreement over allied naval commands. They excluded **Israel** from MEC to avoid angering the Arab states.

In October 1951, the United States, Great Britain, France, and Turkey jointly invited Egypt to join the pact and base it in Cairo. Egyptian leaders, however, not only rejected the MEC proposal but also abrogated their defense treaty with Britain and demanded that British forces withdraw from Egypt. The United States and Britain then invited other Arab governments to join MEC, but they declined because of widespread approval of Egypt's action by their peoples. American officials soon realized that MEC had little chance of success. *See also* MIDDLE EAST DEFENSE ORGANIZATION.

MIDDLE EAST DEFENSE ORGANIZATION (MEDO). A revised version of a discredited security scheme promoted by the United

States in the early 1950s. After Egypt rejected the proposed **Middle East Command (MEC)** idea in late 1951, U.S. and British officials modified the concept in a futile effort to overcome its shortcomings. In the summer of 1952, they renamed it MEDO, called it a planning board rather than a command, and tried to sell the idea to Arab military officers rather than the politicians who seemed preoccupied by **Israel**. But **Egypt** remained hostile to any defense arrangement prior to British evacuation of the Canal Zone, and other Arab states remained reluctant to defy Egypt. The rejection of MEDO convinced U.S. officials that they needed to assume a greater leadership role in security planning for the Middle East rather than rely on Great Britain. It thus set the stage for the **Baghdad Pact** and **Eisenhower Doctrine** of the mid- and late 1950s and other security commitments that followed.

MIDDLE EAST FREE TRADE AREA (MEFTA). A plan, announced by President **George W. Bush** in 2003, to promote free trade between the United States and the Middle East. MEFTA would constitute a series of agreements between the United States and Middle East powers that would encourage trade and investment as a means of generating prosperity and political stability in the Middle East and thereby avert the resort of local peoples to terrorism. In 2003, Bush announced his goal of establishing MEFTA by 2013.

MITCHELL, GEORGE (1933–). Former U.S. senator from Maine who chaired a peace commission appointed by President **William J. Clinton** in late 2000 to propose a plan to quell the second **intifada**. In May 2001, the five-man commission released a peace plan that urged that the Palestinians and **Israel**, first, reaffirm commitments to past agreements, curb violence, and resume security cooperation; second, promote accord through such measures as cessation of settlement construction and renunciation of **terrorism**; and, third, resume peace negotiations. Although Israeli prime minister **Ariel Sharon** and Palestinian leader **Yasser Arafat** endorsed the Mitchell plan, the violence continued unabated.

MOSSADEGH, MOHAMMED (1882–1967). Nationalist prime minister of **Iran** in 1951–1953 who challenged Western interests in his country. Distressed by Great Britain's dominance of Iran's lucrative oil industry, Mossadegh emerged as prime minister and enacted nationalization of the Anglo-Iranian Oil Company (AIOC) in 1951. British leaders contemplated using force to unseat Mossadegh, but President **Harry S. Truman** talked them out of it. Britain instead shut down the AIOC's massive refinery at Abadan and organized a Western embargo of Iranian oil that brought the country's industry to a virtual standstill. But Mossadegh refused to yield, gathering a political following in Tehran that challenged the authority of pro-Western shah **Mohammed Reza Pahlavi**.

On taking office in 1953, President **Dwight D. Eisenhower** moved quickly to resolve the standoff. In May, he rejected an appeal from Mossadegh for financial assistance on the pretext that American taxpayers would not endorse such aid. Rather, Eisenhower decided that Mossadegh's policy threatened American interests. Although Mossadegh was not a communist, he apparently had become dependent on the local Communist (Tudeh) Party for political support. Mossadegh's nationalization of the AIOC undermined Britain's prestige and set a precedent for similar action against other Western firms in the developing world. The instability in Iran impeded the U.S. goal of establishing an anti-Soviet pact among states along the Soviet Union's southern border.

Thus, Eisenhower authorized a U.S.–British covert operation to overthrow Mossadegh. Following a clash with Mossadegh, the shah fled the country on 15 August 1953. When Mossadegh's antiroyalist forces split between Tudeh members and Muslim nationalists, however, Western intelligence officers exploited the schism by raising an anti-Mossadegh mob in Tehran and recruiting key units of the armed forces to support the shah. On 20 August, Mossadegh was arrested by forces loyal to the shah, and days later the shah returned to his throne. Mossadegh was jailed or detained under house arrest until his death in 1967. His legacy inspired Iranians who later rebelled against the shah and criticized the United States.

MUBARAK, HOSNI (1928–). Longtime president of Egypt who developed a moderate foreign policy and close ties to the United States. Born in 1928, Mubarak was educated at military academies and became a pilot in the Egyptian air force. Appointed air force chief of staff (1969) and commander in chief (1972), he commanded the Egyptian air force during the **Arab-Israeli War of 1973**. A close adviser to **Anwar Sadat**, Mubarak became vice president in 1975 and president on the assassination of Sadat in 1981. As the head of the National Democratic Party, Mubarak was reelected in 1987, 1993, and 1999 in pollings with no viable opposition candidates. He was reelected in 2005 in an election in which, under U.S. pressure, he allowed a modest degree of political opposition.

Mubarak's foreign policies have been marked by moderation and friendship with the West. He cooperated with the anti-Soviet security initiatives of President **Ronald Reagan**. He endorsed U.S. aims in the **Persian Gulf War** of 1990–1991 and the postwar sanctions against **Iraq**, and he withheld sharp criticism of U.S. policy in the **Iraq War** of 2003–. Mubarak affirmed the peace treaty with **Israel** that Sadat had signed, and he encouraged the Oslo-based Arab–Israeli peace process of the 1990s. The United States rewarded the Mubarak government with billions of dollars in aid.

Such a foreign policy compounded Mubarak's domestic troubles. Radical groups criticized his friendship with the West and his tolerance of Israel, and some inflicted violence on government targets and on foreign tourists to undermine the regime. **Egyptian Islamic Jihad** and Gamaa Islamiya launched a campaign of **terrorism** that claimed 1,000 victims in 1992–1997, and they attempted to assassinate Mubarak in 1995. Mubarak maintained power through a combination of repression of Islamists and economic reform that preserved popular loyalty to the state. *See also* FOREIGN AID.

MURPHY, ROBERT D. (1894–1978). A career U.S. Foreign Service officer who brokered a settlement of a political crisis in **Lebanon** in 1958. President **Dwight D. Eisenhower** dispatched Murphy, his personal friend who was serving as deputy undersecretary of state, to resolve the political crisis that had prompted Eisenhower to order marines to occupy Beirut in July 1958. Murphy skillfully and tirelessly conducted negotiations involving various Lebanese factions as well as leaders of neighboring states. Ultimately, he arranged for elections that resulted in **Fuad Chehab** replacing **Camille Chamoun** as president. That outcome averted civil war among the Lebanese and enabled the withdrawal of the marines.

– N –

NAGUIB, MOHAMMED (1901–1984). An Egyptian army general and first leader of **Egypt** after the 1952 revolution. Viewed in the West as a moderate and a liberal, Naguib participated in the coup that ousted **King Farouk** in July 1952 and became prime minister of Egypt. Yet he faced a major rival in the more radical colonel **Gamal Abdel Nasser**, who headed the nine-member Revolutionary Command Council. To bolster Naguib, U.S. officials pressured Great Britain to settle an Anglo–Egyptian military bases dispute on terms favorable to Cairo, and they dissuaded Naguib from attempting to make peace with **Israel** for fear he would lose popularity among his own people. During a 1954 power struggle with Nasser, Naguib resigned the prime ministry in February, returned to office as president of Egypt in March, but then was removed from office by Nasser in November.

NASSER, GAMAL ABDEL (1918–1970). Egyptian army officer and political leader with whom the United States developed a tumultuous relationship. A decorated war veteran, Nasser turned to politics in the late 1940s to address what he considered the three major impediments to the Egyptian people: British imperialism, the regime of **King Farouk**, and **Israel**. He conspired with fellow army officers to overthrow King Farouk in July 1952, and he wrested power from a rival revolutionary, General **Mohammed Naguib**, in late 1954.

American officials initially viewed Nasser with cautious optimism. President **Dwight D. Eisenhower** was heartened that Nasser stabilized **Egypt**, prevented the rise of communism as well as Islamic fundamentalism, and embraced U.S. aid and friendship. Nasser's attitude toward the United States soured, however, when Eisenhower refused to supply him substantial military arms and promoted Western defense alliance schemes that seemed to undermine Egyptian sovereignty. The legacy of American backing of Israel also dispirited him. An Anglo-American initiative in 1955–1956 to restore goodwill with Nasser by funding construction of Egypt's Aswan Dam collapsed amidst disagreements on financial and political terms, further straining the relationship.

Even before the Aswan Dam funding episode, Nasser adopted a policy of neutralism that irritated American officials. Invoking a vision of pan-Arab solidarity, he emerged as a critic of Western imperialism, accepted material aid from communist countries, recognized the People's Republic of China, and, in July 1956, nationalized the British- and French-owned Suez Canal Company. That last step provoked the **Suez Crisis**, in which Great Britain, France, and Israel attacked Egypt intent on overthrowing Nasser. Although Eisenhower convinced the attackers to desist and thereby rescued Nasser, U.S.–Egyptian tensions persisted.

In 1958–1962, U.S. leaders enjoyed a brief rapprochement with Nasser. Eisenhower used economic aid to exploit Nasser's emerging rivalry with other Arab leaders and his suspicions of the Soviet Union. President **John F. Kennedy** engaged in an extensive personal correspondence with Nasser and persuaded him to downplay their differences over Israel. But the rapprochement soured after Nasser intervened in the civil war in **Yemen**, backing rebellious forces in opposition to America's partner **Saudi Arabia**.

President **Lyndon B. Johnson** experienced a difficult relationship with Nasser. Johnson criticized Egypt's involvement in Yemen and protested when a series of incidents caused destruction of American property in Cairo. When Nasser personally insulted Johnson, the latter suspended economic aid. During the **Arab-Israeli War of 1967**, Nasser charged that the United States secretly participated in the Israeli attack on his country, severed diplomatic relations with Washington, and expelled thousands of Americans from his country. Nasser condemned American backing of Israel during the **War of Attrition** of 1967–1970. Although Nasser considered making amends with President **Richard M. Nixon** in 1970, their relationship remained tense when Nasser died suddenly of a heart attack in September. *See also* FOREIGN AID.

NATIONAL ASSOCIATION OF ARAB-AMERICANS (NAAA). A political action group established in 1972 to lobby Congress on U.S. policy in the Middle East. The NAAA historically voiced the interests of Arab states in the Arab–Israeli peace process and favored the end of the occupation of **Lebanon** by **Syria**.

NATIONAL SECURITY STRATEGY OF THE UNITED STATES. A policy statement published in September 2002 by the **George W.**

Bush administration that provided a foundation for the **U.S. invasion of Iraq** in March 2003. The statement declared, among other points, that the United States would take preemptive action against threats to its national security and that it would target governments that willfully harbored or aided terrorists. Bush justified his decision to invade **Iraq** by asserting that **Saddam Hussein** controlled weapons of mass destruction and that he might provide such weapons to terrorists.

NETANYAHU, BENJAMIN (1949–). Israeli politician and prime minister in 1996–1999. Born in **Israel**, Netanyahu attended high school and university in the United States and served in the Israeli army in 1967–1972. He joined the conservative Likud Party in the 1980s and, between 1981 and 1992, served as a staff member at the Israeli embassy in Washington, Israeli ambassador to the **United Nations**, and deputy foreign minister, in each post promoting U.S.–Israeli cooperation. Netanyahu took control of the Likud Party in 1993 after the electoral defeat of **Yitzhak Shamir**.

Netanyahu opposed the peace process of the early 1990s promoted by the United States and Israel's Labor Party. He won election as prime minister in May 1996, as his campaign theme of firmness on all security matters found credence in an electorate terrorized by a wave of suicide bombings. As prime minister, he continued the peace process, met Palestinian leader **Yasser Arafat** on occasion, and signed an American-brokered deal to withdraw some Israeli troops from Hebron. But he clearly lacked the passion for peacemaking displayed by **Yitzhak Rabin**, and he implemented certain policies, including the opening of the ancient, recently excavated Hasmonean Tunnel in Jerusalem and a vigorous burst of settlement building in the West Bank, that provoked a violent backlash by Palestinians.

Under enormous pressure from President **William J. Clinton**, Netanyahu signed the **Wye River Memorandum** of October 1998, in which Israel and the **Palestinian National Authority (PNA)** pledged to enact various confidence-building measures and to engage in negotiations leading to a final settlement by 2000. But that step alienated him from both Israeli liberals who favored a vigorous peace process and Israeli conservatives who favored firm measures. Buffeted by allegations of corruption, Netanyahu lost the prime ministry in the May 1999 election.

Netanyahu served in the Likud government of **Ariel Sharon** as foreign minister (2002–2003) and finance minister (2003–2005) before resigning in protest over Sharon's decision to withdraw from Gaza in August 2005. Netanyahu took leadership of the Likud Party in 2005 but proved unable to win the Israeli elections of March 2006.

9/11. Symbol for the devastating terrorist attacks inflicted on the United States on 11 September 2001. Nineteen members of the **al-Qaeda** terrorist network simultaneously hijacked four U.S. domestic airliners. Two of the planes were flown into the twin towers of the World Trade Center in New York City, causing both structures to collapse. A third plane crashed into the Pentagon near Washington, D.C., demolishing a wing of that building. The fourth plane, apparently destined to strike a target in Washington, crashed in a remote area of Pennsylvania after passengers tried to regain control of the aircraft. The 9/11 attacks killed some 3,000 persons and deeply wounded the morale of the American people. The most devastating enemy assault ever on the American homeland and the most destructive act of **terrorism** in world history, 9/11 triggered the **U.S. invasion of Afghanistan** in 2001, indirectly contributed to the **U.S. invasion of Iraq** in 2003, and reshaped the foundation of U.S. national security policy.

NIXON DOCTRINE. A policy statement initially pertaining to East Asia but eventually applied to the Middle East as well. President **Richard M. Nixon** issued the doctrine during a press briefing in Guam in November 1969 and elaborated on it in following years. Recognizing that the Vietnam War had laid bare the limits of American ability to police the world, the Nixon Doctrine declared that while the United States would provide strategic defense against the Soviet nuclear threat, it would equip and rely on various client states to resist revolution and otherwise stabilize each region of the world.

In the Middle East, Nixon viewed **Iran** as his primary client, especially after Great Britain announced that it would relinquish its commitments to security interests east of Suez in 1971. Thus, the president nurtured a close relationship with Shah **Mohammed Reza Pahlavi** and offered to sell any nonnuclear weapon systems the shah desired. In 1972–1977, Iran purchased U.S. weapons valued at $16.2

billion, and U.S. officials formed a close partnership with SAVAK, the shah's secret police force. The overthrow of the shah in 1979 signaled one weakness of the Nixon Doctrine: its reliance on unstable political regimes. *See also* FOREIGN AID.

NIXON, RICHARD M. (1913–1994). American president in 1969–1974 who nurtured close relationships with **Iran** and **Israel**. As part of his global strategy for efficiently containing Soviet communism, Nixon declared under the **Nixon Doctrine** that the United States would equip and rely on various client states to resist revolution and otherwise stabilize each region of the world, and he viewed Iran as his Middle East client. Nixon also hoped to repair the stark **trade** imbalance caused by the American consumption of Iranian oil. Thus, the president nurtured a close relationship with Shah **Mohammed Reza Pahlavi**, offered to sell any nonnuclear weapon systems the shah desired, and directed the Central Intelligence Agency to form a close partnership with SAVAK, the Shah's secret police force.

Nixon also strengthened U.S. ties with Israel. Wary of Soviet political inroads in Arab states, he refrained from pressuring Israeli leaders to consider an offer from Egyptian premier **Gamal Abdel Nasser** to make peace through some settlement brokered by the **United Nations**. Under the influence of National Security Advisor **Henry Kissinger**, the president even resisted the **Rogers Plan**, promoted by Secretary of State **William P. Rogers**, to make peace on the basis of UN Resolution 242 and to settle the **Palestinian refugees** issue. Nixon supported Rogers's diplomacy to end the Egyptian–Israeli **War of Attrition** in August 1970 but only after he assured Israeli prime minister **Golda Meir** that Israel would be forced neither to absorb Palestinian refugees nor to relinquish territory in the absence of a final peace treaty. American officials also encouraged **King Hussein**'s suppression and expulsion of the **Palestine Liberation Organization (PLO)** in the so-called **Black September** episode of 1970–1971 and secured a commitment from Israel to help the king survive the ordeal if necessary.

Nixon's tilt toward Israel contributed to the outbreak of the **Arab-Israeli War of 1973**. The president resisted a plan for peace on the basis of UN Resolution 242, proposed by UN mediator Gunnar Jarring in 1971, and he rejected a proposal by **Egyptian** premier **Anwar**

Sadat that Israel withdraw its forces from the Suez Canal area as a gesture to start a peace process. Nixon adopted Kissinger's view of Israel as a regional client state that, consonant with the Nixon Doctrine, would serve American interests by containing both Soviet communism and Arab radicalism. The president also realized the domestic political advantages of backing Israel on the eve of the presidential election of 1972. Distracted by the war in Vietnam, the pursuit of détente in Beijing and Moscow, and the unfolding Watergate crisis at home in 1972–1973, Nixon also missed warning signs that Egypt contemplated offensive military action to recover the Sinai. The Egyptian–**Syrian** invasion of Israel on 6 October 1973 caught Nixon by surprise.

Increasingly burdened by the Watergate crisis, Nixon delegated authority for Middle East diplomacy to Kissinger during and after the **Arab-Israeli War of 1973**. He approved Kissinger's action of airlifting arms to Israel (perhaps to avert Israel's use of its nuclear weapons to stave off defeat), pushing a fresh cease-fire resolution through the UN Security Council, and warning the Soviets not to carry out a threat to intervene militarily on the Arab side. Nixon also dispatched Kissinger on the so-called **shuttle diplomacy** initiative, which achieved the disengagement of belligerent forces along Israel's borders with Egypt and Syria, the restoration of U.S.–Egyptian diplomatic relations, and the end of the **Arab oil embargo**.

In June 1974, as part of a ploy to salvage his reputation from the Watergate quagmire, Nixon paid the first-ever visit by a U.S. president to Israel. He met Israeli leaders and issued joint declarations affirming friendship between the two states. The domestic effect of Nixon's visit remained modest: Nixon resigned the presidency under threat of impeachment in early August.

NOOR, QUEEN, OF JORDAN (1951–). American-born wife of **King Hussein** of Jordan. Born Lisa Najeeb Halaby in Washington with an Arab-American heritage, the future Queen Noor graduated from Princeton University in 1974 with a degree in architecture and urban planning. She met King Hussein in 1978 while working in Jordan and married him within the year, taking the name Queen Noor al-Hussein (literally "the light of Hussein"). Queen Noor became active in a variety of humanitarian, educational, children's, and peacemaking causes.

NORTH ATLANTIC TREATY ORGANIZATION (NATO). A mutual defense organization established by treaty in 1949 by the United States, Canada, and 10 Western European allies. Its original purpose was to deter and defend against a Soviet attack on any member state. The heart of the alliance was a collective security principle that an attack on any member state would be considered an attack on all. NATO was extended to the Middle East in 1952 when Greece and Turkey joined. By 2004, NATO included 26 countries.

NATO invoked its collective security proviso for the first time ever in reaction to the **9/11** attack on the United States. In August 2003, NATO became involved in Afghanistan, its first major operation outside Europe. NATO officials also opened a dialogue with countries of the southern Mediterranean and Persian Gulf regions about the prospects for future political and military cooperation.

NORTH, OLIVER (1943–). U.S. Marine Corps officer involved in the **Iran-Contra scandal**. A member of the National Security Council staff, North helped arrange the transfer of funds, garnered from arms sales to **Iran**, to the Contra rebels in Nicaragua. When the media reported the arrangement, President **Ronald Reagan** fired North in 1986. In 1987, under a deal providing legal immunity, North revealed many details of the Iran-Contra scandal in testimony to Congress. In 1989, a jury convicted North on three counts of criminal wrongdoing, but an appeals court later overturned the conviction because it was based in part on North's immunized testimony to Congress.

– O –

OCTOBER WAR. *See* ARAB-ISRAELI WAR OF 1973.

OLMERT, EHUD (1945–). Acting prime minister of Israel whose Kadima Party won the Israeli elections of March 2006. Born in Palestine, Olmert served in the Israeli army and earned a law degree. He served in the Knesset in 1973–1998 and also as mayor of Jerusalem in 1993–2003. Reelected to the Knesset in 2003, Olmert held a variety of posts under Prime Minister **Ariel Sharon**, and in November 2005, he joined Sharon in bolting from the Likud Party to establish the new centrist Kadima Party. When Sharon was incapacitated by a stroke in January 2006, Olmert became acting prime minister, in which position he led the Kadima Party to a victory in the Israeli elections of March 2006. As acting and then officially prime minister, Olmert declared that he would continue Sharon's policy of seeking a peace settlement that established a state of **Palestine** on conditions favorable to the preservation of Israel as a Jewish democratic state.

OMAN. A small country located on the Strait of Hormuz, the gateway to the Persian Gulf, with which the United States enjoyed friendly relations. The United States signed a treaty of friendship and navigation with the independent sultanate in 1833 and maintained a consulate in Muscat from 1880 to 1915. As Oman developed ties of friendship with and dependence on the British Empire in the early 20th century, formal U.S. interest in the country waned. After overthrowing his father in 1970, however, Sultan Qaboos bin Said sought to end his country's political isolation and to build ties with the United States. In 1973–1974, the United States and Oman mutually opened embassies. In 1980, the two powers signed a renewable military cooperation agreement in which the United States gained base rights on Omani territory in exchange for more than $1 billion in aid. During the **Persian Gulf War** of 1990–1991, Oman dispatched troops to assist in the liberation of **Kuwait**. Oman also generally supported U.S. efforts to promote Arab–Israeli peace agreements. After the **9/11** terrorist attacks, Oman contributed to the U.S. campaign to staunch the threat of **terrorism** in the region. *See also* FOREIGN AID.

OPERATION DESERT SHIELD. *See* PERSIAN GULF WAR.

OPERATION DESERT STORM. *See* PERSIAN GULF WAR.

ORGANIZATION OF ARAB PETROLEUM EXPORTING COUNTRIES (OAPEC). A consortium of Arab states, with membership limited to countries that earned substantial revenues from the export of petroleum products. **Kuwait, Libya,** and **Saudi Arabia** founded OAPEC in 1968 as a mechanism to foster cooperation among governments to develop an integrated oil infrastructure for the collective good and to advance the energy interests of members of the **Arab League**. Based permanently in Kuwait, OAPEC eventually extended membership to Algeria, **Bahrain**, **Egypt**, **Iraq**, **Qatar**, **Syria**, and the **United Arab Emirates** (Tunisia joined in 1982 but withdrew in 1986). OAPEC was distinct from the **Organization of Petroleum Exporting Countries (OPEC)**.

ORGANIZATION OF THE ISLAMIC CONFERENCE (OIC). An intergovernmental organization of 57 states, founded in 1969 in reaction to the occupation of Jerusalem by **Israel** in 1967. The OIC declared that its purposes included preventing conflict among Islamic countries and peoples, promoting the unity of Islamic states in dealing with international issues and controversies, and sponsoring occasional meetings among heads of state and foreign ministers of Islamic countries. By the 1980s, the OIC had established a permanent secretariat and a complex network of committees. In 2005, the OIC sponsored a conference in **Saudi Arabia** to discuss compelling issues, such as the status of women in Islamic countries and the practice of terrorism by some Islamic extremists.

ORGANIZATION OF PETROLEUM EXPORTING COUNTRIES (OPEC). A cartel formed by oil-producing states for the purpose of wresting control of their oil industries from Western firms and maximizing their oil revenues. OPEC was formed in 1960 by **Iran**, **Iraq**, **Saudi Arabia**, **Kuwait**, and Venezuela. **Qatar**, **Libya**, Indonesia, the **United Arab Emirates**, Algeria, Nigeria, Ecuador, and Gabon joined between 1960 and 1973; Gabon and Ecuador later withdrew from full membership.

In the 1960s and 1970s, OPEC concentrated on nationalizing the assets of Western oil companies in member states, and in the 1970s and 1980s, the cartel negotiated a series of production quotas and price standardization agreements designed to maximize member states' profits. In a backlash against American support for **Israel** during the **Arab-Israeli War of 1973**, OPEC states supported the **Arab oil embargo**, artificially inflating the price of oil products by some 400 percent, causing turmoil in economies around the world. After a second oil shock in 1979, triggered by the **Iranian** revolution, Western countries worked to reduce their dependence on OPEC oil by conservation methods and by seeking new sources of oil in other places.

ORIENTALISM. A construct in Western thinking about the Middle East and Asia that was identified and critiqued by the literary critic and scholar Edward Said, a Palestinian American. According to Said, British and French scholars developed an Orientalist perspective in the 19th century, when they built an elaborate means of understanding the Orient as backward, weak, passive, and irrational, a construct that justified Western colonial conquests across the region. American intellectuals and government officials, Said posited, inherited such a mind-set as they became active in the Middle East after World War II. As a result, the American government and people tended to see Arab peoples as backward, violent, dishonest, and unreliable. Such powerful stereotypes at the core of American culture, in Said's judgment, significantly shaped the broad contours of American policy in the Middle East. Said's thesis proved controversial among some other scholars.

OSLO ACCORD. An agreement, negotiated in 1993, containing terms for an Israeli–Palestinian settlement. Officially called the Declaration of Principles on Interim Self-Government Arrangements, the accord provided that the **Palestine Liberation Organization (PLO)** would renounce **terrorism** and recognize **Israel**, Israel would withdraw from Jericho and the Gaza Strip, and the two parties would thereafter negotiate all points of contention including Jerusalem, borders, **Palestinian refugees**, and settlements and pledge to live in peace. After a series of secret talks, held in Oslo under Norwegian sponsorship in early 1993, Israeli and Palestinian officials initialed the accord in August. Having monitored the talks, President **William J. Clinton** immediately endorsed the accord and invited Israeli prime minister **Yitzhak Rabin** and PLO president **Yasser Arafat** formally to sign it on the lawn of the White House on 13 September. Following that deed, Clinton then nudged Rabin to shake Arafat's extended hand in a historic gesture of peace.

The Oslo accord opened the peace process of the 1990s. Israel and **Jordan** signed a formal peace treaty in October 1994, and Israel began interacting with Morocco, Tunisia, and **Saudi Arabia**. Progress was also made on the Israeli–Palestinian front. In May 1994, the Israel Defense Forces (IDF) departed Gaza and Jericho. In July, Arafat returned to Gaza to loud celebrations and established the **Palestinian National Authority (PNA)**, which soon fielded a police force, printed postage stamps, issued travel documents, and otherwise acted like a state. In October 1995, Israel and the PNA signed the Israeli-Palestinian Interim Agreement on the West Bank and Gaza, alternatively known as the Taba accord or Oslo II, which provided for the withdrawal of the IDF from nine major Palestinian towns. On 20 January 1996, Palestinian voters elected Arafat as president and elected an 88-member legislature. On 24 April, the PLO overwhelmingly voted to amend its charter to excise those passages that called for the violent destruction of Israel. A day later, Israel's Labor Party declared that it no longer opposed Palestinian statehood. Yet this progress toward a full Israeli–Palestinian peace arrangement faltered in the political conflict and violence of the late 1990s.

– P –

PAHLAVI, MOHAMMED REZA, SHAH OF IRAN (1919–1980). A longtime U.S. ally who fell from power in a revolution in 1979. Mohammed Reza Pahlavi succeeded his father **Reza Shah** as shah (king) of Iran in 1941. In the early years of his reign, the young shah successfully weathered two major political challenges, with U.S. assistance. He crushed a Soviet-backed secessionist movement in Azerbaijan province in 1946 after the United States pressured the Soviet Union to withdraw its soldiers from the area, and he prevailed over a domestic rival, nationalist leader and Prime Minister **Mohammed Mossadegh**, who briefly removed the shah from power before falling from office in a coup organized by U.S. and British intelligence officers in 1953.

The shah emerged as a key partner of the United States in subsequent years. He gained U.S. economic aid and military training and membership in the **Baghdad Pact**. In the early 1970s, President **Richard M. Nixon** embraced the shah as his partner under the **Nixon Doctrine** and sold Iran extensive military hardware. The shah also consolidated his political power in Tehran, amassed enormous wealth, ostentatiously displayed regal splendor, and built a repressive police force to protect his throne with censorship and torture. He resisted modest U.S. pressures to liberalize his political system.

By the 1970s, the shah faced signs of trouble. Religious clerics organized an underground resistance movement that grew despite attempts to repress it. Economic turmoil, urban blight, and housing shortages stressed the people of Iran, who increasingly questioned their monarch's partnership with the United States and his wealth and corruption. Diagnosed with cancer in 1974, the shah seemed to lose the strength needed to govern effectively. The opposition became outright revolution in 1978, and the shah went into exile on 16 January 1979, never to return to Iran. His admission to the United States for medical treatment in October 1979 provoked the **Iran Hostage Crisis**. The shah died of cancer in July 1980. *See also* FOREIGN AID.

PAHLAVI, REZA, SHAH OF IRAN (1878–1944). First shah (king) of modern **Iran** who briefly looked on the United States as a counterweight to the British and Russian empires. Born as Reza Kahn, the future king rose through the ranks of the Cossack Brigade and seized political offices in Tehran in the early 1920s, when he pressured first the Russians and then the British to end their occupations of Iranian territory dating from World War I. In 1925, he deposed the last shah of the Qajar dynasty, Ahmad Mirza, and declared himself Reza Shah Pahlavi. For 16 years, Reza Shah worked to modernize, industrialize, and secularize his country, changing its name from Persia to Iran in 1935, and he encouraged Iranian nationalism and challenged British imperial prerogatives. To circumvent British influence, Reza Shah in the early 1920s welcomed a financial mission led by an American, Arthur Millspaugh, designed to reform his country's treasury. In the 1930s, however, Reza Shah developed substantial economic ties, including civil air service, with Nazi Germany. Fearing Reza Shah's pro-German proclivities, Great Britain and the Soviet Union reoccupied Iran in 1941 and forced Reza Shah to abdicate in favor of his son **Mohammed Reza Pahlavi**. Reza Shah died in exile in 1944.

PALESTINE. The territory along the eastern shore of the Mediterranean Sea that became the center point of the **Arab–Israeli conflict**.

Conquered repeatedly over many centuries, Palestine was controlled by the Ottoman Empire from 1516 until British forces occupied it during World War I. Great Britain governed the land as a League of Nations mandate from 1922 to 1948. Conflict ensued when Jewish immigrants motivated by the Zionist dream of restoring the ancient Jewish homeland in Palestine clashed with local Arab Palestinians who resisted such a development. Finding it difficult to pacify the mandate after World War II, Britain relinquished control to the **United Nations**, which approved a plan to **partition** Palestine into an Arab state and a Jewish state. The Jewish community declared the independence of **Israel** over approximately half the mandate, while the Arab Palestinians refrained from accepting partition, trying instead to destroy Israel and seize all the land. Israel survived the **Arab-Israeli War of 1948–1949** and even expanded its borders beyond what had been reserved for it under partition. The remnants of the territory designated for an Arab Palestinian state, known as the West Bank and the Gaza Strip, were occupied by Jordan and Egypt, respectively. While a small fraction of Arab Palestinians remained in Israeli territory and became Israeli citizens, the vast majority became **Palestinian refugees** who dwelled in decrepit refugee camps in nearby states.

After decades of armed conflict between Israel and neighboring Arab countries, the idea of a state of Palestine for the Arab Palestinian people reemerged in international diplomatic discourse in the 1970s and 1980s. The Palestinians had begun to organize politically in the 1950s and 1960s, most notably under the lead of the **Palestine Liberation Organization (PLO)**, which used violence and diplomacy in pursuit of its objective of the destruction of Israel. In 1974, the **Arab League** resolved that the PLO was the sole representative of the Palestinian people. After the spontaneous eruption of the **intifada**, the PLO decided in 1988 to accept the partition plan of 1947, renounce **terrorism**, and demand that Israel withdraw from the West Bank and Gaza Strip in conformity with **United Nations** Resolution 242 of 1967. On 15 November 1988, the PLO declared the existence of a state of Palestine with its capital at Jerusalem. Even though the PLO did not control any territory, about 100 other countries recognized Palestine.

Israeli officials, overcoming their initial skepticism about PLO intentions, met Palestinian leaders at the **Madrid Conference** in 1991 and signed the **Oslo Accord** in 1993. The peace process born at Oslo provided for gradual withdrawal of Israeli occupation forces from most of Gaza and from large segments of the West Bank and for Palestinian autonomy in those areas. Yet political tensions and violence perpetrated by opponents of peacemaking on both sides slowed the progress, and the original target date for a final settlement—4 May 1999—passed with no redeclaration of Palestinian statehood. Additional diplomatic deadlocks and the eruption of the second intifada stymied further progress into the early 2000s.

The United States gradually embraced the idea of a state of Palestine. Although Secretary of State **Henry Kissinger** declared in 1975 that the United States would not recognize the PLO unless it renounced terrorism and accepted the legitimacy of Israel, President **Jimmy Carter** publicly acknowledged that Palestinians deserved a state. After the PLO renounced terrorism and pledged to accept Israel in 1988, U.S. leaders opened a dialogue with it and vigorously promoted the peace process of the 1990s. President **George W. Bush** declared in September 2001 that he envisioned a Palestinian state as part of a comprehensive peace settlement, and he sponsored the **Roadmap peace plan** of 2003, which envisioned a provisional Palestinian state by 2004. In Resolution 1397 of March 2002, the UN Security Council for the first time ever explicitly referred to a state of Palestine.

PALESTINE CONCILIATION COMMISSION (PCC). A **United Nations** agency with U.S. membership that tried futilely to solve the **Arab–Israeli conflict** in the aftermath of the **Arab-Israeli War of 1948–1949**. The UN Security Council created the PCC in December 1948 with U.S., French, and Turkish membership to mediate a permanent Arab–Israeli settlement. After Israel and its Arab adversaries signed armistices in early 1949, the PCC organized a peace conference at Lausanne, Switzerland, in April, and persuaded **Israel**, **Egypt**, **Syria**, **Lebanon**, and **Jordan** to send delegates. But the Arab representatives refused to meet the Israelis in person, and the conference ended in August after the parties deadlocked on such major issues as borders and **Palestinian refugees**. The PCC sponsored additional peace talks in New York in October 1949, in Geneva in January–June 1950, in Jerusalem in June 1950, and in Paris in September–November

1951, but it made no progress toward achieving a peace agreement. The PCC gradually faded into oblivion.

PALESTINE LIBERATION ORGANIZATION (PLO). A political organization among Arab Palestinians that evolved from a revolutionary movement to a quasi-state structure. Palestinians formed the PLO in 1964 under the leadership of Ahmad Shuqeiri and with the support of the **Arab League**. Initially, the PLO called for the destruction of **Israel** and the establishment of a State of **Palestine**, and it formed various militias, ranging from Fatah to the Popular Front for the Liberation of Palestine, to reach that objective through violence. **Yasser Arafat**, the head of Fatah, became chairman of the PLO's Executive Committee in 1969 and remained in control of the organization until his death in 2004.

The PLO militarily fought Israel from the 1960s to the 1980s. It inflicted terrorist attacks on Israeli (and occasionally non-Israeli) targets around the world, and it suffered Israeli preemptive and retaliatory strikes. The PLO was based in the West Bank until Israel occupied that territory in 1967; then in **Jordan**, until **King Hussein** expelled it in 1970; then in **Lebanon**, until Israel occupied that country in 1982; and then in Tunis, until it returned to the West Bank under a new agreement with Israel in 1994. While it fought Israel, the PLO gained increasing international recognition. In 1974, the Arab League and the **United Nations** General Assembly recognized the PLO as the sole representative of the Palestinian people, and in 1976, the UN Security Council permitted the PLO to participate in a debate.

The United States initially viewed the PLO with disdain because of its use of **terrorism** and its meddling in the politics of Jordan and Lebanon. To induce Israel to sign a limited deal with **Egypt** in 1975, the **Gerald R. Ford** administration pledged that it would not negotiate with or recognize the PLO without first consulting Israel. In a quest to promote a general Arab–Israeli peace agreement, President **Jimmy Carter** declared that he would consult the PLO about establishing a Palestinian state if the PLO recognized Israel's right to exist. In July 1979, however, Carter's ambassador to the United Nations, **Andrew Young**, was forced to resign under public criticism after he met informally with Zehdi Labib, the PLO's observer at the United Nations. President **Ronald Reagan** reverted to the firm policy of refusing to deal with the PLO unless it recognized Israel's right to exist. Angered by **Israel's invasion of Lebanon** in 1982, however, Reagan brokered a deal in which U.S. and French troops arrived in Beirut in August 1982 to supervise the relocation of some 11,000 PLO fighters to various distant Arab countries.

American relations with the PLO improved after the organization moderated in the late 1980s. In November 1988, the Palestinian National Council of the PLO declared the independence of Palestine, and the next month, under diplomatic pressure by the United States, the PLO publicly renounced terrorism and recognized Israel's right to exist. In 1989, President **George H. W. Bush** authorized discussions with PLO leaders in Tunis, but he suspended the talks after PLO leaders refused to denounce a terrorist attack on Israeli beaches in May 1990. The PLO's backing of **Iraq** during the **Persian Gulf War** of 1990–1991 also strained U.S.–PLO relations.

American relations with the PLO improved during the 1990s. After the PLO negotiated the **Oslo Accord** in the summer of 1993, President **William J. Clinton** welcomed Arafat to meet Israeli prime minister **Yitzhak Rabin** at the White House. The Oslo Accord and subsequent agreements provided for the establishment of the **Palestinian National Authority (PNA)** to practice self-government in portions of the West Bank and Gaza. Arafat took control of the PNA and established its headquarters in Ramallah. In January 1996, Palestinians democratically elected an 88-member council and elected Arafat as president of the PNA. Three months later, the PLO officially amended its charter to remove language calling for the destruction of Israel. The Clinton and **George W. Bush** administrations worked closely with PLO leaders in the peacemaking diplomacy of the 1990s and early 2000s.

The renewal of Israeli–Palestinian violence in the early 2000s complicated the U.S.–PLO relationship. American officials remained suspicious that Arafat covertly endorsed the violence inflicted on Israel during the Palestinian uprising or **intifada**. They also found troubling Arafat's reluctance to accept the **Roadmap peace plan** and his refusal to cede real political power to **Mahmoud Abbas** or **Ahmed Qureai**, who served as prime ministers of the PNA in 2003–2004. After Arafat's death in November 2004, Palestinians elected Abbas as president of the PNA, raising hopes of an improvement in U.S.–Palestinian relations. The electoral victory of the **Islamic Resistance Movement (Hamas)** in the Palestinian elections of January 2006, however, called into question the future stability of U.S.–PNA relations.

PALESTINIAN NATIONAL AUTHORITY (PNA). A semigovernmental authority created by the Israeli–Palestinian peace process in the 1990s. It was also known as the Palestinian Authority. The **Oslo Accord** of 1993 provided for the establishment of a "Palestinian Interim Self-Governing Authority" to exercise control of territories from which Israeli occupation forces would withdraw. To fulfill this role, leaders of the **Palestine Liberation Organization (PLO)** created the Palestinian National Authority—with executive and legislative branches—in October 1993 and designated PLO chairman **Yasser Arafat** as president of the PNA. In 1994, Arafat returned to the West Bank, appointed a cabinet, and assumed responsibility for administering social services, finance, justice, education, health care, culture, communications, and local security in the territory from which Israeli forces withdrew. (Israel remained responsible for foreign affairs, external security, and the safety of Israeli citizens and settlers.) In democratic elections held on 20 January 1996, Palestinian voters affirmed Arafat as president and elected the 88-member Palestinian Legislative Council. Because the Israeli–Palestinian peace process deadlocked in the late 1990s, the vision of the PNA becoming a national government of a state of **Palestine** remained unfulfilled in the early 2000s.

American officials welcomed the PNA in the 1990s as an instrument vital to the success of the peace process. After the start of the second **intifada**, however, President **George W. Bush** distanced the United States from Arafat on the grounds that he abetted **terrorism** against Israel. The election of **Mahmoud Abbas** as president after the death of Arafat in 2004 stabilized U.S. relations with the PNA. In early 2006, however, the election of an **Islamic Resistance Movement (Hamas)** majority in the Palestinian Legislative Council threatened to unravel U.S. relations with the PNA.

PALESTINIAN REFUGEES. Arab Palestinians (and their descendants) displaced from **Israel** and Israeli-occupied territory. Some

800,000 Palestinians departed from the territory that became Israel during the **Arab-Israeli War of 1948–1949**. An additional 500,000 or so Palestinians became refugees from territories occupied by Israel in the **Arab-Israeli War of 1967**. Given natural population growth, the total population of Palestinian refugees surpassed 4 million by the early 2000s. Although Palestinian refugees became dispersed over time throughout the world, about one-third remained confined to squalid refugee camps, administered by the **United Nations**, in nearby Arab states.

The refugees immediately became the basis for major disagreements among government officials, activists, scholars, and others. Deep debate ensued over whether those persons who left Israel in 1948 took flight under duress imposed by Israeli forces or departed of their own volition. Israeli officials consistently and categorically refused to repatriate substantial numbers of Palestinian refugees, claiming that such immigrants would endanger the security of their state and undermine its Jewish identity and insisting that Arab states absorb the refugee population. Arab states, by contrast, refused to integrate the refugees, charging that Israel bore legal and moral responsibility for their suffering and that Israel therefore must recognize their right of return. The refugees themselves repeatedly demanded Israeli recognition of their right to return to their previous homes, and many retained deeds to land and keys to houses as tangible symbols of their claims. The refugees' situation contributed to the general Arab–Israeli hostility of the 1940s–1980s, especially after refugees organized by the **Palestine Liberation Organization (PLO)** and other groups began organizing violence against Israel in the 1960s. The question of the rights of the refugees was one of the major stumbling blocks that stymied the peace process of the 1990s and triggered the second **intifada** of the early 2000s.

The United States straddled the refugees issue for decades. Concerned that impoverished refugees would embrace communism, U.S. officials of the early Cold War period established the enduring U.S. practice of generously funding **United Nations**–based relief operations, such as the **United Nations Relief and Works Agency (UNRWA)**, which provided basic subsistence to the refugees. The UN General Assembly resolved in 1948 that Palestinian refugees should be permitted to choose between returning to their homes and living in peace with their neighbors or receiving financial compensation for their property losses. Throughout the Cold War, however, U.S. officials refrained from compelling Israel to repatriate significant numbers of refugees, given Israeli firmness on the issue. They also refrained from pressuring the Arab states to absorb the refugees to avoid alienating those powers. The growing willingness of U.S. officials to accept the legitimacy of a state of **Palestine** as a haven for Palestinian people reflected in part a desire to bring the refugee issue to resolution.

PARTITION OF PALESTINE. A proposal to divide the British mandate of Palestine into an Arab state and a Jewish state. British officials contemplated partition schemes prior to World War II but did not implement any of them. After Great Britain indicated that it would abandon the mandate by 1948, the **United Nations Special Committee on Palestine (UNSCOP)**, after extensive study, proposed partition in 1947. The UNSCOP plan also proposed economic interaction between the two states and an international regime to govern Jerusalem. In November 1947, the **United Nations** General Assembly approved UNSCOP's partition plan by a vote of 33 to 13, with 10 abstentions. President **Harry S. Truman** supported the UN resolution, and in subsequent months he deflected State Department pressure to rescind partition in favor of a UN trusteeship scheme.

Partition was never formally implemented. Neither the United Nations nor any state would enforce the plan in the face of Arab–Jewish violence that escalated in **Palestine** in early 1948. **Israel** declared its independence and, in the process of defeating attacks on it, occupied territory in excess of the land allotted to it by partition. Arab Palestinians refrained from declaring statehood, and **Egypt** and **Jordan** occupied the remnants of Palestine designated to the Arab Palestinians. No international regime was ever created to govern Jerusalem.

PERES, SHIMON (1923–). Longtime Labor Party politician and government official of **Israel** who interacted with the United States on numerous occasions. Born in Poland, Peres migrated to **Palestine** in 1934. He served in Israel's military during the **Arab-Israeli War of 1948–1949**, and in 1949–1952, he headed a mission to purchase arms in the United States. As director general of the Ministry of Defense (1952–1959), Peres promoted a close relationship with France, leading to both the outbreak of war during the **Suez Crisis** of 1956 and the genesis of Israel's nuclear weapons program. The **Dwight D. Eisenhower** administration expressed displeasure at Israeli policy in both areas.

Peres thereafter held a variety of government posts, including two stints as prime minister. As minister of defense in 1974–1977, he cooperated with U.S. initiatives leading to the **Disengagement Accords** that followed the **Arab-Israeli War of 1973**. As prime minister in 1984–1986, during the so-called National Unity government in which the Labor and Likud parties rotated leadership, Peres oversaw the withdrawal of Israeli forces in **Lebanon** to a narrow security zone in the south of the country, a move that placated the United States.

Peres endeared himself to the United States while serving as foreign minister in 1992–1995 under Prime Minister **Yitzhak Rabin**. Peres initiated the negotiations with the Palestinians that led to the **Oslo Accord** and other agreements, and he promoted Israel's peace treaty with **Jordan** in 1994. On the assassination of Rabin in November 1995, Peres became prime minister and tried to advance the peace process. But in an election in May 1996, after a series of Palestinian terrorist attacks on Israeli civilians, Israeli voters elected **Benjamin Netanyahu** as prime minister.

PERSIAN GULF WAR. An international conflict in 1990–1991 between **Iraq** and an international coalition led by the United States. The war started in August 1990 when Iraq, under the leadership of **Saddam Hussein**, conquered **Kuwait**. Although Kuwait had backed Iraq during the **Iran–Iraq War** of 1980–1988, Hussein nursed a grudge about the wealth Kuwait had accumulated while Iraq had spent its own treasures on the battlefields, and he accused Kuwait of stealing Iraqi oil from well fields near the border and deflating oil prices to the detriment of Iraqi interests. On 2 August, Iraqi armed forces invaded Kuwait and easily overpowered its tiny army.

President **George H. W. Bush** interpreted Hussein's behavior as a danger to international order in the post–Cold War era and thus resolved to contest it. He first acted to ensure the security of **Saudi Arabia**, which in early August seemed vulnerable to conquest by Iraq. Bush implemented Operation Desert Shield, in which some

100,000 U.S. troops were dispatched to Saudi Arabia by the end of August. The immediate threat to the Saudi kingdom subsided when Hussein relocated several elite units from the frontier to reserve positions in southern Iraq.

Having secured Saudi Arabia, Bush also took steps to reverse Iraq's conquest of Kuwait. He demanded an immediate and unconditional Iraqi withdrawal, imposed sanctions, and secured **United Nations** Security Council Resolution 660, which condemned the Iraqi aggression and demanded withdrawal. When such diplomacy failed to have the desired effect, Bush also began to prepare for military action to liberate Kuwait. In November, he relocated 200,000 U.S. soldiers from Germany to Saudi Arabia and secured UN Security Council Resolution 678, which ordered Iraq to withdraw from Kuwait by 15 January 1991 and authorized member states, if Iraq remained defiant, to use "all necessary means" to achieve that outcome. Bush convinced leaders of 28 other countries to contribute troops to such an operation against Iraq, and yet other powers to bankroll it. In January 1991, Congress authorized Bush to use force to liberate Kuwait.

Bush ordered the start of offensive military action against Iraq—under Operation Desert Storm—on 17 January 1991. American and allied aircraft conducted a massive aerial blitz against command, control, and communications facilities in Iraq and Iraqi-occupied Kuwait and against Iraqi ground troops in Kuwait. Iraq's countermeasures of occupying the Saudi border town of Khafji and launching Scud missiles against Saudi Arabia, **Bahrain**, **Qatar**, and **Israel** proved ineffective at stemming the Allied attacks.

Because Hussein continued to defy the admonitions of the United Nations, Bush decided in February 1991 to launch a ground offensive to liberate Kuwait. On 22 February, he issued an ultimatum that Iraq must leave Kuwait within 24 hours. When Hussein refused to comply, the U.S.-led coalition, directed by **Colin Powell**, launched a major ground offensive, led by General **H. Norman Schwarzkopf Jr.**, on 24 February against Iraqi troops in Kuwait. The Iraqi army collapsed quickly in death, retreat, and surrender; the Allied powers destroyed the bulk of Iraqi armor and artillery; and Kuwait was liberated in a combat phase that lasted exactly 100 hours.

The rapid success in Kuwait naturally raised the prospect of pressing on with the war, occupying Baghdad, and deposing Hussein.

Some observers suggested that danger loomed as long as Hussein remained in power, given his aggressiveness, armed forces, and weapons of mass destruction. But Bush decided that such an offensive against Iraq would exceed the authority granted by the United Nations, shatter the coalition, destabilize the Persian Gulf region, and incur massive casualties. Thus, he opted for a strategy of encouraging Iraqi army officers to overthrow Hussein, a strategy that backfired when Iraqi **Kurds** and Shiites rebelled and the Hussein regime mercilessly crushed their uprisings. Bush thus settled into a long-term plan, continued by the **William J. Clinton** administration, of containing Iraq through political, military, and financial restrictions.

POINDEXTER, JOHN M. (1936–). Navy rear admiral involved in controversial U.S policies in the Middle East in the 1980s and early 2000s. As national security advisor to **Ronald Reagan**, Poindexter personally approved **Oliver North**'s proposal that the proceeds from arms sales to **Iran** would be diverted to the Contra rebels in Nicaragua, an action that became the central issue in the **Iran-Contra scandal**. Poindexter later testified that he consciously decided not to tell Reagan of the action in order to shield the president from legal and political trouble if the operation became publicly known. A jury convicted Poindexter of five felony counts for his role in the scandal, although an appeals court later overturned the convictions on grounds that they were based on testimony given to Congress in exchange for legal immunity.

In 2002, Poindexter returned to federal service as head of the Pentagon's Defense Advanced Research Projects Agency. He promoted a complicated initiative, known as the Policy Analyst Market, designed to predict important political events and terrorist attacks in the Middle East by operating a for-profit, online, public trading program. After Democrats in Congress criticized the initiative, the Pentagon canceled it. Poindexter departed his office in August 2003.

POWELL, COLIN (1937–). A son of immigrants who became a four-star U.S. Army general and served as Chairman of the Joint Chiefs of Staff (JCS) in 1989–1993 and as secretary of state in 2001–2005 (thus becoming the highest-ranking African American in the history of the U.S. government). As chairman of the JCS, the top military position in the U.S. government, Powell proved highly competent in mobilizing the armed services during the **Persian Gulf War** of 1990–1991, and he became quite popular for explaining the U.S. cause to the American people.

As secretary of state under President **George W. Bush**, Powell earned a reputation as a moderate who questioned the wisdom and rationale for preemptive war against **Iraq**. Yet in November 2002, he convinced the **United Nations** Security Council unanimously to pass Resolution 1441, which eventually formed a legal cornerstone of the Bush administration's invasion of Iraq. In a February 2003 address to the United Nations, moreover, Powell echoed Bush's observations that **Saddam Hussein** had come to possess weapons of mass destruction in violation of UN resolutions. That speech helped solidify public backing for the **U.S. invasion of Iraq** in March 2003. During the **Iraq War**, Powell apparently lost influence within the Bush administration to more hawkish officials such as Vice President **Richard Cheney** and Secretary of Defense **Donald Rumsfeld**. Powell resigned his post in November 2004, just after Bush's reelection.

– Q –

AL-QADDAFI, MUAMMAR (1942–). Dictator of **Libya** since 1969. Born in 1942, Qaddafi seized power in a coup against **King Idris** in 1969. Qaddafi entertained illusions of grandeur, seeking to achieve a position of greatness in Africa and the Arab world by separating his country from the West and the East and by building a revolutionary system of people's democracy within the state. In the 1980s, his bold foreign policy—most notably his sponsorship of **terrorism** against the West and **Israel**—resulted in military conflict with the United States. In the 1990s, Qaddafi renounced terrorism and began to reintegrate his country in the Western world. Although secular, Qaddafi occasionally exploited religion to bolster his political power.

QASSIM, ABDUL KARIM (1914–1963). Army general who overthrew the government of **Iraq** in July 1958. Qassim led a bloody coup against pro-Western **King Faisal II** and Prime Minister **Nuri al-Said**. Qassim withdrew Iraq from the U.S.-backed **Baghdad Pact**

in March 1959, and he thereafter leaned toward the Soviet Union for political support. Qassim proved unable to consolidate power and was overthrown by a Baath Party coup in 1963.

QATAR. Small, oil-rich Persian Gulf country with which the United States developed a close relationship in the 1990s. Formerly a British protectorate, Qatar declared its independence in 1971 on Great Britain's strategic withdrawal from the Persian Gulf region. Qatar financed **Iraq** during the **Iran–Iraq War** of 1980–1988, and it endorsed the struggle of the **Palestine Liberation Organization (PLO)** to establish a state of **Palestine** at the expense of **Israel**. The United States opened an embassy in Doha in 1973, but relations remained distant. The United States and Qatar quarreled in 1988–1990 over the latter's unauthorized acquisition of U.S.-made Stinger antiaircraft missiles; Qatar appeased the United States by destroying the weapons in 1990.

The **Persian Gulf War** of 1990–1991 triggered a significant improvement in U.S.–Qatari relations. Qatar condemned the Iraqi invasion of **Kuwait** and criticized the PLO for backing **Iraq**. In June 1992, the United States and Qatar signed a Defense Cooperation Agreement that provided U.S. access rights at military bases in Qatar, enabled the United States to store military hardware on Qatari soil, and enabled combined military drills. By the late 1990s, U.S. tanks were prepositioned in Qatar, and U.S. aircraft carriers called regularly at Qatari ports. While Qatar disagreed with U.S. policy toward Iraq and **Iran** in the early 2000s, the security partnership remained intact.

Qatar derives most of its wealth from the export of petroleum products. The British developed the country's oil industry in the 1930s–1950s. Qatar joined the **Organization of Petroleum Exporting Countries (OPEC)** in 1961, and it nationalized its oil industry in the 1970s. Although several American firms participate in the industry, virtually no Qatari oil was imported to the United States in the early 2000s.

QUREIA, AHMED (1937–). Moderate, charismatic Palestinian statesman who served as the second prime minister of the **Palestine Liberation Organization (PLO)**. Born in Jerusalem, Qureia, also known as Abu Ala, joined the PLO in 1965 and eventually emerged as its top financial officer. By the 1990s, he had a reputation as a moderate, and he participated actively in the 1993 Oslo talks and in subsequent negotiations with Israeli leaders. **Yasser Arafat** named Qureia as prime minister following the resignation of **Mahmoud Abbas** in September 2003, but Qureia soon developed the same quarrels with Arafat that had troubled Abbas. When Arafat died in late 2004, Qureia called on the United States to implement its **Roadmap peace plan**.

QUTB, SAYYID (1906–1966). An Egyptian educator and philosopher whose writings inspired the emergence of Islamic fundamentalism in the late 20th century. While working for the Egyptian Ministry of Education, Qutb was selected in 1948 for an exchange program in the United States designed to foster international goodwill. During two years of residence in Colorado, however, he came to consider U.S. culture as sexually depraved, greedy, and racist; to view U.S. history as a stream of violence and conquest; and to condemn U.S. support of **Israel** as unjust.

On his return to **Egypt**, Qutb joined the Muslim Brotherhood, a fundamentalist group that challenged the power of **King Farouk** and, eventually, Premier **Gamal Abdel Nasser**. After the Muslim Brotherhood attempted to assassinate Nasser in 1954, Qutb was jailed for nearly a decade, and the Brotherhood was suppressed. After a second assassination attempt on Nasser in 1965, Qutb was imprisoned again and hanged in 1966.

Through his publications, many of which were composed in prison, Qutb became a popular voice across the Muslim world during and after his life. In such works as *In the Shadow of the Quran* (30 vols., 1952–1966) and *Milestones* (1964), he condemned modernism and the secularism of regimes such as Nasser's as threats to the existence of Islam. He called on the faithful to wage jihad (holy war), even at risk of their own lives, to replace such secular regimes with a system consistent with fundamentalist Islamic law and ideals. Qutb's writings were translated into all the languages of Muslim states, and reputedly they inspired **Osama bin Laden** and other terrorists to take up arms against Middle East governments and the United States in the 1990s and early 2000s.

AL-QUWATLY, SHUKRY (1892–1967). First president of independent **Syria** who criticized U.S. diplomacy in the Middle East. A nationalist who long labored to free his native country from French control, Quwatly emerged as president of the new republic in 1946 and censured U.S. support of Zionist aspirations in **Palestine** as illegitimate and immoral. He fell from power in 1949 during political unrest triggered by Syria's poor performance in the **Arab-Israeli War of 1948–1949**. After a brief exile, he was reelected president in 1955, and he criticized U.S. backing of the **Baghdad Pact** military alliance. Quwatly's signature on the agreement merging Syria and **Egypt** in the United Arab Republic in 1958 marked the end of his political career.

– R –

RABIN, YITZHAK (1922–1995). Israeli soldier and statesman who emerged as a leading proponent of the peace process of the 1990s. Born in Jerusalem, Rabin joined the Haganah, a prestate Jewish defense force, in 1940 and commanded a brigade in the fight for Jerusalem during the **Arab-Israeli War of 1948–1949**. Over the following two decades, he rose in rank to chief of staff of the Israeli Defense Forces (1964–1968), thereby commanding Israeli soldiers in the **Arab-Israeli War of 1967**. After his retirement from military service in 1968, Rabin served for five years as ambassador to Washington, in which post he nurtured close relations with the United States and secured American military supplies to Israel.

In 1973, Rabin joined the Labor Party of **Israel** and became politically active. He won election to the Knesset in 1973 and served as prime minister in 1974–1977, during which time he cooperated with U.S. initiatives to negotiate the **Disengagement Accords** that followed the **Arab-Israeli War of 1973**. As minister of defense in 1984–1990, Rabin faced the challenge of the first Palestinian **intifada**. He ordered tough measures to suppress the uprising but also came to believe that peace negotiations with the Palestinians were essential.

Elected prime minister of Israel in 1992, Rabin gave priority to the Arab–Israeli peace process. He immediately released Palestinian prisoners, slowed construction of Israeli settlements in the occupied territories, and made other goodwill gestures. More important, he authorized secret negotiations with Palestinian officials in Oslo in early and mid-1993 that resulted in the initialing of a declaration of principles (later known as the **Oslo Accord**) that provided a blueprint for Israeli–Palestinian harmony. At the invitation of President **William J. Clinton**, Rabin joined **Palestine Liberation Organization (PLO)** leader **Yasser Arafat** at the White House to sign the Oslo Accord and to shake hands in a historic gesture of peace. A follow-up agreement of October 1995, alternatively known as the Taba accord or Oslo II, provided for the withdrawal of Israeli troops from nine major Palestinian towns.

Also acting with Clinton's encouragement, Rabin and **King Hussein** of **Jordan** signed the Israeli–Jordanian peace treaty in October 1994. During a diplomatic initiative promoted by the Clinton administration, Rabin also proposed in 1993 that Israel would evacuate the Golan Heights over a five-year period if **Syria** would make peace and normalize relations. But Syria refused the offer.

Rabin's willingness to make peace endeared him to the United States and to a substantial number of Israelis who were tired of perpetual conflict. But it also angered Israeli conservatives who mistrusted the Palestinians or believed that the West Bank must be retained on religious grounds. On 4 November 1995, Yigal Amir, an Israeli extremist claiming to be acting on God's orders to preserve Israeli control of holy lands, assassinated Rabin as he departed a massive peace rally in Tel Aviv.

RAFSANJANI, AKBAR HASHEMI (1934–). Iranian cleric and political leader who shaped U.S. relations with **Iran** in the aftermath of the Iranian revolution. Rafsanjani studied Islam under the Ayatollah **Ruhollah Khomeini** and conspired with Khomeini to overthrow Shah **Mohammed Reza Pahlavi** in 1979. As speaker of the National Assembly (Majlis) in 1980–1989, Rafsanjani was a central player in negotiating arms-for-hostages deals with the **Ronald Reagan** administration, reportedly receiving from **Oliver North** a leather-bound Bible bearing Reagan's signature. He apparently advised Khomeini to decline opportunities to end the **Iran–Iraq War** in the early 1980s but also convinced Khomeini to accept the cease-fire that took effect in 1988. As president of Iran in 1989–1997 (elected in 1989 and reelected in 1993), Rafsanjani promoted development of Iran's nuclear capabilities and burnished his reputation as a tough promoter of Iran's interests overseas.

In the Iranian presidential election of 2005, by contrast, Rafsanjani campaigned as a reformer who would liberalize Iran and seek improved relations with the United States in the tradition of outgoing president **Mohammed Khatami**. Amidst allegations that the clerical establishment corrupted the elections, however, Rafsanjani lost the election to conservative candidate **Mahmoud Ahmadinejad**.

RAMADAN WAR. See ARAB-ISRAELI WAR OF 1973.

REAGAN DOCTRINE. A U.S. policy toward the Third World developed by President **Ronald Reagan** in the 1980s. The doctrine promoted not merely the containment but also the reversal of Soviet power and influence by openly supporting states and movements willing to resist the Soviet Union by political and military means. President Reagan approved the doctrine in a classified National Security Decision Directive in 1983, and he articulated it publicly in his State of the Union Address in 1985. American covert support of the anti-Soviet resistance forces in Afghanistan represented one manifestation of the Reagan Doctrine in practice.

REAGAN, RONALD (1911–2004). Popular, two-term U.S. president who formulated major policies in the Middle East on the basis of two fundamental pronouncements. Under the **Reagan Doctrine**, the president committed the United States to support anti-Soviet forces and promote freedom and democracy around the world. Under the **Strategic Consensus** initiative, he declared an aim to build a pro-American, anti-Soviet bastion in the Middle East by arming and aiding such friendly states as **Egypt**, **Israel**, **Saudi Arabia**, Turkey, and Pakistan.

Reagan successfully applied these two doctrines in Afghanistan, which the Soviet Union had invaded and occupied in 1979. The Reagan administration covertly organized and armed Afghan partisans (as well as mercenaries recruited from around the Muslim world) via secret supply lines through Pakistan; in 1979–1989, U.S. aid topped

$3 billion. Several dozen U.S. soldiers infiltrated Afghanistan, where they trained partisans in resistance tactics. Despite sending more than 100,000 soldiers to Afghanistan and sustaining some 40,000 casualties, the Soviets could not secure control of the country and withdrew from it in 1988.

Reagan's Strategic Consensus policy experienced setbacks, however, in several other situations. It was immediately challenged by the fallout over Israel's June 1981 preemptive aerial attack on a nuclear reactor at Osirak, near Baghdad, **Iraq**. Israel justified the raid on the grounds that the Iraqis would soon devote the reactor to building weapons. But the attack incensed Saudi Arabia, which withdrew its support of efforts by Reagan envoy **Philip Habib** to broker a truce in the battle over **Lebanon**.

In addition, **Israel's invasion of Lebanon** in 1982 not only further angered Arab states but also gravely destabilized Lebanon. Reagan dispatched some 1,200 marines to Beirut as a stabilizing force, but they quickly became the target of attacks, most infamously an October 1983 suicide truck bombing that killed 241 marines. Reagan soon ended the American military presence in Lebanon without achieving stability.

The Reagan administration also faced a delicate situation in **Libya**, whose dictator **Muammar Qaddafi** brazenly endorsed anti-Western **terrorism**. In 1981, Reagan expelled Libyan officials from the United States, embargoed the importation of Libyan oil, and sent the U.S. Sixth Fleet into the disputed Gulf of Sidra off Libya's coast, where U.S. Navy jets downed two Libyan fighters. A prolonged confrontation followed in which Libya reportedly organized several terrorist attacks on American targets, and the United States used military force, sinking several Libyan patrol boats in the Gulf of Sidra in March 1986 and bombing Tripoli and other military sites in April. Qaddafi's government retaliated by exploding a bomb on a Pan Am Airlines jetliner in 1988, killing 270 people.

Reagan enjoyed mixed success in the **Iran–Iraq War** of 1980–1988. By supplying economic aid, military hardware and ships to escort oil tankers, the United States enabled Iraq to resist Iranian military counteroffensives that might have spread Iranian influence across the Persian Gulf region. In 1987–1988, after sending U.S. naval force into the gulf and engaging **Iran** in limited war, Reagan helped broker a compromise cease-fire. Yet Reagan also became ensnared in the **Iran-Contra scandal** when his subordinates surreptitiously sold weapons to Iran and diverted the profits to the Contra rebels in Nicaragua.

Reluctant to risk his anti-Soviet partnership with Israel, Reagan initially took no initiative to solve the **Arab–Israeli conflict**, and he showed little interest in peace plans developed by others. Only the eruption of the **intifada** in December 1987 sparked belated action by the United States. In March 1988, Secretary of State **George P. Shultz** proposed essentially an acceleration of the Camp David peace process and a reaffirmation of the land-for-peace formula of **United Nations** Resolutions 242 and 338. Shultz secured a breakthrough in December 1988—only a month before Reagan left office—when **Palestine Liberation Organization (PLO)** chairman **Yasser Arafat** formally accepted UN Resolutions 242 and 338, renounced terrorism, and pledged to live in peace with Israel, and the Reagan administration reciprocated by agreeing to negotiate with the PLO. That breakthrough set the stage for the peace process of the 1990s.

RED LINE AGREEMENT. A pact among major petroleum firms that established a virtual oil production cartel in the territory of the former Ottoman Empire. Signed in 1928, the Red Line Agreement granted American oil companies a substantial share of ownership of the **Iraq Petroleum Company (IPC)**, and it pledged all IPC partners to share equally rather than compete in future oil exploration and development. The agreement was named for the demarcation of former Ottoman territories, drawn in red pencil on a map of the Middle East during negotiations among oil executives. American firms had initially been excluded from oilfields of **Iraq**, and the State Department had pressed the British in the early 1920s to allow free competition under the American "open-door" policy. When U.S. firms gained a profitable stake in the IPC under the Red Line Agreement, however, the U.S. government eased its pursuit of the open-door policy.

RICE, CONDOLEEZZA (1954–). Top official in the **George W. Bush** administration and an advocate of the president's assertive diplomacy in the Middle East. Born in Birmingham, Alabama, Rice became a professor of political science at Stanford University in 1981 and served as provost there in 1993–1999. President Bush named her assistant to the president for national security affairs in 2001 and secretary of state in 2005. An academic specialist in Russian-Soviet military affairs, Rice had little firsthand experience in Middle East policy at the time of her appointment.

Once in office, Rice strongly advocated the **U.S. invasion of Afghanistan** in 2001 and U.S. operations in the **Iraq War**. At Bush's direction, Rice also assumed direct responsibility for monitoring progress under the **Roadmap peace plan** for promoting Israeli–Palestinian peace. Rice also defended the Bush administration against the criticism that it should have anticipated and thwarted the **9/11** attacks.

RICHARDS, JAMES P. (1894–1979). A member of the U.S. House of Representatives (D-S.C.) in 1933–1957 who served as special assistant to the president for the Middle East in 1957–1958. In the latter capacity, Ambassador Richards toured the Middle East in early 1957 to promote the **Eisenhower Doctrine** among local states. He visited and dispensed tens of millions of dollars in economic and military aid to Turkey, **Iran**, Pakistan, **Iraq**, **Saudi Arabia**, **Lebanon**, and **Libya** in exchange for their acceptances of the Eisenhower Doctrine. He also allocated funds to **Jordan** even though **King Hussein** declined to invite him to Amman, citing revolutionary fervor in his country. Richards avoided **Egypt** and **Syria** because of the anti-U.S. nationalism mounting in each country. He visited **Israel** only under pressure from Congress but failed to reach an aid agreement with that state. *See also* FOREIGN AID.

ROADMAP PEACE PLAN. An Israeli–Palestinian peace plan promoted by the United States and other powers in the early 2000s. The United States, Russia, the European Union, and the **United Nations** (known as "the Quartet") developed the three-step Roadmap in 2001–2002. The plan envisioned in phase 1 (through May 2003) an end to Israeli–Palestinian violence, the building of Palestinian institutions, and a freeze on construction of Israeli housing settlements on the contested terrain of the occupied West Bank and Gaza. During phase 2 (May–December 2003), the Quartet would sponsor a conference to establish a state of **Palestine**, adopt a Palestinian constitution, and discuss such contentious issues as the rights of **Palestinian refugees** and the control of water resources. During phase 3 (2004–2005), the Quartet would host a second conference to negotiate a final settlement between **Israel** and Palestine as well as Israeli peace treaties with **Lebanon** and **Syria**.

President **George W. Bush** vigorously promoted the Roadmap during a visit to the Middle East in June 2003. The plan faced major obstacles, however, including a persistence of Israeli settlement building, Palestinian violence against Israelis and Israeli retributive strikes on Palestinian targets, and unwillingness on both sides to make concessions on the political issues. While widely discussed as a point of reference, the Roadmap remained unfulfilled for several years after its conception.

ROGERS PLAN. A proposal for Arab–Israeli peace promoted by Secretary of State **William P. Rogers** in 1969–1970. Concerned by the sharp escalation in the **War of Attrition** in early 1969, Rogers, on 9 December, proposed an Arab–Israeli peace agreement on the basis of **United Nations** Security Council Resolution 242 (1967) plus a settlement of the **Palestinian refugees** issue. National Security Advisor **Henry Kissinger** quietly discouraged **Israel** from cooperating with Rogers, however, and Israeli leaders rejected the scheme as damaging to their interests and instead escalated the War of Attrition with strategic bombing.

In 1970, Rogers floated a modified plan, sometimes called Rogers Plan B, calling for a cease-fire; affirmation of UN Resolution 242 by **Israel**, **Jordan**, and **Egypt**; and peace negotiations led by UN mediator Gunnar Jarring. Egypt and Jordan immediately accepted these terms. Israel followed suit after President **Richard M. Nixon** assured Prime Minister **Golda Meir** that Israel would be forced neither to absorb Palestinian refugees nor to relinquish territory in the absence of a final peace treaty. The Rogers Plan thereby achieved an end of the War of Attrition, but it did little to settle the **Arab–Israeli conflict** at a fundamental level.

ROGERS, WILLIAM P. (1913–2001). Secretary of state in 1969–1973 whose efforts to promote Arab–Israeli accord were only partially successful. In 1969, Rogers sought to start a Middle East peace process based on **United Nations** Resolution 242 of 1967, but his efforts to promote the so-called **Rogers Plan** were undermined by National Security Advisor **Henry Kissinger**, who convinced President **Richard M. Nixon** to refrain from compelling **Israel** to make peace on compromise terms. In 1970, Rogers enjoyed greater success in arranging an end to the Egyptian–Israeli **War of Attrition**. But his efforts to start peace talks during a visit to the region in 1971 came to naught.

ROOSEVELT, FRANKLIN D. (1882–1945). President in 1933–1945 who laid the cornerstones of certain U.S. policies in the Middle East. Roosevelt virtually neglected the Middle East until the dynamics of World War II compelled U.S. officials to take an interest in the region. The threat of Axis conquest of the region, made real by the German–Italian occupation of North Africa and the invasion of British-occupied **Egypt**, raised fears of a German–Japanese linkup in South Asia that would consolidate Germany's control of the Eastern Hemisphere.

Given the severity of this threat, Roosevelt deferred to Great Britain to shore up Western security interests across the Middle East by assertive means. He approved Britain's overthrow of the pro-German Iraqi nationalist Rashid Ali al-Gaylani, who had seized power in Baghdad in April 1941. Roosevelt also endorsed a move in July 1941 by British and Free French forces to liberate **Syria** and **Lebanon** from the Vichy regime that had endorsed Rashid Ali's regime in **Iraq**, and he supported a joint Anglo–Soviet occupation of **Iran** undertaken in August 1941 to purge the country of Nazi influence and to establish a supply line to the Soviet Union. Furthermore, the U.S. president approved a British display of military force in Cairo in February 1942 that compelled **King Farouk** to appoint a prime minister favorable to Britain rather than one sympathetic to Germany. Roosevelt also refused domestic political pressure to contest Britain's anti-Zionist policy in **Palestine** on the grounds that the United States must not risk undermining British prestige or security in the Middle East during the war.

Roosevelt also directly supported Britain's military defense of Egypt against Axis forces. The United States supplied the British army with tanks that proved crucial to its victory over the German army in the Battle of El Alamein, in western Egypt, in October 1942. The Pentagon thereafter constructed air bases that Britain needed to support its position in Egypt for the duration of the war.

After the British defeated the Germans at El Alamein, Roosevelt contested certain aspects of European colonialism in the Middle East. He declared that he would pursue an open-door policy of equal economic opportunity in the Middle East rather than tolerate British commercial dominance. He also pressured the Free French to relinquish their mandate in Syria and Lebanon, thus helping both states achieve their independence from French colonialism in 1944–1946.

Roosevelt took a special interest in **Saudi Arabia** because the kingdom's oil resources figured significantly in plans for securing the region during the world war and after. In 1943, the president officially declared that the kingdom was a vital security interest, making it eligible for lend-lease assistance, and soon thereafter the Pentagon constructed a military airbase at Dhahran. As Roosevelt returned home from the Yalta Conference in February 1945, he welcomed **King ibn Saud** aboard a U.S. naval vessel for a meeting designed to promote commercial ties and political amity between their two countries. Roosevelt also pledged to ibn Saud that the United States would not change its policy toward Palestine without consulting the leaders of Arab states.

ROSS, DENNIS. Scholar and career diplomat who took major responsibility for the conduct of U.S. diplomacy in the Middle East in 1989–2001. As director of the Policy Planning Staff of the Department of State under President **George H. W. Bush**, Ross helped form the international coalition that the United States led against **Iraq** during the **Persian Gulf War** and advised Secretary of State **James A. Baker** on the Arab–Israeli situation. President **William J. Clinton** appointed Ross as special Middle East coordinator and tasked him to serve as the administration's point man on the actual conduct of U.S. negotiations on Arab–Israeli issues. Working closely with Secretaries of State **Warren R. Christopher** and **Madeleine K. Albright**, Ross engaged in countless rounds of negotiations with **Israel**, **Jordan**, **Syria**, and the Palestinians, and he arranged and participated actively in summit meetings in Washington, D.C.; Wye River and Camp David, Maryland; Shepherdstown, West Virginia; and Geneva, Switzerland. Ross proved instrumental in securing the Israeli-Palestinian Interim Agreement on the West Bank and Gaza of 1995 and the Hebron Accord of 1997 as well as facilitating the Israel–Jordan peace treaty of 1994.

RUMSFELD, DONALD H. (1932–). Government official and four-term congressman from Illinois who served as secretary of defense in 1975–1977 and, after a stint in private business, was again appointed secretary of defense by President **George W. Bush** in 2001. Rumsfeld was known for his hawkish views on American foreign policy, and the events of **9/11** (he was at his desk in the Pentagon when the building was attacked by a hijacked airliner) strengthened his resolve to use force against **terrorism**. At Bush's command, Rumsfeld directed American forces in the **U.S. invasion of Afghanistan** and in the **Iraq War**. In the Iraqi theater, he readily achieved the ouster of **Saddam Hussein**, but critics charged that several of Rumsfeld's decisions about the postinvasion occupation of the country inadvertently abetted instability and anti-American insurgency there. Amid deepening criticism of his handling of the Iraq War, Rumsfeld resigned as secretary of defense in late 2006, after Democrats won control of Congress in midterm elections.

– S –

AL-SADAT, ANWAR (1918–1981). President of **Egypt** in 1970–1981 whose relationship with the United States improved substantially. Sadat belonged to the group of army officers who overthrew **King Farouk** in 1952, and he served in a variety of posts under Premier **Gamal Abdel Nasser** in 1954–1970. Appointed vice president in 1969, Sadat consolidated power as Egyptian premier on the death of Nasser in 1970.

Initially, Sadat's relationship with the United States was frosty. He insisted that the United States pressure **Israel** to withdraw immediately from the Sinai, Egyptian territory that Israel had occupied in the **Arab-Israeli War of 1967**, and he criticized U.S. arms supply to Israel. Sadat hinted that he might use force to liberate the Sinai, but after he expelled 20,000 Soviet advisers from Egypt in 1972, U.S. officials concluded that he lacked the means to do so and that his threats of action were empty.

Yet Sadat surprised the United States and Israel by attacking the Sinai in October 1973, in coordination with a Syrian assault on the Israeli-occupied Golan Heights, thus triggering the **Arab-Israeli War of 1973**. American officials rushed emergency arms supply to Israel to enable it to avoid defeat (and perhaps to deter it from using nuclear weapons), and they delayed imposition of a **United Nations** cease-fire until Israeli forces had counterattacked sufficiently to neutralize the initial Egyptian advance.

Although upset by the American backing of Israel, Sadat cooperated with the postwar **shuttle diplomacy** of Secretary of State **Henry Kissinger**. Sadat signed major **disengagement accords** with Israel in 1974 and 1975, negotiated under Kissinger's direction. He declared Kissinger to be his friend, welcomed President **Richard M. Nixon** on a state visit to Egypt in 1974, lobbied the Arab oil-producing states to rescind the 1973 **Arab oil embargo**, and restored diplomatic relations with the United States in 1974 after a seven-year hiatus.

Sadat also worked closely with President **Jimmy Carter** to achieve a peace treaty with Israel. Sadat visited Israel and launched direct Egyptian–Israeli talks in late 1977, and when those talks bogged down, he joined Israeli prime minister **Menachem Begin** at a summit meeting, hosted by Carter, at which the **Camp David Accords** were negotiated. Sadat and Begin signed a formal peace treaty in March 1979 in Washington at a ceremony over which Carter presided. Carter rewarded Sadat with massive economic and military aid, and Sadat reciprocated by offering the Pentagon military base privileges in Egypt.

Carter and President **Ronald Reagan** viewed Sadat as a counterweight to the Soviet Union, revolutionary **Iran**, and more radical Arab states that vilified Sadat for making peace with Israel. Sadat in turn sought the protection of the United States from his regional rivals. But his peacemaking with Israel and his friendship with the United States isolated him in the Arab community and exposed him to the animosity of extremists. In October 1981, Sadat was assassinated by an Islamic fundamentalist army officer in Cairo.

AL-SAID, NURI (1888–1958). Longtime Iraqi politician killed during the July 1958 revolution in **Iraq**. Trained as an Ottoman military officer, al-Said joined the Arab revolt against Ottoman rule during World War I and thus endeared himself to the Hashemite monarchs who governed Iraq after the war. He served 14 times as prime minister of Iraqi governments in the 1930s–1950s, demonstrating a pro-Western orientation in his foreign policy by signing various Anglo–Iraqi defense treaties and joining the **Baghdad Pact**. His pro-Western disposition contributed to his unpopularity among the Iraqi nationalists. One day after Iraqi army officers overthrew **King Faisal II** in July 1958, al-Said was murdered by a mob in the streets of Baghdad.

SAUD, KING, OF SAUDI ARABIA (1902–1969). Second king of **Saudi Arabia** who advanced the country's friendly relations with the United States. The oldest son of **ibn Saud**, founder of Saudi Arabia, Saud was named successor in 1933. In 1953, he became foreign minister and defense minister, and following his father's death, he was crowned king. But Saud's mismanagement of the crown's assets, his extravagant lifestyle, and his appointments of his sons over his brothers to leading government positions provoked opposition by his brothers, who contested his reign as early as 1958. In 1964, Saud's brothers engineered a coup against him, naming Prince **Faisal** as his successor. Saud died in exile in 1969.

American–Saudi relations experienced turmoil during Saud's reign. In the early 1950s, the king endorsed **Egypt**'s rhetoric about liberating **Palestine** from the control of **Israel**, and he approved a defense pact with Egypt in 1955. He also broke diplomatic relations with Great Britain and France after their assault on Egypt during the **Suez Crisis** of 1956. Under pressure from anti-Western nationalists, he declined certain U.S. aid programs. Saud criticized U.S. policies toward the civil war in **Yemen** in the early 1960s.

Yet Saud eventually restored a friendly relationship with the United States. In 1957, he enjoyed a warm reception from President **Dwight D. Eisenhower** during a visit to the United States. Eisenhower ordered a U.S. Navy 21-gun salute of Saud as his ship reached New York City after Mayor Robert Wagner Jr. refused the traditional ceremonial welcome on the grounds that the king tolerated slavery and practiced anti-Semitism. To reciprocate Eisenhower's welcome, Saud endorsed the **Eisenhower Doctrine** and renewed a deal giving the United States airbase rights in his country.

SAUDI ARABIA. A kingdom on the Arabian Peninsula with which the United States interacted closely over many decades. Abdel Aziz ibn

Saud, a local chieftain, began fighting in 1902 to unify the peninsula, then part of the Ottoman Empire. He defeated such rivals as the Hashimite family, which went on to rule in **Jordan** and **Iraq**, and he declared the Kingdom of Saudi Arabia in 1932, taking the name **King ibn Saud**. Saudi Arabia became a religious state inasmuch as the Saudi family practiced a conservative form of Sunni Islam known as Wahhabism, and the kingdom contained Mecca and Medina, Islam's two most holy cities. A basic law adopted in 1992 affirmed that the Quran was the country's constitution and that its legal codes would be based on Islamic law (Shari'a), administered by religious courts.

The United States first noticed Saudi Arabia because of its oil resources. Standard Oil of California gained rights to explore for oil in 1933, made its first large strike in 1938, and developed the country's oil industry during World War II. In 1944, various firms formed the **Arabian-American Oil Company (ARAMCO)**, which dominated and vastly developed the country's oil industry for a generation after World War II. The Saudi government nationalized ARAMCO in 1973–1980, and as a member of the **Organization of Petroleum Exporting Countries (OPEC)**, it participated in the **Arab oil embargo of 1973**. In the early 2000s, Saudi Arabia remained the world's leading oil producer and exporter; it claimed proven reserves of 260 billion barrels, about 25 percent of the world's total, and it supplied about 14 percent of U.S. oil imports.

The United States and Saudi Arabia developed close political relations during World War II and the early Cold War. President **Franklin D. Roosevelt** established diplomatic relations in 1939, and in 1943 he dispatched U.S. soldiers to Saudi Arabia to provide military training and to build military facilities. Roosevelt met King ibn Saud aboard a U.S. naval vessel in 1945 to affirm their friendship. In a series of deals, President **Harry S. Truman** pledged to provide arms and military training to Saudi Arabia in exchange for permission to use military bases in Saudi Arabia deemed important to achieving U.S. objectives in the Cold War. Under **King Saud**, Saudi Arabia approved the **Eisenhower Doctrine** of 1957, and in 1962 President **John F. Kennedy** supported a Saudi-backed faction battling an Egyptian-backed force in a civil war in **Yemen**.

American–Saudi relations experienced tension in the 1970s. The Saudis had considered U.S. backing of **Israel** a violation of a pledge that Roosevelt had made to ibn Saud in 1945 and had frequently protested U.S. policy on Arab–Israeli issues. After the **Arab-Israeli War of 1967**, **King Fahd** and other Saudi officials were upset that the United States did not compel Israel to relinquish the territories it had occupied, and the U.S. rearmament of Israel during the **Arab-Israeli War of 1973** triggered the OPEC oil embargo and the Saudi nationalization of ARAMCO.

The relationship improved slightly during the 1980s. The **Ronald Reagan** administration named Saudi Arabia as one member of its **Strategic Consensus** coalition in the Middle East and sold Saudi Arabia advanced surveillance aircraft despite a determined effort by pro-Israel lobbyists to convince Congress to block the deal. But continuing anger over American policy toward Israel and a nationalistic backlash against the United States among Saudi citizens deterred the Saudi throne from posing outwardly as a close friend of the United States.

American–Saudi relations hit their high point in the early 1990s. The conquest of **Kuwait** by **Iraq** in 1990 threatened the territorial and economic interests—if not the very survival—of the Saudi state, and thus **King Fahd** welcomed U.S. and other foreign troops both to defend his country and to concentrate forces for the liberation of Kuwait. After the **Persian Gulf War**, U.S. forces remained in Saudi Arabia to conduct Operation Southern Watch, in which the United States enforced restrictions on Iraqi military maneuvers in southern Iraq in 1991–2003. During this long military partnership, U.S. service personnel honored Saudi cultural restrictions on alcohol and immodest dress, while Saudi Arabia allowed U.S. servicewomen to perform their duties in violation of the kingdom's conservative gender codes.

Saudi Arabia also accepted the U.S.-led Arab–Israeli peace process of the 1990s. Having backed the **Palestine Liberation Organization (PLO)** for years, the Saudis felt betrayed by the PLO's pro-Iraq policy during the Persian Gulf War. Thus, Saudi Arabia attended the **Madrid Conference** of October 1991 and endorsed the Oslo peace process that followed. By 1995, Saudi Arabia led the Gulf Cooperation Council in easing its economic embargo against Israel. President **William J. Clinton** rewarded Saudi Arabia with sales of aircraft and other goods, and Saudi Arabia lavishly supported the **Palestinian**

National Authority (PNA) as it took form in the West Bank and Gaza in the late 1990s. In 2002, Crown Prince Abdullah floated a peace plan in which Israel would withdraw from occupied territories and allow the return of **Palestinian refugees**, and the Arab states would recognize Israel. President **George W. Bush** publicly applauded the initiative.

In the 1990s and early 2000s, the problem of **terrorism** strained the U.S.–Saudi relationship. The presence of American forces in Saudi territory during and after the Persian Gulf War irritated Islamic fundamentalists, including the Saudi national **Osama bin Laden**, who organized a campaign of terrorism designed to overthrow the Saudi monarchy and to punish the United States. Terrorists bombed U.S. military facilities in Saudi Arabia in November 1995 and June 1996, killing 26 U.S. personnel, and struck at a housing complex in May 2003, killing 35 people, including eight Americans. American public opinion toward Saudi Arabia soured after revelations that 15 of the 19 hijackers who committed the **9/11** attacks were Saudi nationals, and rumors circulated that the Saudi government had indirectly funded or otherwise supported the perpetrators. Even those Americans who accepted Saudi explanations that the crown worked hard to prevent terrorist attacks wondered if the Saudi state promoted a form of Islam that nurtured anti-Western extremism across the Middle East.

The U.S. and Saudi governments sought to stabilize their relationship in the early 2000s. Saudi Arabia allowed the Pentagon limited use of Saudi facilities for the U.S. invasion of Iraq in 2003, even though, for domestic political reasons, it publicly criticized the invasion. A few months after the invasion of Iraq, the United States relocated most of its personnel in Saudi Arabia to **Qatar**, thus ending a military presence that had generated anti-Americanism among Saudi subjects since 1990. Prodded by the United States, Saudi Arabia also granted modest reforms regarding freedom of the press and political participation. But the enduring threat of terrorism and the trouble that the United States faced in its occupation of Iraq created conditions that had the potential to strain the relationship.

SCHWARZKOPF, H. NORMAN, JR. (1934–). U.S. Army general who commanded U.S. forces during the **Persian Gulf War** of

1990–1991 as commander in chief of U.S. Central Command. Schwarzkopf also directed certain allied forces into battle and coordinated operations with Arab military leaders. The general earned widespread popularity among the American people, as well as the nickname "Stormin' Norman," for his battlefield successes and his tough demeanor displayed in televised news conferences. At the conclusion of Operation Desert Storm, Schwarzkopf made the controversial decision to allow the Iraqi military to fly helicopters in the postwar period, giving **Saddam Hussein** the tactical ability to crush the Shiite and **Kurdish** rebellions that challenged his government after the war. *See also* SCHWARZKOPF, H. NORMAN, SR.

SCHWARZKOPF, H. NORMAN, SR. (1895–1958). U.S. Army officer who shaped U.S. relations with **Iran** in the 1940s and 1950s. Schwarzkopf graduated from West Point in 1917, gained combat experience in Europe during World War I, and served as chief of the New Jersey state police after the war. Schwarzkopf returned to army service in 1940, and in 1942, shortly after Iran was occupied by Soviet, British, and U.S. forces, he was dispatched to Tehran to train a national Iranian police force. Having befriended Shah **Mohammed Reza Pahlavi**, Schwarzkopf remained in touch with the shah during the revolutionary unrest in Iran in the early 1950s and returned to Tehran after the 1953 revolt to train the shah's police officers. Schwarzkopf was father to **H. Norman Schwarzkopf Jr.**, who led U.S. forces in the **Persian Gulf War** of 1990–1991.

SCOWCROFT, BRENT (1925–). Veteran and international affairs expert who served as national security advisor to President **George H. W. Bush**. Highly trusted by the president, Scowcroft encouraged the firm diplomatic and military policies manifest in Operation Desert Shield and Operation Desert Storm, which achieved the liberation of **Kuwait** during the **Persian Gulf War** of 1990–1991. As head of a private international consulting firm in the early 2000s, Scowcroft publicly questioned President **George W. Bush**'s rationale for invading in **Iraq**.

SHAMIR, YITZHAK (1915–). Leader of **Israel** who left a mark on U.S.–Israeli relations in the 1980s and early 1990s. Born in Poland,

Shamir migrated to **Palestine** in 1935 and was twice arrested by British authorities for resistance activities. In the 1950s and 1960s, he served in Israel's intelligence services and thereafter joined the conservative Likud Party. Under Likud-dominated governments and the Labor–Likud national unity government of the 1980s, Shamir served as foreign minister in 1980–1986 and as prime minister in 1983–1984 and 1986–1992.

During the 1980s, Shamir repaired the strain in U.S.–Israeli relations that resulted from the **Israeli invasion of Lebanon**. He negotiated with the United States an agreement on strategic cooperation and a free trade agreement. Yet he also promoted the construction of new settlements in the occupied West Bank, and he resisted various U.S. peace plans promoted by President **Ronald Reagan**, Secretary of State **George Shultz**, and Secretary of State **James Baker**. Shamir mollified the United States by attending the **Madrid Conference** of 1991, but his persistence in encouraging settlement building in the West Bank dismayed U.S. officials and prompted President **George H. W. Bush** to threaten to withhold U.S. aid needed to resettle Russian immigrants pouring into Israel.

Denied another term as prime minister in the Israeli election of 1992, Shamir retired from the Knesset in 1996.

SHARETT MOSHE (1896–1965). Second prime minister of **Israel,** with a reputation for moderation on Arab–Israeli issues. Born in Ukraine as Moshe Shertok, Sharett emigrated to **Palestine** in 1906 and gradually became involved in political activism to establish a Jewish state in Palestine. As head of the political department of the Jewish Agency for Palestine (1933–1948), Sharett advocated support for **Zionism** from Western states, represented Palestine's Jewry before the **Anglo-American Committee of Inquiry**, lobbied for passage of the **United Nations partition** resolution of 1947, and signed the Israeli declaration of statehood. A close confidante of **David Ben-Gurion**, Sharett was appointed Israel's first foreign minister (1948–1956). Sharett also served as prime minister in 1953–1955 between Ben-Gurion's first retirement from and return to that office.

American officials considered Sharett a moderate on Arab–Israeli issues, especially in comparison to Ben-Gurion. As foreign minister, Sharett accepted armistice agreements with four of the five Arab belligerents of the **Arab-Israeli War of 1948–1949**, and he demonstrated a willingness to negotiate permanent peace treaties with Arab leaders. He gained for Israel UN membership and diplomatic recognition by dozens of states, including the United States, and he consciously sought to build a positive image of Israel among the American public, Congress, and the executive branch. Sharett also negotiated various aid packages, including a massive reparations deal with West Germany in 1952, that bolstered Israel's financial foundation.

As prime minister, Sharett was challenged by the eruption of violence along Israel's borders. His moderate response to border incursions by Arab raiders pleased the United States, but it angered conservative Israelis such as Ben-Gurion, who favored a policy of military reprisals against the countries from which raids originated. Ben-Gurion returned from retirement to displace Sharett from the prime ministry in late 1955, and he relieved Sharett as foreign minister in June 1956. Sharett's departure from the Israeli government was a milestone on Israel's road toward its invasion of **Egypt** in October 1956.

SHARM EL-SHEIKH MEMORANDUM. An Israeli–Palestinian agreement of September 1999 calling for resumption of the stalled Oslo peace process. Brokered by Secretary of State **Madeleine Albright**, the deal committed **Israel** and the **Palestine Liberation Organization (PLO)** to seek a framework of a peace settlement by February 2000 and a final settlement by September 2000. The memorandum stimulated a final round of diplomacy that culminated in the failed Camp David summit of 2000.

SHARON, ARIEL (1928–). Controversial Israeli soldier and statesman whose bold and hawkish foreign policy complicated U.S. policy in the Middle East over several decades. Born in **Palestine**, Sharon became a soldier and earned a reputation of toughness, if not brutality, toward Arabs and Palestinians. He led deadly military operations against the **Jordanian** village of Qibya in 1953 and against an **Egyptian** army post at Gaza in 1955, in both cases earning the reproach of the **Dwight D. Eisenhower** administration. Sharon commanded a division of soldiers that captured Jerusalem during the

Arab-Israeli War of 1967, but international criticism of his harsh policies in the occupied West Bank compelled him to resign from the army. He returned from retirement during the national emergency that followed the onset of the **Arab-Israeli War of 1973** and led Israeli forces on their successful counteroffensive against the Egyptian army.

Elected to the Knesset in 1977, Sharon was appointed minister of defense in 1981 by Prime Minister **Menachem Begin**. In that post, Sharon executed the **Israeli invasion of Lebanon** in 1982, exceeding his orders by advancing Israeli forces all the way to Beirut. That offensive earned the reproach of the **Ronald Reagan** administration as destabilizing to **Lebanon** and catastrophic to the Lebanese people. Sharon's offensive forced Palestinian warriors to evacuate Lebanon, but it also led to the massacres of hundreds of Palestinians by Christian militias in refugee camps near Beirut. After an Israeli tribunal found Sharon indirectly responsible for the massacres, he was forced to resign as minister of defense.

Sharon was able to return to positions of influence in Israeli politics after a decade in the shadows. As minister of construction and housing in 1990–1992, he encouraged massive development of Israeli settlements on the occupied West Bank, a move that arguably violated international law, certainly complicated the Israeli–Palestinian quarrels over land, and drew criticism from some U.S. government officials. After a stint as foreign minister (1998–1999), Sharon emerged as leader of the Likud Party and sharply criticized the efforts of Prime Minister **Ehud Barak** to make peace with **Yasser Arafat** under the leadership of President **William J. Clinton**. After the failure of Barak's negotiations with Arafat at Camp David in the summer of 2000, Sharon, in a political gimmick designed to affirm his hard-line credentials, marched across the Temple Mount in late September under a heavy police guard and vowed in a speech that Israel would never surrender the land that held the Al-Aqsa Mosque. Within 24 hours, Palestinians rioted across the West Bank in protest, triggering the second **intifada** and dashing U.S. hopes of an early peace settlement.

Sharon then exploited Israelis' mounting insecurity at Palestinian violence and terrorist attacks to defeat Barak in an election in February 2001 and to win reelection in 2003. As prime minister, Sharon ordered drastic measures to suppress the intifada and secure Israel from **terrorism**, including mass arrests, the virtual confinement of Arafat for two years in his bunker in Ramallah, and the construction of a concrete security barrier that infringed on Palestinian land rights inside the West Bank. When President **George W. Bush** promoted the **Roadmap peace plan** in 2003, Sharon pledged to cooperate, to accept in principle a Palestinian state with contiguous borders, and to dismantle some settlements in the West Bank. Neither Sharon nor his Palestinian counterparts, however, budged on such issues as the control of Jerusalem and the rights of **Palestinian refugees**.

In 2005, Sharon slightly moderated his policies toward Palestinians. In August, he ordered the compulsory withdrawal of Israeli settlers from the Gaza Strip. In November, he formed Kadima ("Forward" in Hebrew), a new, centrist political party, for the purpose of formulating a peace settlement that established a state of Palestine, respecting the peace and security of Israel, and exonerated Israel from repatriation of Palestinian refugees. After Sharon suffered a debilitating stroke that left him permanently incapacitated in January 2006, acting prime minister **Ehud Olmert** took control of Kadima, which won the Israeli elections of March 2006.

SHULTZ, GEORGE P. (1920–). Secretary of state in 1982–1989 who made a mark on two facets of U.S. diplomacy in the Middle East. First, he strongly opposed proposals from members of the National Security Council (NSC) to sell weapons to **Iran**, and when the NSC staff proceeded with such deals on a covert basis, leading to the **Iran-Contra scandal**, Shultz bitterly condemned the operation as a threat to American foreign policy and a blow to American democratic principles. He vigorously defended President **Ronald Reagan** by charging that NSC staff members deliberately misled him, softening the intense public criticism of the president.

Shultz also addressed the Arab–Israeli peace process. In response to the **intifada**, he proposed in March 1988 a peace plan under which **Israel** would withdraw from the occupied territories and the Palestinians (represented by **Jordan** since the United States refused to recognize the **Palestine Liberation Organization (PLO)** would renounce **terrorism** and recognize Israel). Despite active efforts by Shultz to sell the plan during several visits to the region, Israel and

Jordan seemed cool to the idea, and the plan collapsed when **King Hussein** relinquished to the Palestinians all claims to the West Bank in July.

Yet Shultz achieved a modest diplomatic breakthrough in late 1988. He denied an application from **Yasser Arafat** for a U.S. visa to visit New York City for the purpose of addressing the **United Nations** General Assembly on the grounds that Arafat had ties to terrorist groups. Unhappy with Shultz's action, the General Assembly reconvened in Geneva and welcomed Arafat there. Yet Arafat also seemed to give in to U.S. pressure. He formally accepted UN Resolutions 242 and 338, renounced **terrorism** and pledged to recognize Israel, and called for a UN-sponsored conference among the Palestinians, Israel, and neighboring states. Shultz promptly declared that the United States would speak to the PLO. That breakthrough set the stage for the peacemaking diplomacy of the **George H. W. Bush** administration.

SHUTTLE DIPLOMACY. An exhaustive diplomatic initiative conducted by Secretary of State **Henry A. Kissinger** in the aftermath of the **Arab-Israeli War of 1973**. Aiming to launch a peace process from the ashes of the hostilities, Kissinger repeatedly visited Arab states and **Israel** from October 1973 to the summer of 1974 and hosted a five-power (the United States, the Soviet Union, Israel, **Jordan**, and **Egypt**) conference at Geneva in December 1973. Kissinger aimed for **disengagement accords** providing for the withdrawal of Arab and Israeli troops in the war zones and insertion of UN peacekeepers along both fronts. He achieved an Egyptian–Israeli accord, signed on 18 January 1974, and a Syrian–Israel deal, signed on 31 May. Along the way, Kissinger also reestablished U.S. diplomatic relations with Egypt, which had been severed since 1967, and he convinced Arab states to resume shipments of oil to Western states in March 1974. *See also* SINAI II AGREEMENT.

SINAI II AGREEMENT. An agreement between **Egypt** and **Israel** reached in September 1975 under the **shuttle diplomacy** of **Henry Kissinger**. The deal broadened the **United Nations** buffer zone established in 1974 to include the strategically sensitive Mitla and Gidi passes, from which Israel withdrew. Both Israel and Egypt established monitoring/early warning stations in the passes, Egypt's built by the United States and staffed by American civilians. Israel withdrew from the oil fields at Abu Rodeis. Egypt and Israel accepted limits on the numbers of tanks, artillery, and personnel stationed near the UN zone, and both powers agreed to work toward a final settlement through peaceful means rather than war.

SIX DAY WAR. *See* ARAB-ISRAELI WAR OF 1967.

STRATEGIC CONSENSUS. A policy of the **Ronald Reagan** administration designed to stabilize the Middle East. The Reagan administration envisioned a partnership linking the United States to friendly regional powers such as **Egypt**, **Israel**, **Saudi Arabia**, Turkey, and Pakistan. By arming and aiding these countries, the administration would aim to build a pro-American, anti-Soviet bastion in the Middle East and contain the revolutionary fervor of **Iran**.

Events soon proved the limits to the Strategic Consensus. A series of Saudi–Israeli clashes in 1981 revealed that the policy disregarded intraregional tensions. Nor did the policy recognize the growing tide of Islamic fundamentalism sweeping the region, manifest in the assassination of Egyptian president **Anwar Sadat** in 1981 by extremists who opposed his peace treaty with Israel and his friendliness toward the United States. **Israel's invasion of Lebanon** in 1982, which resulted in a debilitating U.S. occupation of Beirut in 1982–1983, further destabilized the region. Reagan's decision to deal firmly with the mounting threat of **terrorism** by bombing **Libya** in 1986 exacerbated anti-American feelings across parts of the region.

SUEZ CRISIS. A complicated international crisis that triggered a brief war in **Egypt** in late 1956 and proved to be one of the most perilous events of the Cold War. The crisis began in July when Egyptian premier **Gamal Abdel Nasser** nationalized the British- and French-owned Suez Canal Company. Previously aggravated by Nasser's machinations against their imperial interests, British and French leaders decided to use the threat of force to compel Nasser to return the canal company.

During the ensuing four-month standoff, President **Dwight D. Eisenhower** sought to avert a military clash and settle the canal dispute with diplomacy. He feared that an Anglo–French military strike would spawn anti-Western nationalism across the region and give the Soviet Union an opportunity for political gain. Eisenhower directed Secretary of State **John Foster Dulles** to defuse the crisis through public statements, negotiations, two international conferences, and deliberations at the **United Nations**. By late October, however, these efforts proved fruitless, and Anglo–French preparations for war continued.

Meanwhile, Great Britain and France secretly colluded with **Israel** to launch a tripartite attack on Egypt. Under the ruse, Israel would invade the Sinai, Britain and France would issue ultimatums ordering Egyptian and Israeli troops to withdraw from the Suez Canal Zone, and when Nasser (as expected) rejected the ultimatums, the European powers would occupy the Canal Zone and depose Nasser. American officials failed to anticipate the collusion scheme before Israel invaded the Sinai on 29 October. Within days, Israeli forces approached the Suez Canal, and the European powers issued the contrived ultimatum and launched air strikes against Egypt.

Caught off guard by the start of hostilities, Eisenhower took steps to end the war quickly. He imposed sanctions on the colluding powers, achieved a **United Nations** cease-fire resolution, and organized a UN Emergency Force (UNEF) to disengage the combatants.

Yet before Eisenhower's diplomacy had effect, the crisis moved into a dangerous phase. British and French paratroopers landed along the Suez Canal on 5 November, and Soviet leaders threatened to intervene in the fighting and to retaliate against London and Paris with weapons of mass destruction. Prudently, Eisenhower ordered the Pentagon to prepare for world war even as he increased pressure on the colluding powers to desist. A UN-brokered cease-fire agreement took effect on 7 November, and tensions gradually eased. British and French forces departed Egypt in December, and Israeli forces withdrew from the Sinai by March 1957.

The Suez Crisis had a profound impact on the Middle East and on the responsibilities that the United States assumed there. It badly tarnished Britain's and France's prestige and thus undermined their traditional authority in the region. Nasser attained a new level of prestige among Arab peoples, and the region's remaining pro-Western regimes seemed vulnerable to pro-Nasser uprisings. The prospect of an Arab–Israeli peace process declined sharply, and the Soviet Union enjoyed an improved image among certain Arab states. In reaction to these consequences of the Suez Crisis, the United States declared the **Eisenhower Doctrine** in early 1957.

SYRIA. Former province of the Ottoman Empire and mandate of France with which the United States developed a checkered relationship in the years following World War II. During the 19th century, Americans nurtured cultural connections with Syria, which then encompassed present-day **Lebanon**, by establishing the **American University of Beirut (AUB)** and other such institutions in the area. After a British army liberated Syria from the control of Vichy France in 1941, the United States supported the independence of Lebanon (1944) and Syria (1946), earning the appreciation of the Syrian people. Despite tensions surrounding the Arab–Israeli conflict, early leaders of Syria signaled a willingness to side with the West in the Cold War; for example, Prime Minister Hassan Abdel Razzak el Hakim openly endorsed the **Middle East Command** proposal in the early 1950s.

Yet U.S.–Syrian relations crumbled in the 1950s. American leaders feared that radical, pan-Arab ideology, embraced by many Syrians, threatened the pro-Western orientation of the Middle East. Syrians, for their part, vented their anger about the establishment of **Israel** and their fear of its expansionism by criticizing the United States for supporting that state. In 1956–1957, U.S. observers detected rising communist influence in Syria as its government accepted Soviet weapons, denounced the **Eisenhower Doctrine**, suppressed conservative opposition, and apparently fomented a revolt in **Jordan**. In August 1957, the Syrian regime foiled an apparent U.S. covert operation to unseat it. Worried that the Soviet Union might annex Syria or subvert neighboring pro-Western regimes, President **Dwight D. Eisenhower** nudged Turkey to overthrow the government in Damascus. An ensuing war scare abated only when **Egypt** and Syria merged into the United Arab Republic (UAR) on 1 February 1958. Although surprised and concerned by this merger, Eisenhower promptly recognized the UAR on the hunch that the merger would stymie communist influence in Damascus.

American–Syrian relations remained tense after Syria withdrew from the UAR in 1961. As it developed ties with the Soviet Union (and the Untied States armed Israel), Syria confronted Israel in a series of battles that triggered the **Arab-Israeli War of 1967**. The loss of the Golan Heights to Israel in that war embittered Syrians against Israel and, by extension, the United States. Syrian threats on Jordan during the **Black September** episode of 1970 further antagonized the United States. The **Arab-Israeli War of 1973** strained Syrian–U.S. relations and drove Damascus into further dependency on the Soviet Union.

The United States also regretted Syria's intervention in the civil war in Lebanon. Seeking to counter Israeli and Egyptian influence, Syria occupied central Lebanon in 1976 and bolstered Lebanese Muslim and Palestinian forces, the latter of which waged attacks into northern Israel. That policy provoked Israeli counterstrikes, most notably an **Israeli invasion of Lebanon** in June 1982. American forces sent to disengage Israeli forces from Beirut came under attack by local militias, and in late 1983, President **Ronald Reagan** ordered aerial counterassaults on Syrian targets east of Beirut. In addition, Syria berated Egypt for breaking Arab unity by making peace with Israel in 1979, and it apparently backed or at least sympathized with kidnappers who seized American hostages in Lebanon and terrorists who attacked Western targets in various theaters.

The United States and Syria developed a limited rapprochement in the 1990s after the collapse of the Soviet Union undermined Syria's base of support and supply. In 1990–1991, Syria endorsed the U.S.-led international effort to reverse the Iraqi conquest of **Kuwait** during the **Persian Gulf War**. President **Hafez al-Assad**, who dominated Syria from 1970 to 2000, endorsed the U.S.-led Arab–Israeli peace process, attending the **Madrid Conference** of October 1991 and negotiating with Israel and the United States on terms of a peace settlement through the 1990s. That peace process bore little fruit, however, as Assad and his Israeli counterparts failed to reach a settlement. Evidence that Assad continued to sponsor violence against Western and Israeli interests undercut U.S. confidence in Syria. **Bashar Assad**, who succeeded his father as president in 2000, seemed more moderate, but improvement in U.S.–Syrian relations was delayed by the turmoil of the second **intifada** in Israeli-occupied territory and by the U.S. war on **terrorism** and the invasion of **Iraq**.

– T –

TALABANI, JALAL (1933–). Leader of the Patriotic Union of Kurdistan, which vied for control of Iraqi Kurdistan in the 1990s. *See also* **BARZANI, MASSOUD; KURDS.**

TARIKI, ABDULLAH (1925–1997). A Saudi oil engineer who sparked a transformation in the American-dominated oil industry of **Saudi Arabia**. Tariki received a master's degree in oil engineering from the University of Texas and thereby earned the reputation as the first Saudi to understand the oil business. In 1954, he became the Saudi director general of petroleum and mineral affairs, a position from which he managed relations between his government and the **Arabian-American Oil Company (ARAMCO)**. Inspired by the nationalism espoused by **Egypt** in the late 1950s, Tariki pressed ARAMCO to raise its profitability, to increase the revenues paid to the kingdom, and to prepare for a transition to Saudi Arabia's control of its oil resources. In 1959, Tariki organized the First Arab Petroleum Congress in Cairo to build unity among Arab oil producers, and in 1960 he welcomed the founding of the **Organization of Petroleum Exporting Countries (OPEC)**. Yet Tariki failed to gain control of OPEC as he sought, and he fell out of favor with the Saudi crown. In 1962, he was dismissed from office and took up exile in Beirut, where he lobbied for years for Arab control of oil production.

TENET, GEORGE (1953–). Director of central intelligence (DCI) in 1997–2004. Appointed by President **William J. Clinton**, Tenet remained in office after the inauguration of President **George W. Bush** in 2001, and in June 2001 the DCI earned laurels for negotiating a brief cease-fire in the Israeli–Palestinian violence. Tenet came under criticism, however, after the Central Intelligence Agency failed to anticipate the **9/11** terrorist attacks on the United States. Tenet also lost credibility when it became clear that his strong assurances to Bush that Iraqi dictator **Saddam Hussein** possessed weapons of mass destruction—assurances that helped justify the decision to invade **Iraq** in 2003—were eventually proven false. Under mounting political pressure, Tenet resigned his post, citing personal reasons, in July 2004.

TERRORISM. Generally, acts of violence undertaken for political or religious purposes. Efforts to define terrorism precisely or to identify groups or behaviors as terrorist have generated controversy and debate. The U.S. Department of State defines terrorism as "premeditated, politically motivated violence perpetrated against noncombatant targets by subnational groups or clandestine agents, usually intended to influence an audience." Terrorism has been practiced worldwide since ancient history and has been applied in pursuit of domestic and international aims.

In the Middle East, terrorism has challenged U.S. foreign policymakers since the middle of the 20th century. Acts of terrorism perpetrated by Arab groups were designed to weaken the state of **Israel**, to deter the United States from politically backing Israel, and to undermine pro-Western Arab regimes. The kidnapping and murder of Israeli athletes at the 1972 Olympic Games in Munich serves as one example of many such deeds. Certain actions by Zionists, such as the bombing of the King David Hotel in Jerusalem in 1946, and other actions by Israelis, such as the murder of **United Nations** mediator **Folke Bernadotte** in 1948, also constituted terrorism. After the 1979 revolution in **Iran**, the government in Tehran was widely accused of abetting terrorism in **Lebanon** and elsewhere. The number of terrorist incidents worldwide declined during the 1990s, although the attacks that occurred tended to be more deadly, politically spectacular, and related to the Middle East.

Terrorism became a central concern of U.S. officials after the **9/11** attack on the United States. Perpetrated by the **al-Qaeda** network under **Osama bin Laden**, that attack symbolized a growing tendency for terrorists motivated by religious ideology to inflict violence for political and religious reasons. In the aftermath of the 9/11 attack, the United States generally prosecuted a war on terrorism by bolstering law enforcement and intelligence, imposing financial restrictions, mobilizing foreign states to detain suspects, and launching an **invasion of Afghanistan** to depose the Taliban regime and suppress al-Qaeda. The **U.S. invasion of Iraq** in 2003 was also partially motivated by counterterrorism concerns, although some experts suggested that the war did more to generate terrorism than to stem it. *See also* BLACK SEPTEMBER; EGYPTIAN ISLAMIC JIHAD; HIZBALLAH; ISLAMIC RESISTANCE MOVEMENT (HAMAS).

TRADE WITH THE MIDDLE EAST, U.S. The sale of goods between the United States and the countries of the Middle East. In the early 2000s, trade with Middle East powers comprised only about 5 percent of total U.S. foreign trade. Yet Middle East oil and gas constituted key commodities imported into the United States, accounting for about one-fifth of U.S. oil and gas imports and one-tenth of those products consumed in the United States. Various Middle East countries also exported significant quantities of textiles and apparel to the American market. Key U.S. exports to Middle East states included transportation equipment and agricultural products. *See also* MIDDLE EAST FREE TRADE AREA.

TRANSJORDAN. *See* JORDAN.

TRIPARTITE DECLARATION. A statement issued on 25 May 1950 by the United States, Great Britain, and France to declare a collective policy on arms supply and security in the Middle East. The three Western powers—the traditional suppliers of military hardware to the Middle East—declared that they would supply weapons to Middle East states "for the purposes of assuring their internal security and their legitimate self-defense and to permit them to play their part in the defense of the area as a whole." Each state seeking arms would pledge nonaggression against its neighbors, and if any state broke its nonaggression pledge, then the three Western powers would "immediately take action, both within and outside the **United Nations**, to prevent such violation."

Western officials designed the Tripartite Declaration to serve several objectives. Acting in the shadow of the **Arab-Israeli War of 1948–1949**, they hoped to prevent the renewal of hostilities. They also sought to avert an Arab–Israeli arms race that would exhaust the limited financial resources of local states. Finally, they aimed broadly to promote the security of the Middle East against Soviet encroachments by aligning local states in a broad coalition.

The Tripartite Declaration had limited long-term consequence. In the early 1950s, the United States occasionally cited it during moments of crisis to deter states from provoking war. But the decision by **Egypt** in 1955 to purchase weapons from communist countries broke the West's historic monopoly on arms supply, while Arab–Israeli tensions persisted and triggered the **Suez Crisis** in 1956. As the first American commitment to the security of the Middle East, however, the declaration set an important precedent for future American involvement in the region. *See also* FOREIGN AID.

TRUMAN DOCTRINE. A highly significant U.S. national security policy declared by President **Harry S. Truman** in 1947. After World War II, Truman was deeply worried by the prospect of communist victory in a civil war in Greece, by Soviet demands for political concessions from the government of Turkey, and by Great Britain's mounting inability to fulfill its traditional role of protector of Western interests in those two countries. Facing an economy-minded, Republican-controlled Congress, the Democratic president alarmed the American people about the situation in Greece by characterizing it as a conspiracy by foreign communists to undermine a friendly government. "I believe that it must be the policy of the United States," Truman declared to Congress on 12 March 1947, in words that would become known as the Truman Doctrine, "to support free peoples who are resisting attempted subjugation by armed minorities or by outside pressures." The gambit worked, as Congress appropriated $400 million in aid for Greece and Turkey and both countries remained noncommunist. Truman's success encouraged him to practice similar anti-Soviet containment measures in Europe and elsewhere, and it drew greater U.S. interest to security issues in the Middle East.

TRUMAN, HARRY S. (1884–1972). President from 1945 to 1953 who laid several foundations of U.S. policy in the Middle East for the Cold War era. First, Truman established the doctrine of anti-Soviet containment in the region. In 1946, he pressured the Soviet Union to withdraw its occupation troops from northern **Iran**, bolstering the integrity of **Shah Mohammed Reza Pahlavi**, who would reign as an American partner for more than three decades. He also encouraged Turkey to resist Soviet demands for strategic concessions, and under the **Truman Doctrine** of 1947, he provided massive aid to Turkey and Greece that stabilized those two countries and aligned them in the Western orbit for the duration of the Cold War. Truman enrolled Turkey and Greece in the **North Atlantic Treaty Organization (NATO)** in 1952 and launched several other initiatives, such as the

Tripartite Declaration and the **Middle East Command** initiative, that were designed to deny the Soviet Union political or military influence in the Middle East.

Second, Truman established an enduring legacy of U.S. development of Middle East oil. He developed a long-lasting friendship with **Saudi Arabia** that served the American interest of preserving access to Middle East oil for both domestic and military purposes. Working in collaboration with Britain, Truman laid the groundwork for an oil production and distribution system across the region that tied the United States to the region for decades to come.

Third, Truman positioned the United States at the center of the **Arab–Israeli conflict**. For a variety of political, diplomatic, and cultural reasons, he endorsed the migration of Jews to **Palestine** and the establishment of the state of **Israel** in 1948, steps that earned the United States the enduring goodwill of Israel and enduring bitterness of the Arab community. He also took modest steps to end the **Arab-Israeli War of 1948–1949** and to resolve the controversies that lingered after the war, thus becoming the first in a long line of American leaders who tried to advance the Arab–Israeli peace process.

Finally, Truman was the first U.S. president who faced the challenge of dealing with nationalism in newly emergent Third World states. During his presidency, **Gamal Abdel Nasser** led a group of army officers who took over the government of **Egypt**, and **Mohammed Mossadegh** briefly dominated the government of Iran and nationalized that country's Western-owned oil industry. Truman administration officials handled such leaders with a mixture of firmness and appeasement, beginning a long American search for the best formula for the new challenges of the era of decolonization and Third World revolution.

– U –

UNITED ARAB EMIRATES (UAE). A federation of seven independent Arab sheikhdoms situated on the southeastern edge of the Arabian Peninsula with which the United States developed a close security partnership in the 1990s. Having achieved independence from Great Britain in 1971, the UAE opened diplomatic relations with the

United States in 1972. American firms participated in the exploitation of the UAE's vast oil resources, building a sense of amity between the two states. Some tensions developed in the 1970s when the UAE participated in the **Arab oil embargo** of 1973–1974 and broke relations with **Egypt** after it made peace with **Israel** in 1979.

Yet relations began to improve in 1990 when UAE fear of aggression by **Iraq** compounded an older concern with revolutionary **Iran**. During the **Persian Gulf War** of 1990–1991, the UAE offered base rights to U.S. combat forces, dispatched troops to participate in the liberation of **Kuwait**, and contributed $1 billion to the allied war effort. As the United States imposed its containment policy against Iraq in 1992–2003, the UAE extended the base rights and contributed some $15 million per year to the American operations. Although it publicly opposed the **U.S. invasion of Iraq** in 2003, the UAE allowed U.S. forces destined for Iraq to stage on its territory. In 2000, the United States sold the UAE advanced military weaponry valued at more than $8 billion.

The UAE's relationship with the **al-Qaeda** terrorist network caused some concern to U.S. officials. The UAE recognized the Taliban regime in Afghanistan in 1996–2001, and two of the 19 hijackers involved in the **9/11** attacks were UAE nationals. After 9/11, the UAE cooperated with the United States by arresting suspected terrorists and closing down al-Qaeda money-laundering operations. Yet popular American suspicions of the UAE remained deep, evident in a public uproar in early 2006 that forced the **George W. Bush** administration to cancel a deal in which a UAE firm would have purchased a corporation that managed several maritime ports in the United States.

UNITED NATIONS ORGANIZATION. An international organization founded at the end of World War II in 1945. Comprised of a Security Council, a General Assembly, and various executive offices and councils, the United Nations aspired to promote international peace, stability, cooperation, and human progress.

The United Nations became deeply involved in the **Arab–Israeli conflict** in the 1940s. The General Assembly approved the Palestine **partition plan** in 1947 despite strong opposition among Arab powers, and when war resulted, the United Nations achieved cease-fire agreements in early 1949 and sought, futilely, to broker formal peace agreements thereafter. The United Nations also tried to mitigate specific problems resulting from the Arab–Israeli conflict. It established the **UN Relief and Works Agency for Palestine Refugees in the Near East (UNRWA)** to care for the millions of **Palestinian refugees** uprooted as a result of Arab–Israeli violence. The UN Emergency Force (UNEF) was formed during the **Suez Crisis** of 1956 and deployed to the Sinai peninsula to ease Israeli withdrawal from **Egypt**. United Nations soldiers also served as inspectors during the civil insurrection in **Lebanon** in 1958 and as peacekeepers along the Israeli–Syrian border and in south Lebanon in the 1970s and subsequent decades. The United Nations joined the United States, the European Union, and Russia as a formal cosponsor of the **Roadmap peace plan** of the early 2000s.

The United Nations also became politically involved in the Arab–Israeli conflict, often on the side of the Arab states and peoples. In 1974, the General Assembly recognized the rights of Palestinians to national independence and granted observer status to the **Palestine Liberation Organization (PLO)**. In 1975, the General Assembly also passed, over vigorous Israeli and U.S. opposition, a resolution calling **Zionism** a form of racism. The resolution was rescinded in 1991 as an enticement for Israel to attend the **Madrid Conference**. The United States was frequently seen as Israel's protector at the United Nations, exercising its veto to protect Israel from severe resolutions in the Security Council.

The United Nations also passed resolutions regarding Middle East issues that served as legal foundations for diplomatic policy by the United States and other countries. Security Council Resolution 242 of 1967 established the principle of land for peace as a basis for a permanent settlement of the Israeli–Palestinian dispute. Several other resolutions gave legal sanction to the policies of President **George H. W. Bush** during the **Persian Gulf War** of 1990–1991 and to the U.S. policies to contain Iraq in the 1990s and early 2000s.

UNITED NATIONS RELIEF AND WORKS AGENCY FOR PALESTINE REFUGEES IN THE NEAR EAST (UNRWA). A **United Nations** agency created with U.S. support to care for **Palestinian refugees**. The United Nations established UNRWA in December

1949 to provide for the material needs of the 800,000 Palestinians who had become refugees during the **Arab-Israeli War of 1948–1949**. Although it was designed as a temporary agency, its mandate was routinely renewed every three years because the status of Palestinian refugees remained unsolved as a political issue. By the early 2000s, UNRWA provided educational, health care, and welfare benefits to more than 3 million registered refugees and their descendants and operated on an annual budget of more than $300 million. The United States supported the creation and renewal of UNRWA and paid much of its operating costs, despite some domestic political backlash against the financial expense, in recognition of the humanitarian role it played.

UNITED NATIONS SPECIAL COMMITTEE ON PALESTINE (UNSCOP). A **United Nations** agency that surveyed the **Palestine** situation in 1947 and recommended a plan to partition the territory into a Jewish and an Arab state. The UN General Assembly created UNSCOP in April 1947 after the British referred the issue of Palestine to that body. As the 11-member committee studied the situation in Palestine, Jewish leaders lobbied for partition while Palestinian leaders boycotted the proceedings. In August, an eight-member majority recommended partition, with independence to follow a two-year transition period. Although the **Harry S. Truman** administration remained uninvolved in the UNSCOP investigation, it voted for the **partition plan** when the United Nations approved it in November 1947.

USS *LIBERTY*. A U.S. Navy intelligence-gathering ship attacked by Israeli military forces on 8 June 1967 during the **Arab-Israeli War of 1967**. The *Liberty* was sailing off the coast of **Egypt**, likely monitoring electronic signals pertaining to the war between **Israel** and its Arab neighbors. After reconnoitering the ship over several hours, Israeli warplanes bombed and strafed the *Liberty*, and Israeli patrol boats struck it with several torpedoes. The attack left 34 U.S. sailors and other personnel dead and 172 wounded, and the ship was nearly lost. For reasons that remain unclear, President **Lyndon B. Johnson** called off a counterstrike by nearby naval units. Israel later explained the incident as a result of errors in reconnaissance and communications and apologized for it, and Johnson accepted the apology and refrained from publicly investigating the episode. The incident had little effect on U.S.–Israeli official relations, although for years afterward certain groups of U.S. military veterans and other Americans remained dissatisfied with the official explanations and alleged in books, articles, and other venues that Israel deliberately attacked the ship to prevent it from detecting evidence of controversial Israeli wartime actions, including a massacre of Egyptian prisoners of war.

– V –

VANCE, CYRUS (1917–). Secretary of state in 1977–1980 who counseled President **Jimmy Carter** on key aspects of Middle East policy. A rival to National Security Advisor **Zbigniew Brzezinski** for access to the president, Vance also lost stature when Carter appointed personal emissary Robert Strauss to oversee Egyptian–Israeli peace talks. On **Iran**, Vance advocated that the United States early accommodate the revolutionary movement of the Ayatollah **Ruhollah Khomeini**. Once Khomeini took power and seized American hostages, Vance favored resolution of the **Iran Hostage Crisis** by diplomatic means, and after Carter ordered the ill-fated rescue mission of April 1980, Vance resigned his post.

– W –

WAR OF ATTRITION. A low-intensity but persistent armed clash between **Egypt** and **Israel** fought in 1967–1970. Eager to recover from the humiliation of the **Arab-Israeli War of 1967**, Egyptian premier **Gamal Abdel Nasser** contested Israeli forces in occupation of the Sinai Peninsula. In March 1969, Egyptian units launched massive artillery and air strikes on Israeli forces east of the Suez Canal. Responding with similar measures, Israel quickly achieved air superiority and the ability to strike Egyptian targets virtually at will. By January 1970, Israeli war jets bombed targets deep in Egyptian territory with the purposes of signaling Israel's firmness, securing the frontier, and triggering Nasser's downfall. But Nasser reacted by traveling to Moscow to secure modern arms and 15,000 Soviet soldiers as advisers (including 200 pilots). By June 1970, Soviet pilots fought Israeli airmen in dogfights near the Suez Canal, and casualties mounted on both sides of the waterway.

Internal divisions limited the ability of the **Richard M. Nixon** administration to deal with the War of Attrition. Secretary of State **William P. Rogers** eagerly sought to broker a settlement in concert with European powers and the Soviet Union. But National Security Advisor **Henry A. Kissinger**, who disliked Rogers and mistrusted the Soviets, quietly discouraged Israel from working with the secretary of state. Israeli leaders rejected the **Rogers Plan** of December 1969 as damaging to their interests and instead escalated the War of Attrition with strategic bombing.

Rogers achieved more success in 1970. In June, he proposed a second peace plan that Egypt and **Jordan** accepted. Israel followed suit after Nixon assured Israel that it would be forced neither to absorb **Palestinian refugees** nor to relinquish territory in the absence of a final peace treaty. On these terms, the War of Attrition ended on 7 August. Despite suffering heavy casualties and stoking tensions, Nasser reached his goals of restoring his political image, gaining Soviet weapons, proving the limits of Israeli superiority, and triggering U.S. involvement in peacemaking.

WEINBERGER, CASPAR W. (1917–2006). Secretary of defense (1981–1987) who influenced President **Ronald Reagan**'s policies in the Middle East. Weinberger favored Reagan's inclination to deal forcefully with **Libya** and he oversaw U.S. military operations against Libya in 1981 and 1986. He also secured Reagan's approval for the policy of reflagging oil tankers of **Kuwait** as U.S. vessels and providing U.S. Navy escorts for them, an important act of American intervention in the **Iran–Iraq War**. Weinberger opposed, by contrast, the decision to send marines into **Lebanon** in 1982–1983, arguing that those soldiers lacked a clear mission and that no U.S. vital interests were at stake.

Weinberger claimed that he opposed the provision of arms to **Iran** and that he knew nothing about the illegal activities committed during the **Iran-Contra scandal**. In 1992, he was indicted on four felony counts, including obstruction of justice and perjury, for his actions related to the scandal. President **George H. W. Bush** issued a pardon that shielded Weinberger from prosecution.

WILSON, THOMAS WOODROW (1856–1924). President of the United States (1913–1921) who contemplated U.S. official involvement in the Middle East. A Democrat elected with a reputation for domestic reform, Wilson devoted much of his presidency to shaping American diplomatic and military involvement in World War I (1914–1919) in Europe. He expressed his vision for the postwar world order in the Fourteen Points Address of 1918, advocating such principles as self-determination and calling specifically for the autonomy of the various nationalities living under Ottoman rule. Wilson dispatched the **King-Crane Commission** to study political dynamics in the Middle East and recommend steps to implement his ideals. Before the commission completed its work, however, Wilson became consumed with political challenges in Europe and at home, and thus little came of the King-Crane initiative.

WYE RIVER MEMORANDUM. An Israeli–Palestinian agreement signed under the sponsorship of President **William J. Clinton** in 1998. In an effort to resuscitate the peace process stalled since 1995, Clinton invited Palestinian president **Yasser Arafat** and Israeli prime minister **Benjamin Netanyahu** to a meeting at the Wye River Conference Center in Maryland in October 1998. With Clinton arbitrating, the two leaders negotiated a memorandum providing that **Israel** would transfer an additional 13 percent of the West Bank to Palestinian control, ensure safe passage of Palestinians between Gaza and the West Bank, and release certain Palestinian prisoners from Israeli jails and that the **Palestinian National Authority (PNA)** would renounce **terrorism**, imprison certain perpetrators of violence against Israel, and undertake various measures to prevent attacks by Palestinian extremists. The memorandum also committed both powers to cooperate in certain civil and economic enterprises and to resume the final status talks by 4 May 1999.

The Wye River Memorandum restarted the stalled peace process for a brief time. Clinton visited Gaza in December 1998 to witness the Palestinian National Council's vote to remove from its charter those passages calling for the destruction of Israel. In May 1999, Labor candidate **Ehud Barak** won election as prime minister of Israel, and he and Arafat engaged in vigorous although fruitless final status talks under American leadership in 2000.

– Y –

YAMANI, AHMED ZAKI (1930–). Saudi Arabian minister of petroleum and mineral resources in 1962–1986 who significantly shaped pricing and other policies of the **Organization of Petroleum Exporting Countries (OPEC)**. Born in Mecca and trained at Harvard University Law School, Yamani exercised such power that he was known in financial circles around the world as Mr. Oil. He engineered the **Arab oil embargo** of 1973–1974 that resulted in the quadrupling of oil prices and led to severe economic dislocation for the United States and other Western states. **King Fahd** dismissed Yamani as oil minister in 1986 after a controversy within the kingdom over petroleum prices.

YEMEN. A small state on the southern edge of the Arabian Peninsula with which the United States has had limited contact. Yemen was formed in 1990 when South Yemen and North Yemen merged. South Yemen traced its roots to a protectorate that the British Empire secured around the port of Aden in the 19th century. North Yemen secured its independence from the Ottoman Empire in 1919, established diplomatic relations with the United States in 1946, and joined the **United Nations** in 1947. North Yemen joined **Egypt** and **Syria** in forming the short-lived United Arab Republic (1958–1961). The merger of the two Yemens in 1990 survived a secessionist movement among southerners that triggered a brief civil war in 1994. In 2000, Yemen and **Saudi Arabia** formally delimited their mutual border.

North Yemen posed a challenge to the United States during the presidency of **John F. Kennedy**. In 1962, rebels overthrew the country's monarchy, declared the Yemen Arab Republic, and turned to Egyptian premier **Gamal Abdel Nasser** for political and military support. The deposed monarchists fought a counterrevolutionary war backed by Saudi Arabia and **Jordan**. Intent on improving ties with Nasser, Kennedy recognized the new government in December 1962 even though the move irritated his Saudi friends. Fighting ebbed in 1967 after Nasser withdrew his military forces from the country. In 1970, the Saudis recognized the Yemen Arab Republic and curtailed their support of the royalists, a move that helped end the civil war. American relations with North Yemen were broken in 1967–1972 because of Yemeni anger about the role of the United States in the **Arab-Israeli War of 1967**, but in succeeding years North Yemen received substantial U.S. foreign aid.

South Yemen attracted little attention in the United States as long as it remained a protectorate of the British Empire. Trouble developed in the relationship, however, after Great Britain, increasingly targeted by domestic terrorist attacks, abandoned the protectorate in 1967. The United States promptly recognized the independence of South Yemen, officially known as the People's Democratic Republic of Yemen, but it criticized the country's Marxist orientation, dependence on the Soviet Union, and support of **terrorism**. American relations with South Yemen were severed in October 1969. South Yemen agreed to the 1990 merger with North Yemen in large part because the strength of its Soviet patron had waned.

American relations with the newly unified Yemen experienced strain. Yemen happened to occupy the Arab seat in the UN Security Council and used that post to oppose U.S. policies during the **Persian Gulf War** of 1990–1991. The United States thus dramatically curtailed its economic aid to the country. In October 2000, terrorists believed to be affiliated with **al-Qaeda** bombed the U.S. Navy destroyer USS *Cole* as it refueled in Aden Harbor, killing 17 U.S. sailors. In subsequent years, the United States resumed economic aid to Yemen as Yemen cracked down on terrorists within the country and cooperated in broad counterterrorism initiatives in the Middle East. *See also* FOREIGN AID.

YOM KIPPUR WAR. *See* ARAB-ISRAELI WAR OF 1973.

YOUNG, ANDREW J. (1932–). American ambassador to the **United Nations** who was forced to resign after he held unauthorized meetings with representatives of the **Palestine Liberation Organization (PLO)**. President **Jimmy Carter** had appointed Young—a Christian clergyman, civil rights activist, and member of Congress—to the post in New York as an indication of his administration's commitment to advancing the interests of the Third World, and Young soon gained a reputation for criticizing Western policies. Disclosure of Young's meeting with the PLO generated sufficient domestic political pressure for Carter to ask for the ambassador's resignation.

– Z –

AL-ZARQAWI, ABU MUSAB (1966–2006). Jordanian-born terrorist killed in June 2006 in a targeted American air strike near Baqubah, north of Baghdad, **Iraq**. A high school dropout and petty criminal in his youth, al-Zarqawi ventured to Afghanistan in the late 1980s to resist Soviet occupation forces in partnership with **Osama bin Laden**. In the 1990s, al-Zarqawi spent seven years in prison in **Jordan** for revolutionary activity. He later fled to Afghanistan, where he reconnected with bin Laden and trained terrorists at camps protected by the Taliban regime.

By 2004, al-Zarqawi had entered Iraq, where he merged his own radical terrorist groups with **al-Qaeda** forces and waged relentless violence against U.S. forces and Iraqi Shiites. He was blamed for hundreds of attacks and suicide bombings designed to provoke civil war between Sunnis and Shiites and to undermine the U.S. occupation of the country. Al-Zarqawi became notorious for beheading his captives and posting videotapes of such deeds on the Internet. American officials offered a $25 million bounty for the capture or killing of al-Zarqawi. His death generated celebrations among members of the Iraqi government but also a new round of terrorist attacks by his allies and supporters.

AL-ZAWAHIRI, AYMAN (1951–). Savvy terrorist who emerged as a major threat to the United States in the 1990s. Zawahiri was born into a prominent Egyptian family of scholars and diplomats, and he was educated as a surgeon. Having flirted as a teenager with the outlawed Muslim Brotherhood, a fundamentalist group, Zawahiri joined the **Egyptian Islamic Jihad** in 1979 and embraced **terrorism**. He was imprisoned in **Egypt** in 1981–1984 for involvement in the conspiracy to assassinate President **Anwar Sadat**. In the mid-1980s, Zawahiri ventured to Afghanistan to battle Soviet occupation forces, becoming a close associate of **Osama bin Laden**, and through the 1990s, Zawahiri helped bin Laden build the **al-Qaeda** terrorist network. Zawahiri masterminded terrorist strikes against Egypt, including the failed assassination attempt on President **Hosni Mubarak** in 1995. In 1998, Zawahiri and bin Laden merged Egyptian Islamic Jihad and al-Qaeda, and Zawahiri became al-Qaeda's deputy leader and chief ideologue.

American officials identified Zawahiri as a major threat in the late 1990s. In 1998, he signed, with bin Laden, an edict calling on Muslims to kill American soldiers and civilians. He was believed to have helped plan the August 1998 bombings of two U.S. embassies in Africa and the **9/11** terrorist attacks in the United States. Zawahiri avoided capture during the **U.S. invasion of Afghanistan** in 2001, and he remained elusive for years thereafter despite massive U.S. efforts to find him. From seclusion, Zawahiri periodically released video and audio messages encouraging the al-Qaeda faithful to continue waging war on the United States, Egypt, Pakistan, and the new regime in **Iraq**.

ZINNI, ANTHONY. Career Marine Corps officer who commanded the U.S. Central Command in 1997–2000 and served as presidential emissary on Israeli–Palestinian issues in 2001–2003. The Central Command post placed Zinni in charge of 36,000 U.S. soldiers based in **Saudi Arabia** and arrayed largely against **Iraq**. As an envoy of President **George W. Bush**, Zinni ventured several times to the Middle East to pressure Israel and the Palestinians to honor the terms of the peace plan formulated by **George Mitchell**, to no avail. Zinni emerged as a prominent critic of the **U.S. invasion of Iraq** in 2003.

ZIONISM. A political ideology favoring the return of the Jewish people from their worldwide diaspora to their ancient homeland in **Palestine** and the establishment of a political state there. Reflecting an ancient cultural connection to Palestine deeply rooted in Jewish scriptures, Zionism spread widely in the 19th century among European Jews, who were inspired by vigorous versions of European nationalism, who experienced various degrees of anti-Semitic oppression, and who had the financial means to fulfill the Zionist vision. Publication of Theodor Herzl's *The Jewish State* in 1896 spread Zionism across Europe. By the early 1900s, tens of thousands of European Jews migrated to Palestine and purchased land and built political and economic institutions there, and Nazi persecution triggered an even greater wave of migration in the 1930s. While Jews accounted for than 10 percent of Palestine's population in 1900, by 1947 they made up nearly one-third of Palestine's estimated 1.9 million residents. Zionism inspired the Jews of Palestine to struggle for the statehood of **Israel**, achieved in 1948, and it thereafter transitioned into Israeli nationalism.

Zionism spread belatedly to the United States. As late as the 1930s, most American Jews were anti-Zionist because they feared that they might be compelled to emigrate to Palestine against their will. German persecution of Jews, which culminated in genocide in the early 1940s, convinced most American Jews to embrace Zionism as a means of safeguarding the surviving remnants of European Jewry. Zionism also became popular among non-Jewish Americans, especially evangelical Christians, who viewed Jews as religious forebears; political liberals, who sympathized with the victims of Nazi Germany; and nativists, who opposed the immigration of European Jews to the United States. The widespread popularity of Zionism in American public opinion helped convince President **Harry S. Truman** to endorse the creation of Israel in 1948. *See also* CHRISTIAN ZIONISM.

Appendix: U.S. Presidents and Secretaries of State

Franklin D. Roosevelt (March 1933–April 1945)
   Cordell Hull (March 1933–November 1944)
   Edward Stettinius Jr. (December 1944–June 1945)

Harry S. Truman (April 1945–January 1953)
   James F. Byrnes (July 1945–January 1947)
   George C. Marshall (January 1947–January 1949)
   Dean G. Acheson (January 1949–January 1953)

Dwight D. Eisenhower (January 1953–January 1961)
   John Foster Dulles (January 1953–April 1959)
   Christian A. Herter (April 1959–January 1961)

John F. Kennedy (January 1961–November 1963)
   Dean Rusk (January 1961– November 1963)

Lyndon B. Johnson (November 1963–January 1969)
   Dean Rusk (November 1963–January 1969)

Richard M. Nixon (January 1969–August 1974)
   William Rogers (January 1969–September 1973)
   Henry Kissinger (September 1973–August 1974)

Gerald R. Ford (August 1974–January 1977)
   Henry Kissinger (August 1974–January 1977)

James Carter (January 1977–January 1981)
   Cyrus R. Vance (January 1977–April 1980)
   Edmund Muskie (May 1980–January1981)

Ronald Reagan (January 1981–January 1989)
    Alexander P. Haig (January 1981–July 1982)
    George P. Shultz (July 1982–January 1989)

George H. W. Bush (January 1989–January 1993)
    James A. Baker III (January 1989–August 1992)
    Lawrence S. Eagleburger (December 1992–January 1993)

William J. Clinton (January 1993–January 2001)
    Warren Christopher (January 1993–January 1997)
    Madeleine Albright (January 1997–January 2001)

George W. Bush (January 2001–)
    Colin Powell (January 2001–January 2005)
    Condoleezza Rice (January 2005–)

Bibliography

This bibliography provides a concise and representative sample of the vast literature published on the history of U.S. diplomacy in the Middle East. Many of the available sources on the U.S. experience in the Middle East are tendentious; this bibliography aims to guide readers seeking further information to sources that reflect scholarly objectivity and detachment rather than polemics. While worthy resources have been published in Arabic, Hebrew, and Persian, moreover, this bibliography, as part of a book intended for an English-speaking audience, is limited by definition to works published in that language.

Researchers seeking primary sources may find a plethora of records in published form. The U.S. Department of State's venerable *Foreign Relations of the United States* series, available in print and online, contains thousands of documents that reveal the making of Middle East policy in the 1940s–1960s. Israel's Ministry of Foreign Affairs published a similar series of volumes, *Documents on the Foreign Policy of Israel*, which covers the same years. Various publications of the National Security Archive contain valuable U.S. government records on specific topics. (Professional historians seeking the original records in archival form should visit such depositories as the National Archives of the United States in College Park, Maryland; various presidential libraries located around the country; the British Public Record Office in London; the Israel State Archive in Jerusalem; and the David Ben-Gurion Library in Sde Boqer, Israel.)

Many excellent reference works assist readers looking for information about the U.S. experience in the Middle East. Published under the auspices of the Society for Historians of American Foreign Relations and edited by Robert L. Beisner, the two-volume *American Foreign Relations since 1600: A Guide to the Literature* provides a comprehensive and annotated catalog of major books and articles in the field of American foreign relations history, including the Middle East. Scarecrow Press has published and is regularly updating a series of reference works on individual countries as well as such topics as warfare, intelligence, organizations, and ethnic groups, which are covered in this book. The historical dictionaries on Israel, Egypt, Saudi Arabia, and the Arab–Israeli conflict, listed here, are particularly noteworthy.

Several books, listed in the sections that follow, deserve special mention as recommended. Excellent overviews of the American experience in the Middle East include Peter L. Hahn, *Crisis and Crossfire: The United States and the Middle East since 1945*; Douglas Little, *American Orientalism: The United States and the Middle East since 1945*; and David Lesch, ed., *The Middle East and the United States: A Historical and Political Reassessment*.

Among the best memoirs by makers of American foreign policy are Jimmy Carter, *The Blood of Abraham*; George Bush and Brent Scowcroft. *A World Transformed*; James Addison Baker, *The Politics of Diplomacy: Revolution, War, and Peace, 1989–1992*; Colin L. Powell, *My American Journey*; Madeleine Korbel Albright, *Madam Secretary*; and Dennis Ross, *The Missing Peace: The Inside Story of the Fight for Middle East Peace*.

While the literature on U.S. diplomacy in the Middle East before World War II is relatively thin, several books are notable in providing important perspectives. Among these are James A. Field, *From Gibraltar to the Middle East: America and the Mediterranean World, 1776–1882*; Ruth Kark, *American Consuls in the Holy Land, 1832–1914*; Bruce Kuklick, *Puritans in Babylon: The Ancient Near East and American Intellectual Life, 1880–1930*; Lester I. Vogel, *To See a Promised Land: Americans and the Holy Land in the Nineteenth Century*; and Yaakov S. Ariel, *On Behalf of Israel: American Fundamentalist Attitudes toward Jews, Judaism, and Zionism, 1865–1945*.

Those interested in U.S. policy regarding the Cold War in the Middle East and the Arab–Israeli conflict during its first four decades would be advised to study Melvyn P. Leffler, *A Preponderance of Power: National Security, the Truman Administration, and the Cold War*; William Roger Louis, *The British Empire in the Middle East, 1945–1951: Arab Nationalism, the United States, and Postwar Imperialism*; Peter L. Hahn, *The United States, Great Britain, and Egypt, 1945–1956: Strategy and Diplomacy in the Early Cold War*; Michael J. Cohen, *Palestine and the Great Powers, 1945–1948*; Peter L. Hahn, *Caught in the Middle East: U.S. Policy toward the Arab-Israeli Conflict, 1945–1961*; Michael B. Oren, *Six Days of War: June 1967 and the Making of the Modern Middle East*; and William B. Quandt, *Decade of Decisions: American Policy toward the Arab-Israeli Conflict, 1967–1976*.

There are also several excellent studies of bilateral relations between the United States and Middle East countries. Such works include Salim Yaqub, *Containing Arab Nationalism: The Eisenhower Doctrine and the Middle East*; Nathan J. Citino, *From Arab Nationalism to OPEC: Eisenhower, King Saud, and the Making of U.S.–Saudi Relations*; Irene L. Gendzier, *Notes from the Minefield: United States Intervention in Lebanon and the Middle East, 1945–1958*; Zach Levey, *Israel and the Western Powers, 1952–1960*; and Warren Bass, *Support Any Friend: Kennedy's Middle East and the Making of the U.S.-Israel Alliance.*

A major concern of American leaders and diplomats, Iran has also attracted the attention of many scholars. The following books deserve wide reading: James A. Bill, *The Eagle and the Lion: The Tragedy of American-Iranian Relations*; Richard W. Cottam, *Iran and the United States: A Cold War Case Study*; Mark J. Gasiorowski, *U.S. Foreign Policy and the Shah: Building a Client State in Iran*; Mary Ann Heiss, *Empire and Nationhood: The United States, Great Britain, and Iranian Oil, 1950–1954*; and Gary Sick, *All Fall Down: America's Tragic Encounter with Iran.*

The Persian Gulf War of 1990–1991 and the U.S. invasion of Iraq in 2003 have stimulated a veritable cottage industry of publishing. Among the best works on these two conflicts are Michael R. Gordon and Bernard E. Trainor, *The Generals' War: The Inside Story of the Conflict in the Gulf*; Dilip Hiro, *Desert Shield to Desert Storm: The Second Gulf War*; Bob Woodward, *The Commanders*; Michael R. Gordon and Bernard E. Trainor, *Cobra 2: The Inside Story of the Invasion and Occupation of Iraq*; and John Keegan, *The Iraq War.*

In recent years, specialists in the history of American foreign policy have examined cultural and other nonofficial aspects of the American people's encounter with the world. Among the books that take such approaches with regard to the Middle East are Edward W. Said, *Orientalism*; Melani McAlister, *Epic Encounters: Culture, Media, and U.S. Interests in the Middle East, 1945–2000*; Paul Boyer, *When Time Shall Be No More: Prophecy Belief in Modern American Culture*; Kathleen Christison, *Perceptions of Palestine: Their Influence on U.S. Middle East Policy*; and Michelle Mart, *Eye on Israel: How America Came to View the Jewish State as an Ally.*

Finally, it is worth mentioning that browsers on the Internet may profit by visiting several noteworthy websites. Reliable news coverage is provided by the *New York Times* and the BBC, while *al-Jazeera* and the *Jerusalem Post* present the news through lenses reflecting Arab and Israeli interests, respectively. The Avalon Project at Yale University offers myriad primary sources on Middle East political and diplomatic history. Thoughtful commentaries on current events are posted at the Council on Foreign Relations and the Informed Comment websites listed here.

Because scholars often publish their findings in articles before books, readers seeking the latest research may also peruse a number of top-flight scholarly journals. Recommended titles include *Diplomatic History*, *Foreign Affairs*, and *Middle East Journal*. A special issue of the *Organization of American Historians Magazine of History*, published in May 2006 and cited here, contains a blend of scholarly essays and lesson plans designed to guide secondary teachers in their classrooms.

REFERENCE WORKS

AbuKhalil, As'ad. *Historical Dictionary of Lebanon*. Lanham, Md.: Scarecrow Press, 1998.

Adamec, Ludwig W. *Historical Dictionary of Islam*. Lanham, Md.: Scarecrow Press, 2001.

Anderson, Sean K., and Stephen Sloan. *Historical Dictionary of Terrorism*. Lanham, Md.: Scarecrow Press, 2002.

Arnold, Guy. *Historical Dictionary of the Non-Aligned Movements and Third World*. Lanham, Md.: Scarecrow Press, 2006.

Beisner, Robert L., ed. *American Foreign Relations since 1600: A Guide to the Literature*. 2 vols. Santa Barbara, Calif.: ABC-CLIO, 2003.

Bennett, A. LeRoy. *Historical Dictionary of the United Nations*. Lanham, Md.: Scarecrow Press, 1995.

Bryson, Thomas A., ed. *United States/Middle East Diplomatic Relations, 1784–1978: An Annotated Bibliography*. Metuchen, N.J.: Scarecrow Press, 1979.

Burrowes, Robert D. *Historical Dictionary of Yemen*. Lanham, Md.: Scarecrow Press, 1995.

Clements, Frank A. *Historical Dictionary of Arab and Islamic Organizations*. Lanham, Md.: Scarecrow Press, 2001.

Commins, David. *Historical Dictionary of Syria*. Lanham, Md.: Scarecrow Press, 2004.

Davis, Simon, and Joseph Smith. *Historical Dictionary of the Cold War*. Lanham, Md.: Scarecrow Press, 2000.

Dougherty, Beth, and Edmund A. Ghareeb. *Historical Dictionary of Iraq*. Lanham, Md.: Scarecrow Press, 2004.

Goldberg, David H., and Bernard Reich. *Political Dictionary of Israel*. Edited by Jon Woronoff. Lanham, Md.: Scarecrow Press, 2000.

Goldschmidt, Arthur, and Robert Johnston. *Historical Dictionary of Egypt*. Lanham, Md.: Scarecrow Press, 2003.

Gubser, Peter. *Historical Dictionary of the Hashemite Kingdom of Jordan*. Lanham, Md.: Scarecrow Press, 1991.

Gunter, Michael M. *Historical Dictionary of the Kurds*. Lanham, Md.: Scarecrow Press, 2003.

Hiro, Dilip. *Dictionary of the Middle East*. New York: St. Martin's Press, 1996.

Kahana, Ephraim. *Historical Dictionary of Israeli Intelligence*. Lanham, Md.: Scarecrow Press, 2006.

Kumaraswamy, P. R. *Historical Dictionary of the Arab-Israeli Conflict*. Lanham, Md.: Scarecrow Press, 2006.

Kuniholm, Bruce R. *The Palestinian Problem and United States Policy: A Guide to Issues and References*. Claremont, Calif.: Regina Books, 1994.

——. *The Persian Gulf and United States Policy: A Guide to Issues and References*. Claremont, Calif.: Regina Books, 1994.

Lin, Lin, and Seth Spaulding. *Historical Dictionary of the United Nations Educational, Scientific and Cultural Organization (UNESCO)*. Lanham, Md.: Scarecrow Press, 1997.

Lorentz, John H. *Historical Dictionary of Iran*. Lanham, Md.: Scarecrow Press, 1995.

Medoff, Rafael, and Chaim I. Waxman. *Historical Dictionary of Zionism*. Lanham, Md.: Scarecrow Press, 2000.

Moussalli, Ahmad. *Historical Dictionary of Islamic Fundamentalist Movements in the Arab World: Iran and Turkey*. Lanham, Md.: Scarecrow Press, 1999.

Nazzal, Nafez Y., and Laila A. Nazzal. *Historical Dictionary of Palestine*. Lanham, Md.: Scarecrow Press, 1997.

Newell, Clayton R. *Historical Dictionary of the Persian Gulf War, 1990–1991*. Lanham, Md.: Scarecrow Press, 1998.

Peck, Malcolm C. *Historical Dictionary of the Gulf Arab States*. Lanham, Md.: Scarecrow Press, 1996.

Peterson, J. E. *Historical Dictionary of Saudi Arabia*. Lanham, Md.: Scarecrow Press, 2003.

Reich, Bernard. *Historical Dictionary of Israel*. Lanham, Md.: Scarecrow Press, 1992.

Reich, Bernard, and Sanford R. Silverburg, eds. *U.S. Foreign Relations with the Middle East and North Africa: A Bibliography*. Lanham, Md.: Scarecrow Press, 1999.

Shavit, David, ed. *The United States in the Middle East: A Historical Dictionary*. New York: Greenwood Press, 1988.

St. John, Ronald Bruce. *Historical Dictionary of Libya*. Lanham, Md.: Scarecrow Press, 2006.

Turner, Michael A. *Historical Dictionary of United States Intelligence*. Lanham, Md.: Scarecrow Press, 2005.

DOCUMENT COLLECTIONS

American-Arab Affairs Council. *Selected Documents Pertaining to U.S.-Arab Relations*. Washington, D.C.: American-Arab Affairs Council, 1990.

Gambone, Michael D., ed. *Documents of American Diplomacy from the American Revolution to the Present*. Westport, Conn.: Greenwood Press, 2002.

Israel. Ministry of Foreign Affairs. *Documents on the Foreign Policy of Israel.* Jerusalem: Ministry of Foreign Affairs, 1976–1997.

Khalidi, Walid, ed. *From Haven to Conquest: Readings in Zionism and the Palestine Problem until 1948.* Washington, D.C.: Institute for Palestine Studies, 1987.

Laqueur, Walter, and Barry Rubin, eds. *The Israel-Arab Reader: A Documentary History of the Middle East Conflict.* 6th ed. New York: Penguin Books, 2001.

Lukacs, Yehuda, ed. *The Israeli-Palestinian Conflict: A Documentary Record.* New York: Cambridge University Press, 1992.

National Commission on Terrorist Attacks upon the United States. *The 9/11 Commission Report: Final Report of the National Commission on Terrorist Attacks upon the United States.* New York: Norton, 2004.

National Security Archive. *Iran: The Making of U.S. Policy, 1977–1980.* Microfiche. Alexandria, Va.: Chadwyck-Healey, 1990.

———. *The Iran-Contra Affair: The Making of a Scandal, 1983–1988.* Microfiche. Alexandria, Va.: Chadwyck-Healey, 1990.

———. *Iraqgate: Saddam Hussein, U.S. Policy, and the Prelude to the Persian Gulf War (1980–1994).* Microfiche. Alexandria, Va.: Chadwyck-Healey, 1995.

U.S. Department of State. *Foreign Relations of the United States.* Washington, D.C.: U.S. Government Printing Office, 1948–.

OVERVIEWS

Bard, Mitchell Geoffrey. *The Water's Edge and Beyond: Defining the Limits to Domestic Influence on United States Middle East Policy.* New Brunswick, N.J.: Transaction Books, 1991.

Brands, H. W. *Into the Labyrinth: The United States and the Middle East, 1945–1993.* New York: McGraw-Hill, 1994.

Bryson, Thomas A. *American Diplomatic Relations with the Middle East, 1784–1975: A Survey.* Metuchen, N.J.: Scarecrow Press, 1977.

Friedman, Thomas L. *From Beirut to Jerusalem.* New York: Farrar, Straus & Giroux, 1989.

Golan, Galia. *Soviet Policies in the Middle East: From World War Two to Gorbachev.* New York: Cambridge University Press, 1990.

Hahn, Peter L. *Crisis and Crossfire: The United States and the Middle East since 1945.* Washington, D.C.: Potomac Books, 2005.

Kaplan, Robert D. *The Arabists: The Romance of an American Elite.* New York: Free Press, 1993.

Kaufman, Burton I. *The Arab Middle East and the United States: Inter-Arab Rivalry and Superpower Diplomacy.* New York: Twayne, 1996.

Kolko, Gabriel. *Confronting the Third World: United States Foreign Policy, 1945–1980.* New York: Pantheon, 1998.

Lenczowski, George. *American Presidents and the Middle East.* Durham, N.C.: Duke University Press, 1990.

Lesch, David W., ed. *The Middle East and the United States: A Historical and Political Reassessment.* Boulder, Colo.: Westview Press, 1999.

Little, Douglas. *American Orientalism: The United States and the Middle East since 1945.* Chapel Hill: University of North Carolina Press, 2002.

Nizameddin, Talal. *Russia and the Middle East: Towards a New Foreign Policy.* New York: St. Martin's Press, 1999.

Parker, Richard Bordeaux. *The Politics of Miscalculation in the Middle East.* Bloomington: Indiana University Press, 1993.

Rodman, Peter W. *More Precious Than Peace: The Cold War and the Struggle for the Third World.* New York: C. Scribner's Sons, 1994.

Rossi, Lorenza. *Who Shall Guard the Guardians Themselves? An Analysis of U.S. Strategy in the Middle East since 1945.* New York: Lang, 1998.

Sayigh, Yezid, and Avi Shlaim, eds. *The Cold War and the Middle East.* Oxford: Clarendon Press, 1997.

Shlaim, Avi. *War and Peace in the Middle East: A Critique of American Policy.* New York: Whittle, 1994.

Tillman, Seth P. *The United States in the Middle East, Interests and Obstacles.* Bloomington: Indiana University Press, 1982.

GOVERNMENT OFFICIALS

Albright, Madeleine Korbel. *Madam Secretary.* New York: Miramax Books, 2003.

AlRoy, Gil C. *The Kissinger Experience: American Policy in the Middle East.* New York: Horizon, 1975.

Baker, James Addison. *The Politics of Diplomacy: Revolution, War, and Peace, 1989–1992.* New York: Putnam, 1995.

Brands, H. W. *The Wages of Globalism: Lyndon Johnson and the Limits of American Power.* New York: Oxford University Press, 1995.

Brzezinski, Zbigniew. *Power and Principle: Memoirs of the National Security Advisor, 1977–1981.* New York: Farrar, Straus & Giroux, 1983.

Bush, George, and Brent Scowcroft. *A World Transformed.* New York: Knopf, 1988.

Carter, Jimmy. *The Blood of Abraham.* Boston: Houghton Mifflin, 1985.

———. *Keeping Faith: Memoirs of a President.* New York: Bantam Books, 1982.

Christopher, Warren. *Chances of a Lifetime.* New York: Scribner, 2001.

———. *In the Stream of History: Shaping Foreign Policy for a New Era.* Stanford, Calif.: Stanford University Press, 1998.

Clarke, Richard A. *Against All Enemies: Inside America's War on Terror.* New York: Free Press, 2004.

Clinton, Bill. *My Life.* New York: Alfred A. Knopf, 2004.

Dann, Uriel. *King Hussein and the Challenge of Arab Radicalism: Jordan 1955–1967.* New York: Oxford University Press, 1989.

Farid, Abdel Magid. *Nasser: The Final Years.* Reading, United Kingdom: Ithaca Press, 1994.

Finklestone, Joseph. *Anwar Sadat: Visionary Who Dared.* Portland, Ore.: Frank Cass, 1996.

Franks, Tommy, with Malcom McConnelly. *American Soldier.* New York: Regan Books, 2004.

Gazit, Mordechai. *President Kennedy's Policy toward the Arab States and Israel: Analysis and Documents.* Tel Aviv: Shiloah Center for Middle Eastern and African Studies, Tel Aviv University, 1983.

Ghanayem, Ishaq I., and Alden H. Voth. *The Kissinger Legacy: American Middle East Policy.* New York: Praeger, 1984.

Golan, Matti. *The Secret Conversations of Henry Kissinger: Step-by-Step Diplomacy in the Middle-East.* Translated by Ruth Geyra Stern and Sol Stern. New York: Quadrangle, 1976.

Haig, Alexander Meigs. *Caveat: Realism, Reagan, and Foreign Policy.* New York: Macmillan, 1984.

Hart, Alan. *Arafat: A Political Biography.* Rev. ed. London: Sidgwick and Jackson, 1994.

Inbar, Efraim. *Rabin and Israel's National Security.* Baltimore, Md.: Johns Hopkins University Press, 1999.

Isaacson, Walter. *Kissinger: A Biography.* New York: Simon & Schuster, 1992.

Johnson, Lyndon B. *The Vantage Point: Perspectives of the Presidency, 1963–1969.* New York: Holt, Rinehart and Winston, 1971.

Karsh, Efraim, and Inari Rautsi. *Saddam Hussein: A Political Biography.* New York: Free Press, 1991.

Moin, Baqer. *Khomeini: Life of the Ayatollah.* New York: St. Martin's Press, 2000.

North, Oliver L., with William Novak. *Under Fire: An American Story.* New York: HarperCollins, 1991.

Powell, Colin L. *My American Journey.* New York: Random House, 1995.

Reagan, Ronald. *An American Life.* New York: Simon & Schuster, 1990.

Ross, Dennis. *The Missing Peace: The Inside Story of the Fight for Middle East Peace.* New York: Farrar, Straus & Giroux, 2004.

Saikal, Amin. *The Rise and Fall of the Shah.* Princeton, N.J.: Princeton University Press, 1980.

Shawcross, William. *The Shah's Last Ride: The Fate of an Ally.* New York: Simon & Schuster, 1988.

Shultz, George Pratt. *Turmoil and Triumph: My Years as Secretary of State.* New York: Scribner's, 1993.

Stephens, Robert. *Nasser: A Political Biography.* New York: Simon & Schuster, 1971.

Vance, Cyrus R. *Hard Choices: Critical Years in America's Foreign Policy.* New York: Simon & Schuster, 1983.

Weinberger, Caspar. *Fighting For Peace: Seven Critical Years in the Pentagon.* New York: Warner, 1990.

U.S. DIPLOMACY TO WORLD WAR I

Bryson, Thomas A. *Tars, Turks, and Tankers: The Role of the United States Navy in the Middle East, 1800–1979.* Metuchen, N.J.: Scarecrow Press, 1980.

Daniel, Robert L. *American Philanthropy in the Near East, 1820–1960.* Athens: Ohio University Press, 1970.

Field, James A. *From Gibraltar to the Middle East: America and the Mediterranean World, 1776–1882.* Chicago: Imprint Publications, 1991.

Gordon, Leland James. *American Relations with Turkey, 1830–1930: An Economic Interpretation.* Philadelphia: University of Pennsylvania Press, 1932.

Grabill, Joseph L. *Protestant Diplomacy and the Near East: Missionary Influence on American Policy, 1810–1927.* Minneapolis: University of Minnesota Press, 1971.

Kark, Ruth. *American Consuls in the Holy Land, 1832–1914.* Detroit, Mich.: Wayne State University Press, 1994.

Kuklick, Bruce. *Puritans in Babylon: The Ancient Near East and American Intellectual Life, 1880–1930.* Princeton, N.J.: Princeton University Press, 1996.

Sha'ban, Fuad. *Islam and Arabs in Early American Thought: Roots of Orientalism in America.* Durham, N.C.: Acorn Press, 1991.

Vogel, Lester I. *To See a Promised Land: Americans and the Holy Land in the Nineteenth Century.* University Park: Pennsylvania State University Press, 1997.

Wright, Lenoir Chambers. *United States Policy toward Egypt, 1831–1914.* New York: Exposition Press, 1969.

INTERWAR YEARS

Ariel, Yaakov S. *On Behalf of Israel: American Fundamentalist Attitudes toward Jews, Judaism, and Zionism, 1865–1945.* Brooklyn, N.Y.: Carlson Publishing, 1991.
Baram, Philip J. *The Department of State in the Middle East, 1919–1945.* Philadelphia: University of Pennsylvania Press, 1978.
Brecher, Frank W. *Reluctant Ally: United States Foreign Policy toward the Jews from Wilson to Roosevelt.* New York: Greenwood Press, 1991.
Cohen, Naomi W. *The Year after the Riots: American Responses to the Palestine Crisis of 1929–30.* Detroit, Mich.: Wayne State University Press, 1988.
Davidson, Lawrence. *America's Palestine: Popular and Official Perceptions from Balfour to Israeli Statehood.* Gainesville: University Press of Florida, 2001.
DeNovo, John A. *American Interests and Policies in the Middle East, 1900–1939.* Minneapolis: University of Minnesota Press, 1963.
Fromkin, David. *A Peace to End All Peace: Creating the Modern Middle East, 1914–1922.* New York: H. Holt, 1989.
Grose, Peter. *Israel in the Mind of America.* New York: Alfred A. Knopf, 1983.
Howard, Harry N. *The Partition of Turkey: A Diplomatic History, 1913–1923.* New York: Fertig, 1966.
Sachar, Howard M. *The Emergence of the Middle East: 1914–1924.* New York: Alfred A. Knopf, 1969.

WORLD WAR II

Bryson, Thomas A. *Seeds of Mideast Crisis: The United States Diplomatic Role in the Middle East during World War II.* Jefferson, N.C.: McFarland, 1981.
Rubin, Barry. *The Great Powers in the Middle East, 1941–1947: The Road to the Cold War.* London: Frank Cass, 1980.

EARLY COLD WAR

Cohen, Michael Joseph. *Fighting World War Three from the Middle East: Allied Contingency Plans, 1945–1954.* London: Frank Cass, 1997.
Devereux, David R. *The Formulation of British Defence Policy towards the Middle East, 1948–56.* New York: St. Martin's Press, 1990.
Kuniholm, Bruce Robellet. *The Origins of the Cold War in the Near East: Great Power Conflict and Diplomacy in Iran, Turkey, and Greece.* Princeton, N.J.: Princeton University Press, 1980.

Leffler, Melvyn P. *A Preponderance of Power: National Security, the Truman Administration, and the Cold War.* Stanford, Calif.: Stanford University Press, 1992.

Louis, William Roger. *The British Empire in the Middle East, 1945–1951: Arab Nationalism, the United States, and Postwar Imperialism.* New York: Oxford University Press, 1984.

ARAB NATIONALISM AND AMERICAN RESPONSES

Ajami, Fouad. *The Arab Predicament: Arab Political Thought and Practice since 1967.* New York: Cambridge University Press, 1992.

———. *The Dream Palace of the Arabs: A Generation's Odyssey.* New York: Pantheon Books, 1998.

Ashton, Nigel John. *Eisenhower, Macmillan, and the Problem of Nasser: Anglo-American Relations and Arab Nationalism, 1955–59.* New York: Macmillan, 1996.

Balfour-Paul, Glen. *The End of Empire in the Middle East: Britain's Relinquishment of Power in Her Last Three Arab Dependencies.* New York: Cambridge University Press, 1991.

Behbehani, Hashim. *The Soviet Union and Arab Nationalism, 1917–1966.* New York: KPI, 1986.

Doran, Michael. *Pan Arabism before Nasser: Egyptian Power Politics and the Palestine Question.* New York: Oxford University Press, 1999.

Gerges, Fawaz A. *The Superpowers and the Middle East: Regional and International Politics, 1955–1967.* Boulder, Colo.: Westview Press, 1994.

Hourani, Albert. *A History of the Arab Peoples.* Cambridge, Mass.: Harvard University Press, 1991.

Persson, Magnus. *Great Britain, the United States, and the Security of the Middle East: The Formation of the Baghdad Pact.* Lund, Sweden: Lund University Press, 1998.

Podeh, Elie. *The Quest for Hegemony in the Arab World: The Struggle over the Baghdad Pact.* New York: Brill, 1995.

Stivers, William. *America's Confrontation with Revolutionary Change in the Middle East, 1948–83.* New York: St. Martin's Press, 1986.

Stookey, Robert. *America and the Arab States: An Uneasy Encounter.* New York: Wiley, 1975.

Takeyh, Ray. *The Origins of the Eisenhower Doctrine: The US, Britain, and Nasser's Egypt, 1953–57.* New York: St. Martin's Press, 2000.

Viorst, Milton. *Sandcastles: The Arabs in Search of the Modern World.* New York: Alfred A. Knopf, 1994.

Yaqub, Salim. *Containing Arab Nationalism: The Eisenhower Doctrine and the Middle East.* Chapel Hill: University of North Carolina Press, 2004.

CULTURAL APPROACHES, MEDIA, AND ORIENTALISM

Boyer, Paul. *When Time Shall Be No More: Prophecy Belief in Modern American Culture.* Cambridge, Mass.: Belknap Press of Harvard University Press, 1992.
Ghareeb, Edmund, ed. *Split Vision: The Portrayal of Arabs in the American Media.* Rev. and expanded ed. Washington, D.C.: American-Arab Affairs Council, 1983.
Kamalipour, Yahya R., ed. *The U.S. Media and the Middle East: Image and Perception.* Westport, Conn.: Greenwood Press, 1995.
Lewis, Bernard. *Islam and the West.* New York: Oxford University Press, 1993.
McAlister, Melani. *Epic Encounters: Culture, Media, and U.S. Interests in the Middle East, 1945–2000.* Berkeley: University of California Press, 2001.
Safty, Adel. *From Camp David to the Gulf: Negotiations, Language and Propaganda, and War.* New York: Black Rose, 1992.
Said, Edward W. *Culture and Imperialism.* New York: Alfred A. Knopf, 1993.
———. *Orientalism.* New York: Vintage, 1988.
Sha'ban, Fuad. *Islam and Arabs in Early American Thought: Roots of Orientalism in America.* Durham, N.C.: Acorn Press, 1995.
Suleiman, Michael W. *The Arabs in the Mind of America.* Brattleboro, Vt.: Amana Books, 1988.
Terry, Janice J. *Mistaken Identity: Arab Stereotypes in Popular Writing.* Washington, D.C.: American-Arab Affairs Council, 1985.
Vogel, Lester Irwin. *To See a Promised Land: Americans and the Holy Land in the Nineteenth Century.* University Park: Pennsylvania State University Press, 1993.

ISLAMIC REVIVAL

Esposito, John L. *The Islamic Threat: Myth or Reality?* 3rd ed. New York: Oxford University Press, 1999.
Gerges, Fawaz A. *America and Political Islam: Clash of Cultures or Clash of Interests?* New York: Cambridge University Press, 1999.
Wright, Robin. *Sacred Rage: The Wrath of Militant Islam.* New York: Simon & Schuster, 2001.

SUEZ CRISIS

Cooper, Chester L. *The Lion's Last Roar: Suez, 1956.* New York: Harper and Row, 1978.
Kingseed, Cole C. *Eisenhower and the Suez Crisis of 1956.* Baton Rouge: Louisiana State University Press, 1995.
Kunz, Diane B. *The Economic Diplomacy of the Suez Crisis.* Chapel Hill: University of North Carolina Press, 1991.
Kyle, Keith. *Suez.* New York: St. Martin's Press, 1991.
Louis, William Roger, and Roger Owen, eds. *Suez 1956: The Crisis and Its Consequences.* New York: Oxford University Press, 1989.
Lucas, Scott. *Divided We Stand: Britain, the U.S. and the Suez Crisis.* London: Hodder and Stoughton, 1991.
Neff, Donald. *Warriors at Suez: Eisenhower Takes America into the Middle East.* New York: Simon & Schuster, 1981.

ARAB–ISRAELI CONFLICT

Arens, Moshe. *Broken Covenant: American Foreign Policy and the Crisis between the U.S. and Israel.* New York: Simon & Schuster, 1995.
Bar-Siman-Tov, Yaacov. *The Israeli-Egyptian War of Attrition, 1969–1970: A Case Study of Limited Local War.* New York: Columbia University Press, 1980.
Bickerton, Ian J., and Carla L. Klausner. *A Concise History of the Arab-Israeli Conflict.* Englewood Cliffs, N.J.: Prentice Hall, 1991.
Caplan, Neil. *Futile Diplomacy.* 4 vols. London: Frank Cass, 1983–1997.
Chomsky, Noam. *Fateful Triangle: The United States, Israel, and the Palestinians.* Boston: South End Press, 1999.
Cobban, Helena. *The Israeli-Syrian Peace Talks: 1991–96 and Beyond.* Washington, D.C.: United States Institute of Peace Press, 1999.
Dupuy, Trevor N. *Elusive Victory: The Arab-Israeli Wars, 1947–1974.* 3rd ed. Dubuque, Iowa: Kendall/Hunt, 1992.
Eisenburg, Laura Zittrain, and Neil Caplan. *Negotiating Arab-Israeli Peace: Patterns, Problems, and Possibilities.* Bloomington: Indiana University Press, 1998.
Finkelstein, Norman G. *Image and Reality of the Israel-Palestine Conflict.* New ed. New York: Verso, 2001.
Feuerwerger, Marvin C. *Congress and Israel: Foreign Aid Decision-Making in the House of Representatives, 1969–1976.* Westport, Conn.: Greenwood Press, 1979.
Freiberger, Steven Z. *Dawn over Suez: The Rise of American Power in the Middle East, 1953–1957.* Chicago: Dee, 1992.

Gilboa, Eytan. *American Public Opinion toward Israel and the Arab-Israeli Conflict.* Lexington, Mass.: Lexington Books, 1987.

Ilan, Amitzur. *Bernadotte in Palestine, 1948: A Study in Contemporary Humanitarian Knight-Errantry.* Basingstoke: Macmillan, 1989.

Korn, David A. *Stalemate: The War of Attrition and Great Power Diplomacy in the Middle East, 1967–1970.* Boulder, Colo.: Westview Press, 1992.

Lowi, Miriam R. *Water and Power: The Politics of a Scarce Resource in the Jordan River Basin.* New York: Cambridge University Press, 1993.

Morris, Benny. *Righteous Victims: A History of the Zionist-Arab Conflict, 1881–1999.* New York: Alfred A. Knopf, 1999.

Quandt, William B. *Camp David: Peacemaking and Politics.* Washington, D.C.: Brookings Institution Press, 1986.

———. *Decade of Decisions: American Policy toward the Arab-Israeli Conflict, 1967–1976.* Washington, D.C.: Brookings Institution Press, 1993.

———. *Peace Process: American Diplomacy and the Arab-Israeli Conflict since 1967.* Rev. ed. Washington, D.C.: Brookings Institution Press, 2001.

Rabinovich, Itamar. *The Brink of Peace: The Israeli-Syrian Negotiations.* Princeton, N.J.: Princeton University Press, 1998.

———. *The Road Not Taken: Early Arab-Israeli Negotiations.* New York: Oxford University Press, 1991.

———. *Waging Peace: Israel and the Arabs at the End of the Century.* New York: Farrar, Straus & Giroux, 1999.

Reich, Bernard. *Quest for Peace: U.S.-Israel Relations and the Arab-Israeli Conflict.* New Brunswick, N.J.: Transaction Books, 1977.

Saunders, Harold H. *The Other Walls: The Politics of the Arab-Israeli Peace Process.* Rev. ed. Princeton, N.J.: Princeton University Press, 1991.

Savir, Uri. *The Process: 1,100 Days That Changed the Middle East.* New York: Random House, 1998.

Shlaim, Avi. *The Iron Wall: Israel and the Arab World.* New York: Norton, 2000.

Shpiro, David H. *From Philanthropy to Activism: The Political Transformation of American Zionism in the Holocaust Years, 1933–1945.* New York: Pergamon Press, 1994.

Spiegel, Steven L. *The Other Arab-Israeli Conflict: Making America's Middle East Policy from Truman to Reagan.* Chicago: University of Chicago Press, 1985.

Spiegel, Steven L., ed. *The Arab-Israeli Search for Peace.* Boulder, Colo.: Lynne Rienner, 1992.

Stein, Kenneth W. *Heroic Diplomacy: Sadat, Kissinger, Carter, Begin, and the Quest for Arab-Israeli Peace.* New York: Routledge, 1999.

Tessler, Mark. *A History of the Israeli-Palestinian Conflict.* Bloomington: Indiana University Press, 1994.

Tivnan, Edward. *The Lobby: Jewish Political Power and American Foreign Policy.* New York: Simon & Schuster, 1987.

ARAB-ISRAELI WAR OF 1967

Bar-Zohar, Michael. *Embassies in Crisis: Diplomats and Demagogues behind the Six-Day War.* Translated by Monroe Stearns. Englewood Cliffs, N.J.: Prentice Hall, 1970.
Gerges, Fawaz A. "The 1967 Arab-Israeli War: U.S. Actions and Arab Perceptions." In *The Middle East and the United States: A Historical and Political Reassessment,* edited by David W. Lesch. Boulder, Colo.: Westview Press, 1999.
Mutawi, Samir A. *Jordan in the 1967 War.* New York: Cambridge University Press, 1987.
Neff, Donald. *Warriors for Jerusalem: The Six Days That Changed the Middle East.* New York: Simon & Schuster, 1984.
Oren, Michael B. *Six Days of War: June 1967 and the Making of the Modern Middle East.* New York: Oxford University Press, 2002.
Parker, Richard B., ed. *The Six-Day War: A Retrospective.* Gainesville: University Press of Florida, 1996.

ARAB-ISRAELI WAR OF 1973

Bulloch, John. *The Making of a War: The Middle East from 1967 to 1973.* London: Longman, 1974.
Dowty, Alan. *Middle East Crisis: U.S. Decision-Making in 1958, 1970 and 1973.* Berkeley: University of California Press, 1984.
Heikal, Mohamed. *The Road to Ramadan.* New York: Quadrangle, 1975.
Israelyan, Victor. *Inside the Kremlin during the Yom Kippur War.* University Park: Pennsylvania State University Press, 1995.
Neff, Donald. *Warriors against Israel: America Comes to the Rescue in 1973.* Brattleboro, Vt.: Amana Books, 1988.
Parker, Richard B., ed. *The October War: A Retrospective.* Gainesville: University Press of Florida, 2001.

EGYPT

Burns, William J. *Economic Aid and American Policy toward Egypt, 1955–1981.* Albany: State University of New York Press, 1985.

Dekmejian, R. Hrair. *Egypt under Nasir: A Study in Political Dynamics.* Albany: State University of New York Press, 1971.
Hahn, Peter L. *The United States, Great Britain, and Egypt, 1945–1956: Strategy and Diplomacy in the Early Cold War.* Chapel Hill: University of North Carolina Press, 1991.
Holland, Matthew F. *America and Egypt: From Roosevelt to Eisenhower.* Westport, Conn.: Praeger, 1996.
Tripp, Charles, and Roger Owen, eds. *Egypt under Mubarak.* New York: Routledge, 1989.

IRAN

Arjomand, Said Amir. *The Turban for the Crown: The Islamic Revolution in Iran.* New York: Oxford University Press, 1988.
Bakhash, Shaul. *The Reign of the Ayatollahs: Iran and the Islamic Revolution.* Rev. ed. New York: Basic Books, 1990.
Bani-Sadr, and Abol Hassan. *My Turn to Speak: Iran, the Revolution and Secret Deals with the U.S.* Washington, D.C.: Brassey's, 1991.
Bill, James A. *The Eagle and the Lion: The Tragedy of American-Iranian Relations.* New Haven, Conn.: Yale University Press, 1988.
Buhite, Russell D. *Lives at Risk: Hostages and Victims in American Foreign Policy.* Wilmington, Del.: Scholarly Resources, 1995.
Christopher, Warren, et al., eds. *American Hostages in Iran: The Conduct of a Crisis.* New Haven, Conn.: Yale University Press, 1985.
Cottam, Richard W. *Iran and the United States: A Cold War Case Study.* Pittsburgh: University of Pittsburgh Press, 1988.
David, Charles-Philippe, Nancy Ann Carrol, and Zachary A. Selden. *Foreign Policy Failure in the White House: Reappraising the Fall of the Shah and the Iran-Contra Affair.* Lanham, Md.: University Press of America, 1993.
Dorman, William A., and Mansour Farhang. *The U.S. Press and Iran: Foreign Policy and the Journalism of Deference.* Berkeley: University of California Press, 1987.
Gasiorowski, Mark J. *U.S. Foreign Policy and the Shah: Building a Client State in Iran.* Ithaca, N.Y.: Cornell University Press, 1991.
Goode, James F. *The United States and Iran, 1946–51: The Diplomacy of Neglect.* New York: St. Martin's Press, 1989.
———. *The United States and Iran: In the Shadow of Musaddiq.* New York: St. Martin's Press, 1997.
Heiss, Mary Ann. *Empire and Nationhood: The United States, Great Britain, and Iranian Oil, 1950–1954.* New York: Columbia University Press, 1997.

Honeggar, Barbara. *October Surprise.* New York: Tudor, 1989.
Fawcett, Louise L'Estrange. *Iran and the Cold War: The Azerbaijan Crisis of 1946.* New York: Cambridge University Press, 1992.
Keddie, Nikki R., and Mark J. Gasiorowski, eds. *Neither East nor West: Iran, the Soviet Union, and the United States.* New Haven, Conn.: Yale University Press, 1990.
Keddie, Nikki R., with Yann Richard. *Roots of Revolution: An Interpretive History of Modern Iran.* New Haven, Conn.: Yale University Press, 1981.
Kemp, Geoffrey. *Forever Enemies? American Policy and the Islamic Republic of Iran.* New York: Carnegie Endowment, 1994.
Ledeen, Michael A., and William Lewis. *Debacle: The American Failure in Iran.* New York: Alfred A. Knopf, 1981.
Lytle, Mark H. *The Origins of the Iranian-American Alliance, 1941–1953.* New York: Holmes and Meier, 1987.
Moses, Russell Leigh. *Freeing the Hostages: Reexamining U.S.-Iranian Negotiations and Soviet Policy, 1979–1981.* Pittsburgh: University of Pittsburgh Press, 1996.
Palmer, Michael A. *Guardians of the Gulf: A History of America's Expanding Role in the Persian Gulf, 1833–1992.* New York: Free Press, 1992.
Peimani, Hooman. *Iran and the United States: The Rise of the West Asian Regional Grouping.* Westport, Conn.: Praeger, 1999.
Ramazani, R. K. *Iran's Foreign Policy, 1941–1973: A Study of Foreign Policy in Modernizing Nations.* Charlottesville: University Press of Virginia, 1975.
———. *Revolutionary Iran: Challenge and Response in the Middle East.* Baltimore, Md.: Johns Hopkins University Press, 1986.
Rubin, Barry. *Paved with Good Intentions: The American Experience and Iran.* New York: Oxford University Press, 1980.
Sick, Gary. *All Fall Down: America's Tragic Encounter with Iran.* New York: Random House, 1985.
———. *October Surprise: America's Hostages in Iran and the Election of Ronald Reagan.* New York: Random House, 1991.
Woodward, Bob. *Veil: The Secret Wars of the CIA, 1981–1987.* New York: Simon & Schuster, 1987.

IRAQ

Batatu, Hanna. *The Old Social Classes and the Revolutionary Movements of Iraq: A Study of Iraq's Old Landed and Commercial Classes and of Its Communists, Ba'athists, and Free Officers.* Princeton, N.J.: Princeton University Press, 1978.

Bulloch, John, and Harvey Morris. *No Friends but the Mountains: The Tragic History of the Kurds.* New York: Oxford University Press, 1992.

Farouk-Sluglett, Marion, and Peter Sluglett. *Iraq since 1958: From Revolution to Dictatorship.* Rev. ed. New York: I. B. Tauris, 2001.

Friedman, Alan. *Spider's Web: The Secret History of How the White House Illegally Armed Iraq.* New York: Bantam, 1993.

Gordon, Michael R., and Bernard E. Trainor. *Cobra 2: The Inside Story of the Invasion and Occupation of Iraq.* New York: Pantheon, 2006.

Hazelton, Fran, ed. *Iraq since the Gulf War: Prospects for Democracy.* London: Zed, 1994.

Jentleson, Bruce W. *With Friends Like These: Reagan, Bush, and Saddam, 1982–1990.* New York: Norton, 1994.

Karabell, Zachary, and Philip D. Zelikow. *Prelude to War: U.S. Policy toward Iraq, 1988–1990.* Cambridge, Mass.: Kennedy School of Government, Harvard University, 1994.

Keegan, John. *The Iraq War.* New York: Alfred A. Knopf, 2004.

Khadduri, Majid, and Edmund Ghareed. *War in the Gulf, 1990–91: The Iraq-Kuwait Conflict and Its Implications.* New York: Oxford University Press, 1997.

Khalil, Samir Al. *Republic of Fear: The Politics of Modern Iraq.* Updated ed. Berkeley: University of California Press, 1990.

Palmer, Michael A. *Guardians of the Gulf: A History of America's Expanding Role in the Persian Gulf, 1833–1992.* New York: Free Press, 1992.

Smolansky, Oles M., and Bettie M. Smolansky. *The USSR and Iraq: The Soviet Quest for Influence.* Durham, N.C.: Duke University Press, 1991.

Timmerman, Kenneth R. *The Death Lobby: How the West Armed Iraq.* Boston: Houghton Mifflin, 1991.

Wurmser, David. *Tyranny's Ally: America's Failure to Defeat Saddam Hussein.* Washington, D.C.: AEI Press, 1999.

ISRAEL

Alteras, Isaac. *Eisenhower and Israel: U.S.-Israeli Relations, 1953–1960.* Gainesville: University Press of Florida, 1993.

Bain, Kenneth Ray. *The March to Zion: United States Policy and the Founding of Israel.* College Station: Texas A&M University Press, 1979.

Ball, George W., and Douglas B. Ball. *The Passionate Attachment: America's Involvement with Israel, 1947 to the Present.* New York: Norton, 1992.

Bar-On, Mordechai. *In Pursuit of Peace: A History of the Israeli Peace Movement.* Washington, D.C.: United States Institute of Peace Press, 1996.

Bass, Warren. *Support Any Friend: Kennedy's Middle East and the Making of the U.S.-Israel Alliance.* New York: Oxford University Press, 2003.
Benson, Michael T. *Harry S. Truman and the Founding of Israel.* Westport, Conn.: Praeger, 1997.
Ben-Zvi, Abraham. *Decade of Transition: Eisenhower, Kennedy, and the Origins of the American-Israeli Alliance.* New York: Columbia University Press, 1998.
——. *The United States and Israel: The Limits of the Special Relationship.* New York: Columbia University Press, 1993.
Berman, Aaron. *Nazism, the Jews, and American Zionism, 1933–1948.* Detroit: Wayne State University Press, 1990.
Blitzer, Wolf. *Territory of Lies: The Exclusive Story of Jonathan Jay Pollard, the American Who Spied on His Country for Israel and How He Was Betrayed.* New York: Harper and Row, 1989.
Brecher, Michael, with Benjamin Geist. *Decisions in Crisis: Israel 1967 and 1973.* Berkeley: University of California Press, 1980.
Cockburn, Andrew, and Leslie Cockburn. *Dangerous Liaison: The Inside Story of the U.S.-Israeli Covert Relationship.* New York: HarperCollins, 1991.
Cohen, Avner. *Israel and the Bomb.* New York: Columbia University Press, 1998.
Druks, Herbert J. *John F. Kennedy and Israel.* Westport, Conn.: Praeger, 2005.
——. *The U.S. and Israel, 1945–1990.* New York: Speller, 1991.
Ennes, James M., Jr. *Assault on the Liberty: The True Story of the Israeli Attack on an American Intelligence Ship.* New York: Random House, 1979.
Feldman, Shai. *Israeli Nuclear Deterrence: A Strategy for the 1980s.* New York: Columbia University Press, 1982.
Findley, Paul. *They Dare to Speak Out: People and Institutions Confront Israel's Lobby.* Chicago: Lawrence Hill Books, 1985.
Green, Stephen. *Living by the Sword: America and Israel in the Middle East, 1968–87.* Brattleboro, Vt.: Amana Books, 1988.
——. *Taking Sides, America's Secret Relations with a Militant Israel.* New York: William Morrow, 1984.
Hahn, Peter L. *Caught in the Middle East: U.S. Policy toward the Arab-Israeli Conflict, 1945–1961.* Chapel Hill: University of North Carolina Press, 2004.
Hersh, Seymour M. *The Samson Option: Israel's Nuclear Arsenal and American Foreign Policy.* New York: Random House, 1991.
Hussain, Asaf. *The United States and Israel: Politics of a Special Relationship.* Islamabad: Quaid-I-Azam University Press, 1991.
Klieman, Aaron S. *Israel and the World after 20 Years.* Washington, D.C.: Pergamon-Brassey's, 1990.
Klinghoffer, Judith A. *Vietnam, Jews, and the Middle East: Unintended Consequences.* New York: St. Martin's Press, 1999.

Levey, Zach. *Israel and the Western Powers, 1952–1960.* Chapel Hill: University of North Carolina Press, 1997.

Mansour, Camille. *Beyond Alliance: Israel and U.S. Foreign Policy.* Translated by James A. Cohen. New York: Columbia University Press, 1994.

Mart, Michelle. *Eye on Israel: How America Came to View the Jewish State as an Ally.* Albany: State University of New York Press, 2006.

Melman, Yossi, and Dan Raviv. *Friends in Deed: Inside the U.S.-Israel Alliance.* New York: Hyperion, 1994.

Netanyahu, Benjamin. *A Durable Peace: Israel and Its Place among the Nations.* Rev. ed. New York: Warner Books, 2000.

Pollock, David. *The Politics of Pressure: American Arms and Israeli Policy since the Six Day War.* Westport, Conn.: Greenwood Press, 1982.

Reich, Bernard. *Securing the Covenant: United States-Israeli Relations after the Cold War.* Westport, Conn.: Greenwood Press, 1995.

———. *The United States and Israel: Influence in the Special Relationship.* New York: Praeger, 1984.

Rubenberg, Cheryl A. *Israel and the American National Interest: A Critical Examination.* Urbana: University of Illinois Press, 1986.

Sachar, Howard M. *A History of Israel: From the Rise of Zionism to Our Time.* 2nd ed. New York: Alfred A. Knopf, 1996.

Safran, Nadav. *Israel, the Embattled Ally.* Cambridge, Mass.: Harvard University Press, 1981.

Schiff, Ze'ev, and Ehud Ya'ari. *Israel's Lebanon War.* Translated by Ina Friedman. New York: Simon & Schuster, 1984.

Schoenbaum, David. *The United States and the State of Israel.* New York: Oxford University Press, 1993.

Sheffer, Gabriel, ed. *U.S.-Israeli Relations at the Crossroads.* Portland, Ore.: Frank Cass, 1997.

Slonim, Shlomo. *Jerusalem in America's Foreign Policy, 1947–1997.* Boston: Kluwer Law International, 1998.

JORDAN

Al Madfai, Madiha Rashid. *Jordan, the United States, and the Middle East Peace Process, 1974–1991.* New York: Cambridge University Press, 1993.

Day, Arthur R. *East Bank/West Bank: Jordan and the Prospects for Peace.* New York: Council on Foreign Relations, 1986.

Lynch, Marc. *State Interests and Public Spheres: The International Politics of Jordan's Identity.* New York: Columbia University Press, 1999.

Salibi, Kamal. *The Modern History of Jordan.* New York: I. B. Tauris, 1993.

LEBANON

El-Khazen, Farid. *The Breakdown of the State in Lebanon, 1967–1976*. Cambridge, Mass.: Harvard University Press, 2000.
Fisk, Robert. *Pity the Nation: The Abduction of Lebanon*. New York: Atheneum, 1990.
Friedman, Thomas L. *From Beirut to Jerusalem*. Updated with a new chapter. New York: Doubleday, 1995.
Gendzier, Irene L. *Notes from the Minefield: United States Intervention in Lebanon and the Middle East, 1945–1958*. New York: Columbia University Press, 1997.
Gilmour, David. *Lebanon: The Fractured Country*. New York: St. Martin's Press, 1983.
Hallenbeck, Ralph A. *Military Force as an Instrument of U.S. Foreign Policy: Intervention in Lebanon, August 1982–February 1984*. New York: Praeger, 1991.
Hiro, Dilip. *Lebanon: Fire and Embers: A History of the Lebanese Civil War*. New York: St. Martin's Press, 1993.
Hudson, Michael C. *The Precarious Republic: Political Modernization in Lebanon*. New York: Random House, 1968.
Korbani, Agnes G. *U.S. Intervention in Lebanon, 1958 and 1982*. New York: Praeger, 1991.
Picard, Elizabeth. *Lebanon, a Shattered Country: Myths and Realties of the Wars in Lebanon*. Translated by Franklin Philip. New York: Holmes and Meier, 1996.
Rabinovich, Itamar. *The War for Lebanon, 1970–1985*. Rev. ed. Ithaca, N.Y.: Cornell University Press, 1985.
Salem, Elie A. *Violence and Diplomacy in Lebanon: The Troubled Years, 1982–1988*. New York: St. Martin's Press, 1995.

NORTH AFRICA

Anderson, Lisa. *The State and Social Transformation in Tunisia and Libya, 1830–1980*. Princeton, N.J.: Princeton University Press, 1986.
Connelly, Matthew. *A Diplomatic Revolution: Algeria's Fight for Independence and the Origins of the Post–Cold War Era*. New York: Oxford University Press, 2002.
Cooley, John K. *Libyan Sandstorm*. New York: Holt, Rinehart and Winston, 1982.
Davis, Brian L. *Qaddafi, Terrorism, and the Origins of the U.S. Attack on Libya*. New York: Praeger, 1990.

ElWarfally, Mahmoud G. *Imagery and Ideology in U.S. Policy toward Libya, 1969–1982*. Pittsburgh: University of Pittsburgh Press, 1988.

Gallagher, Charles F. *The United States and North Africa: Morocco, Algeria, and Tunisia*. Cambridge, Mass.: Harvard University Press, 1963.

Haley, P. Edward. *Qaddafi and the United States since 1969*. New York: Praeger, 1984.

Hall, Luella J. *The United States and Morocco, 1776–1956*. Metuchen, N.J.: Scarecrow Press, 1971.

Horne, Alistair. *A Savage War of Peace: Algeria 1954–1962*. Rev. ed. New York: Penguin, 1987.

Stone, Martin. *The Agony of Algeria*. New York: Columbia University Press, 1997.

Willis, Michael. *The Islamist Challenge in Algeria: A Political History*. New York: New York University Press, 1997.

OIL

Bromley, Simon. *American Hegemony and World Oil: The Industry, the State System, and the World Economy*. Cambridge: Polity Press, 1991.

Casillas, Rex J. *Oil and Diplomacy: The Evolution of American Foreign Policy in Saudi Arabia, 1933–1945*. New York: Garland, 1987.

Gause, F. Gregory, III. *Oil Monarchies: Domestic and Security Challenges in the Arab Gulf States*. New York: Council on Foreign Relations Press, 1994.

Han, Vo Xuan. *Oil, the Persian Gulf, and the United States*. Westport, Conn.: Praeger, 1994.

Hollis, Rosemary, ed. *Oil and Regional Developments in the Gulf*. London: RIIA, 1998.

Nash, Gerald D. *United States Oil Policy, 1890–1964: Business and Government in Twentieth Century America*. Pittsburgh: University of Pittsburgh Press, 1968.

Sampson, Anthony. *The Seven Sisters: The Great Oil Companies and the World They Made*. New York: Viking, 1975.

Shwadran, Benjamin. *The Middle East, Oil, and the Great Powers*. 3rd ed. New York: Wiley, 1974.

Stivers, William. *Supremacy and Oil: Iraq, Turkey, and the Anglo-American World Order, 1918–1930*. Ithaca, N.Y.: Cornell University Press, 1982.

Stoff, Michael B. *Oil, War, and American Security: The Search for a National Policy on Foreign Oil, 1941–1947*. New Haven, Conn.: Yale University Press, 1980.

Yergin, Daniel. *The Prize: The Epic Quest for Oil, Money, and Power*. New York: Simon & Schuster, 1991.

PALESTINE

Arzt, Donna E. *Refugees into Citizens: Palestinians and the End of Arab-Israeli Conflict*. New York: Council on Foreign Relations Press, 1997.
Christison, Kathleen. *Perceptions of Palestine: Their Influence on U.S. Middle East Policy*. Berkeley: University of California Press, 1999.
Cohen, Michael J. *Palestine and the Great Powers, 1945–1948*. Princeton, N.J.: Princeton University Press, 1982.
Dannreuther, Roland. *The Soviet Union and the PLO*. New York: St. Martin's Press, 1998.
Haron, Miriam Joyce. *Palestine and the Anglo-American Connection, 1945–1950*. New York: Peter Lang, 1986.
Kochavi, Arieh J. *Post-Holocaust Politics: Britain, the United States and Jewish Refugees, 1945–1948*. Chapel Hill: University of North Carolina Press, 2001.
Kolinsky, Martin. *Law, Order, and Riots in Mandatory Palestine, 1928–35*. New York: St. Martin's Press, 1993.
Leeuwen, Marianne van. *Americans and the Palestinian Question: The US Public Debate on Palestinian Nationhood, 1973–1988*. Atlanta: Rodopi, 1993.
Mishal, Shaul, and Avraham Sela. *The Palestinian Hamas: Vision, Violence, and Coexistence*. New York: Columbia University Press, 2000.
Neff, Donald. *Fallen Pillars: U.S. Policy towards Palestine and Israel since 1945*. Washington, D.C.: Institute for Palestine Studies, 1995.
Quandt, William B., Fuad Jabber, and Ann M. Lesch. *The Politics of Palestinian Nationalism*. Berkeley: University of California Press, 1973.
Rabie, Muhammed. *Palestine to Israel: From Mandate to Independence*. London: Frank Cass, 1988.
———. *U.S.-PLO Dialogue: Secret Diplomacy and Conflict Resolution*. Gainesville: University Press of Florida, 1995.
Rubin, Barry. *Revolution until Victory? The Politics and History of the PLO*. Cambridge, Mass.: Harvard University Press, 1994.
———. *The Transformation of Palestinian Politics: From Revolution to State-Building*. Cambridge, Mass.: Harvard University Press, 1999.
Shadid, Mohammed K. *The United States and the Palestinians*. New York: St. Martin's Press, 1981.
Sicherman, Harvey. *Palestinian Autonomy, Self-Government and Peace*. Boulder, Colo.: Westview Press, 1993.
Smith, Charles D. *Palestine and the Arab-Israeli Conflict*. 4th ed. New York: St. Martin's Press, 2001.
Suleiman, Michael W., ed. *U.S. Policy on Palestine: From Wilson to Clinton*. Normal, Ill.: Association for Arab-American, University Graduates, 1995.

Victor, Barbara. *A Voice of Reason: Hanan Ashrawi and Peace in the Middle East.* New York: Harcourt Brace, 1994.

PERSIAN GULF

Hiro, Dilip. *The Longest War: The Iran–Iraq Military Conflict.* New York: Routledge, 1991.
Joyce, Miriam. *Kuwait, 1945–1996: An Anglo-American Perspective.* London: Cass, 1998.
Kupchan, Charles A. *The Persian Gulf and the West: The Dilemmas of Security.* Boston: Allen and Unwin, 1987.
Palmer, Michael A. *Guardians of the Gulf: A History of America's Expanding Role in the Persian Gulf, 1833–1992.* New York: Free Press, 1992.
Yetive, Steve A. *America and the Persian Gulf: The Third Party Dimension in World Politics.* Westport, Conn.: Praeger, 1995.

PERSIAN GULF WAR

Atkinson, Rick. *Crusade: The Untold Story of the Persian Gulf War.* Boston: Houghton Mifflin, 1993.
Brune, Lester H. *America and the Iraqi Crisis, 1990–1992: Origins and Aftermath.* Claremont, Calif.: Regina Books, 1993.
Bulloch, John, and Harvey Morris. *Saddam's War: The Origins of the Kuwait Conflict and the International Response.* Boston: Faber & Faber, 1991.
Clark, Ramsey. *The Fire This Time: U.S. War Crimes in the Gulf.* New York: Thunder's Mouth Press, 1992.
Clawson, Patrick L., ed. *Iraq Strategy Review: Options for U.S. Policy.* Washington, D.C.: Washington Institute for Near East Policy, 1998.
Cooley, John K. *Payback: America's Long War in the Middle East.* Washington D.C.: Brassey's, 1991.
Cordesman, Anthony H., and Abraham R. Wagner. *Lessons of Modern War. Vol. 4: The Gulf War.* Boulder, Colo.: Westview Press, 1996.
DeCosse, David E., ed. *But Was It Just? Reflections on the Morality of the Persian Gulf War.* New York: Doubleday, 1992.
Ekeus, Rolf. *The Iraq Experience and Multilateral Approaches to Controlling Nuclear Proliferation.* Livermore, Calif.: Lawrence Livermore National Laboratory, University of California, 1993.

Freedman, Lawrence, and Efraim Karsh. *The Gulf Conflict, 1990–1991: Diplomacy and War in the New World Order.* Princeton, N.J.: Princeton University Press, 1993.

Friedman, Norman. *Desert Victory: The War for Kuwait.* Updated ed. Annapolis, Md.: Naval Institute Press, 1992.

Gordon, Michael R., and Bernard E. Trainor. *The Generals' War: The Inside Story of the Conflict in the Gulf.* Boston: Little, Brown, 1995.

Graham-Brown, Sarah. *Sanctioning Saddam: The Politics of Intervention in Iraq.* New York: I. B. Tauris, 1999.

Graubard, Stephen R. *Mr. Bush's War: Adventures in the Politics of Illusion.* New York: Hill & Wang, 1992.

Hawley, T. M. *Against the Fires of Hell: The Environmental Disaster of the Gulf War.* San Diego, Calif.: Harcourt Brace Jovanovich, 1992.

Hilsman, Rober. *George Bush vs. Saddam Hussein: Military Success! Political Failure?* Novato, Calif.: Lyford Books, 1992.

Hiro, Dilip. *Desert Shield to Desert Storm: The Second Gulf War.* New York: Routledge, 1992.

Johnson, James Turner, and George Weigel. *Just War and the Gulf War.* Washington, D.C.: Ethics and Public Policy Center, 1991.

Khadduri, Majid, and Edmund Ghareeb. *War in the Gulf, 1990–91: The Iraq-Kuwait Conflict and Its Implications.* New York: Oxford University Press, 1997.

Miller, Judith, and Laurie Mylroie. *Saddam Hussein and the Crisis in the Gulf.* New York: Times Books, 1990.

Scales, Robert H., Jr. *Certain Victory: The U.S. Army in the Gulf War.* Washington, D.C.: Office of the Chief of Staff, United States Army, 1993.

Schubert, Frank N., and Theresa L. Kraus. *The Whirlwind War: The United States Army in Operations Desert Shield and Desert Storm.* Washington, D.C.: Center of Military History, United States Army, 1995.

Sciolino, Elaine. *The Outlaw State: Saddam Hussein's Quest for Power and the Gulf Crisis.* New York: Wiley, 1991.

Sifry, Micah L., and Christopher Cerf, eds. *The Gulf War Reader: History, Documents, Opinions.* New York: Times Books, 1991.

Smith, Jean Edward. *George Bush's War.* New York: Henry Holt, 1992.

Teicher, Howard, and Gayle Radley Teicher. *Twin Pillars to Desert Storm: America's Flawed Vision in the Middle East From Nixon to Bush.* New York: Morrow, 1993.

Whicker, Marcia Lynn, James P. Pfiffner, and Raymond A. Moore, eds. *The Presidency and the Persian Gulf War.* Westport, Conn.: Praeger, 1993.

Woodward, Bob. *The Commanders.* New York: Simon & Schuster, 1991.

SAUDI ARABIA

Abir, Mordechai. *Saudi Arabia: Government, Society, and the Gulf Crisis.* New York: Routledge, 1993.

Aburish, Said K. *The Rise, Corruption, and Coming Fall of the House of Saud.* New York: St. Martin's Press, 1995.

Emerson, Steven. *The American House of Saud: The Secret Petrodollar Connection.* New York: F. Watts, 1985.

Hart, Parker T. *Saudi Arabia and the United States: Birth of a Security Partnership.* Bloomington: Indiana University Press, 1998.

Holden, David, and Richard Johns. *The House of Saud: The Rise and Rule of the Most Powerful Dynasty in the Arab World.* New York: Holt, Rinehart and Winston, 1982.

Long, David E. *The United States and Saudi Arabia: Ambivalent Allies.* Boulder, Colo.: Westview Press, 1985.

Safran, Nadav. *Saudi Arabia: The Ceaseless Quest for Security.* Cambridge, Mass.: Belknap Press of Harvard University Press, 1985.

Wilson, Peter W., and Douglas F. Graham. *Saudi Arabia: The Coming Storm.* Armonk, N.Y.: M. E. Sharpe, 1994.

SYRIA

Batatu, Hanna. *Syria's Peasantry, the Descendants of Its Lesser Rural Noables, and Their Politics.* Princeton, N.J.: Princeton University Press, 1999.

Devlin, John F. *Syria: Modern State in an Ancient Land.* Boulder, Colo.: Westview Press, 1983.

Lesch, David W. *Syria and the United States: Eisenhower's Cold War in the Middle East.* Boulder, Colo.: Westview Press, 1992.

Rabinovich, Itamar. *Syria under the Ba'th, 1963–1966: The Army Party Symbiosis.* Jerusalem: Israel Universities Press, 1972.

Saunders, Bonnie F. *The United States and Arab Nationalism: The Syrian Case, 1953–1960.* Westport, Conn.: Praeger, 1996.

TERRORISM

Alexander, Yonah, ed. *Middle East Terrorism: Current Threats and Future Prospects.* New York: G. K. Hall, 1994.

Bergen, Peter L. *Holy War, Inc.: Inside the Secret World of Osama Bin Laden.* New York: Free Press, 2001.
Hoffman, Bruce. *Inside Terrorism.* New York: Columbia University Press, 1998.
Martin, David C., and John L. Walcott. *Best Laid Plans: The Inside Story of America's War against Terrorism.* New York: Harper and Row, 1988.
Seale, Patrick. *Abu Nidal: Gun for Hire.* New York: Random House, 1992.
Turner, Stansfield. *Terrorism and Democracy.* Boston: Houghton Mifflin, 1991.

TURKEY

Abramowitz, Morton, ed. *Turkey's Transformation and American Policy.* New York: Century Foundation Press, 2000.
Barkey, Henri J., ed. *Reluctant Neighbor: Turkey's Role in the Middle East.* Washington, D.C.: United States Institute of Peace Press, 1996.
Bolukbasi, Suha. *The Superpowers and the Third World: Turkish-American Relations and Cyprus.* Lanham, Md.: University Press of America, 1988.
Fuller, Graham E., and Ian O. Lesser, with Paul B. Henze and J. F. Brown, eds. *Turkey's New Geopolitics: From the Balkans to Western China.* Boulder, Colo.: Westview Press, 1993.
Hale, William. *Turkish Politics and the Military.* New York: Routledge, 1994.
Harris, George S. *Troubled Alliance: Turkish-American Problems in Historical Perspective, 1945–1971.* Washington, D.C.: American Enterprise Institute for Public Policy Research, 1972.
Howard, Harry N. *Turkey, the Straits, and U.S. Policy.* Baltimore: Johns Hopkins University Press, 1974.
Pope, Nicole, and Hugh Pope. *Turkey Unveiled: A History of Modern Turkey.* Woodstock, N.Y.: Overlook Press, 1997.
Stearns, Monteagle. *Entangled Allies: U.S. Policy toward Greece, Turkey, and Cyprus.* New York: Council on Foreign Relations Press, 1992.
Watanabe, Paul Y. *Ethnic Groups, Congress, and American Foreign Policy: The Politics of the Turkish Arms Embargo.* Westport, Conn.: Greenwood Press, 1984.

YEMEN

Almadhagi, Ahmed Noman Kassim. *Yemen and the United States: A Study of a Small Power and Super-State Relationship, 1962–1994.* New York: I. B. Tauris, 1996.

Burrowes, Robert D. *The Yemen Arab Republic: The Politics of Development, 1962–1986*. Boulder, Colo.: Westview Press, 1987.

Halliday, Fred. *Arabia without Sultans: A Political Survey of Instability in the Arab World*. New York: Vintage, 1975.

———. *Revolution and Foreign Policy: The Case of South Yemen, 1967–1987*. New York: Cambridge University Press, 1990.

McMullen, Christopher J. *Resolution of the Yemen Crisis, 1963: A Case Study in Mediation*. Washington, D.C.: Institute for the Study of Diplomacy, Georgetown University, 1980.

O'Ballance, Edgar. *The War in the Yemen*. Hamden, Conn.: Archon, 1971.

Yodfat, Aryeh Y. *The Soviet Union and the Arabian Peninsula: Soviet Policy towards the Persian Gulf and Arabia*. New York: St. Martin's Press, 1983.

INTERNET RESOURCES

Al-Jazeera News. http://english.aljazeera.net/HomePage

Avalon Project: The Middle East 1916–2001: A Documentary Record. www.yale.edu/lawweb/avalon/mideast/mideast.htm

BBC News: Middle East. http://news.bbc.co.uk/2/hi/middle_east

Council on Foreign Relations. www.cfr.org/region/397/middle_east.html

History in the News: Middle East. www.albany.edu/history/middle-east

Informed Comment: Thoughts on the Middle East, History, and Religion. www.juancole.com

Internet Islamic History Sourcebook. www.fordham.edu/halsall/islam/islamsbook.html

Israel. Ministry of Foreign Affairs. www.mfa.gov.il/mfa

Jerusalem Post. www.jpost.com

Middle East Media Research Institute. www.memri.org

Middle East Network Information Center, Univeristy of Texas. http://inic.utexas.edu/menic.html

Middle East Research and Information Project. www.merip.org

New York Times. www.nytimes.com/pages/world/middleeast/index.html

U.S. Central Intelligence Agency. World Fact Book. www.cia.gov/cia/publications/factbook

U.S. Department of State. *Foreign Relations of the United States*. www.state.gov/r/pa/ho/frus

JOURNALS AND MAGAZINES

Diplomatic History
Foreign Affairs
International History Review
International Journal of Middle East Studies
Journal of Israeli History
Middle East Journal
Organization of American Historians Magazine of History, special issue on *The U.S. and the Middle East* 20, no. 3 (May 2006).

About the Author

Peter L. Hahn is professor of history at Ohio State University and executive director of the Society for Historians of American Foreign Relations. He is author of *Crisis and Crossfire: The United States and the Middle East since 1945* (2005), *Caught in the Middle East: U.S. Policy toward the Arab-Israeli Conflict, 1945–1961* (2004), and *The United States, Great Britain, and Egypt, 1945–1956: Strategy and Diplomacy in the Early Cold War* (1991) and coeditor (with Mary Ann Heiss) of *Empire and Revolution: The United States and the Third World since 1945* (2001). In 1998, Hahn won the Stuart L. Bernath Lecture Prize, and in 1995 he held a Fulbright Senior Research Fellowship in Jerusalem. Hahn earned his Ph.D. in 1987 at Vanderbilt University, where he defended his dissertation with distinction, and he earned his B.A. summa cum laude in 1982 from Ohio Wesleyan University.